17724

D1587880

AGE MATTERS

To Martin, Ben, Timmy, Matt and Rupert and Oliver

Age Matters

Employing, Motivating and Managing Older Employees

KEREN SMEDLEY AND HELEN WHITTEN

GOWER

Published by
Gower Publishing Limited
Gower House
Croft Road
Aldershot
Hampshire GU11 3HR
England

Gower Publishing Company
Suite 420
101 Cherry Street
Burlington,
VT 05401-4405
USA

Keren Smedley and Helen Whitten have asserted their moral right under the Copyright, Designs and Patents Act, 1988, to be identified as the authors of this work.

British Library Cataloguing in Publication Data
Smedley, Keren
    Age matters: employing, motivating and managing older
    employees
    1. Middle-aged persons – Employment 2. Older people –
    Employment 3. Employees – Training of 4. Age discrimination
    in employment
    I. Title II. Whitten, Helen
    658.3'00844

    ISBN 0 566 08680 8

Library of Congress Cataloging-in-Publication Data
Smedley, Keren.
    Age matters: employing, motivating and managing older employees / by Keren Smedley and Helen Whitten.
       p. cm.
    Includes index
    ISBN: 0-566-08680-8
    1. Older people--Employment--Great Britain. 2. Personnel management--Great Britain. 3. Age and employment--Great Britain. 4. Age discrimination--Great Britain. I. Whitten, Helen. II. Title.

    HF5549.5.O44S64 2006
    658.30084'6--dc22

                                                                              2005034909

Printed and bound in Great Britain by TJ International Ltd, Padstow, Cornwall.

Contents

SECTION THREE:
PRACTICAL STEPS TO ACHIEVING AN
AGE-INCLUSIVE CULTURE

SECTION FOUR:
TRAINING AND IMPLEMENTATION

Acknowledgements

Rupert Eales-White for sharing his Change Preference Model.

Kathleen Reddington for her unstinting help with typing, proofreading, and encouragement.

Margaret Mannell for insight into the inner workings of HR.

Rob Parker for his help in research.

Our parents, grandparents and other older role models who have inspired our thinking.

Our friends who have shared many discussions on the ageing of the baby boomers.

Introduction

The day was coming to a close at XYZ Organization. In his office on the third floor, Simon, a 58-year-old man, sat despondently looking at the calculations he had been making about his current financial position. When he had analysed the figures it dawned on him that his niggling fear that he would not be able to realize his dream of retiring at 60 was a stark reality. He still had dependent children and anxieties about whether he was going to have to support a very elderly mother. He was bored with his job which he had done for what felt like 150 years. He was fed up with continuous change and could not imagine how he could face another seven years at work. He picked up the telephone.

Further down the corridor his manager, Bill, aged 38, looked at another email from Simon, rolled his eyes up to heaven and sighed. Yet again this was a piece of work that was badly done, and showed no care and attention. Bill knew that Simon was perfectly capable of doing this job standing on his head but was putting no effort in. Bill had tried numerous times to discuss this with Simon and offered him strategies to improve his work. Simon had repeatedly said that he was going to retire at 60 and was too old to learn new ways.

Bill sat wondering how long it would be before one of the team rang him again to tell him that Simon was not pulling his weight.

At that moment Sally from Human Resources (HR) unexpectedly put her head around the door and said, 'Have you got a moment?'

'Yes,' Bill said, 'I am glad you're here – I have just had another stroppy email from Simon but the only saving grace is that he will be gone within 18 months.'

Sally said, 'Well that is what I came to talk to you about. Simon has just called me. He has decided to extend his retirement to 65 and the new legislation makes him perfectly entitled to do this.'

Bill put his hands in his head, 'What on earth am I going to do about this? I need your help...'

Possible outcome

Simon stays on in his role for another seven years, disgruntled, and causing negativity within his team and the organization. Bill, an excellent ambitious manager tipped for senior management, becomes demotivated, realizes that he is spending 60 per cent of his emotional and thinking time on this problem and leaves for a new job.

In 2006 new EU legislation is being passed to outlaw discrimination on the basis of age. At the same time as this law is introduced it is predicted that 45–59 year olds will form the largest group in the labour force and by 2007 it is expected that there will be more people of pensionable age than children under 16. This will have wide-reaching consequences for your organization.

We have written this book specifically for those of you responsible for people management because we realize that, in this role, everybody will expect you to understand the law and its implications. You will also need to know specifically how this will affect your organization. This book is a practical guide to finding your way speedily around this new diversity issue. It will provide you with strategies to:

- ensure that business performance and productivity are maintained;
- support individuals throughout the implementation of the legislation;
- manage and motivate an older workforce.

In more than 20 years' experience as management consultants and coaches in organizations we have become aware that it is relatively straightforward to write policies and develop new systems. It is a much harder challenge to implement these because it is very difficult to change everyday behaviours and attitudes in the workplace. Our knowledge and expertise are in behavioural and attitudinal change and this book aims to offer pertinent information, guidelines and suggestions as to how to put policy into practice, alongside both the changes in the law and the demographic change.

The purpose of this book is to:

- highlight the pertinent legal issues and possible pitfalls;
- identify the consequences to your organization of the demographic change;
- explore the issues that face the fastest-growing sector of the working population, the older worker;
- offer the management and behavioural skills needed to implement these changes successfully;
- provide templates for cascading the implementation of the law and awareness-raising sessions on developing an age-inclusive organization;
- consider the HR policies and procedures affected by the new law.

WHY IS THIS RELEVANT TO YOU?

The Age Employment Regulations will mean that it is illegal to discriminate on the basis of age. This will revolutionize working practices and impact all areas of employment. These will include:

- recruitment
- retirement
- pay, benefits and pensions
- health and sickness
- pensions

- redundancy and dismissal
- harassment and discrimination
- performance management
- work-life balance and flexible working
- promotion and career development
- succession planning
- training and lifelong learning
- organizational culture.

The consequences of changes in demography and society mean that:

- there will be a significantly larger number of older people in the workforce;
- not enough young people to replace them;
- people having to continue to work as a result of inadequate pensions;
- longer life expectancy can lead people to work longer.

We will be investigating these and other topics in more detail throughout the book.

THE BUSINESS CASE

In order to influence your decision makers and implement new strategies it is essential that you are able to articulate the business case for this law and explain how social change is impacting individual performance.

Employers stand to gain significant benefits from ensuring they adopt non-ageist employment practices. This is particularly relevant against a backdrop of skills shortages and a changing demographic situation, where older workers will be forming a larger proportion of the workforce.

Many employers have already found that employing an age-diverse workforce brings business benefits and savings through fostering a skilled and well-balanced workforce. Businesses report the following:

- improved rates for keeping staff
- higher staff morale
- fewer short-term staff absences
- higher productivity
- a better public image
- access to a wider customer base
- a wider range of skills and experience
- retained 'corporate memory'.
  (www.agepositive.gov.uk)

Age discrimination will be unlawful and the Employers' Forum for Age (EFA) estimate that age discrimination litigation could cost employers £193 million in the first year. This alone is enough reason for directors and decision makers to take this issue seriously.

PEOPLE ISSUES

One of the most difficult issues for managers and Human Resources personnel is to ensure that the workforce is motivated and working effectively and efficiently in order to meet its goals and objectives and, where appropriate, profits. Following extensive consultation last year, the Government has concluded that legislation should:

- set a default retirement age of 65, but also create a right for employees to request working beyond a compulsory retirement age, which employers will have a duty to consider;
- ensure close monitoring of the retirement age provisions so that evidence is available for a formal review of the default retirement age five years from implementation;
- allow employers to objectively justify earlier retirement ages if they can show it is appropriate and necessary.

It will therefore be unlawful to dismiss an employee under 65 on grounds of early retirement and if they request to stay on post-65 you will need to justify your reasons for any decision.

Prior to the introduction of this legislation many organizations have limped through a period of an older worker's demotivation knowing that they will be able to retire them on their 60th or 65th birthday. As illustrated in our scenario about Bill and Simon at the beginning of this chapter, this will no longer be an option so new strategies will have to be put into place. This will lead to a large number of difficult management issues if not handled well.

The combination of the burgeoning older population, longevity and economic decline in the stock markets has left pension coffers with insufficient funds to provide adequate means for retirees. Many of the workforce whilst unable to retire fully because of pension provision may well want or need to work full time or part time.

A key area that senior managers and HR departments will need to address is leadership and succession planning within the organization. Unless the issue of reducing numbers of the 30–49 year olds is addressed there will be a gap in the leadership generation. This is a global issue and therefore organizations throughout the world are likely to face this problem of a top-heavy workforce.

YOUR ROLE

As people managers, it is essential for you to understand the effects of external factors such as law and demography on productivity and performance. In our experience we have found that people are often unable to get the decision makers to listen in time to what needs to be done. This can lead to rushed and badly thought out policies, which would have been much more effective if the appropriate amount of time had been spent on them. This book will help you to understand the issues and enable you to influence your key stakeholders to take timely action and meet the needs of the organization.

HOW TO USE THIS BOOK

This book has been written to help you easily find a way through this subject and to find helpful examples and exercises that enable you to meet the legislation and the needs of your workforce.

In order to achieve this, the book is divided into four sections:

Section One: Age Discrimination and its Context

Section Two: Managing and Motivating the Older Worker

Section Three: Practical Steps to Achieving an Age-Inclusive Culture

Section Four: Training and Implementation.

This book has been written in self-contained sections to enable you to focus on whichever aspect of the problem is prevalent at the time.

We have combined context and theory with specific true-life examples and exercises, checklists and questionnaires to help you achieve the attitudinal and behavioural changes required for your business.

The exercises in the book are there for you to use and can be photocopied and modified in whichever way you wish. It has been written as an active tool for you and not as a tome to be read once and left on the shelf. We hope you find it useful.

Keren Smedley and Helen Whitten

Age Discrimination and Its Context

Age Discrimination: The Next Diversity Issue

Maria works full time at XYZ plc. She has worked there for a number of years. Over the years she has made a lot of friends from work. Once a month a group of women all of a similar age from a variety of workplaces meet, usually in the pub, to catch up on life and put the world to rights.

Maria bought herself a drink and sat down in the pub. Her friends Salma and Flora joined her. They are all women in their mid to late 50s who have known one another for some time.

Salma opens the conversation by saying, 'You know there have been difficulties in my company? Well, it is pretty clear that they are going to make me redundant and as I am coming up to 60 I am not at all sure what my redundancy pay will be. More's the point, though, how will I ever find a job at my age?'

Maria chips in, 'And even if you do they are forever hinting that you are not worth training or promoting because you're past it.'

Flora adds, 'Listening to us is really odd. We used to talk like this 20 years ago when we were trying to go back to work when we had had children and we were saying, "It is going to be so hard to get jobs as women with children". Things have changed and although there is some discrimination still against women it is not as bad as it used to be. Maybe that is how it will be about age one day.'

Possible outcomes

Two demoralized and depressed women.
Organizations losing out on valuable talent, knowledge and skills.

From October 2006 discrimination on the basis of age is illegal. Since 1975 the UK has introduced a number of discrimination laws, including race, sexual orientation, religion or belief, disability and sex discrimination. The latest one to be introduced will be the Age Employment Regulations in 2006. All of these Acts endeavour to ensure that everyone is treated as equals but on the understanding that they are, nonetheless, different.

The concept of diversity encompasses acceptance and respect. It means understanding that each individual is unique and recognizing and respecting our individual differences. Elaine Sihera, author of *Managing the Diversity Maze*, made history in the House of Commons when she successfully presented the first thought-provoking annual Diversity Lecture in the House of Commons in 2004.

> *The essential need of every human being, without exception, is to be appreciated and valued. True diversity aims to fulfil that need. Appreciating the definition of the word itself is therefore not sufficient. One has to also recognise the part perception and respect plays in achieving equity and the difficulties in maintaining effective diversity practice due to tribal instincts and the vagaries of human nature.*

Many organizations are multicultural gatherings assuming they are truly diverse ones. Sihera continued:

> *The difference is very subtle. People of different cultures are expected to fit in with the majority culture, to be absorbed into it without their values and norms being appreciated in return. A truly diverse gathering appreciates difference, values that difference, recognises the variety of perceptions involved and addresses fears and concerns, from whatever quarter. True diversity does not stifle dissent or comment. Only by acknowledging another's perception can we gain vital understanding of their world and educate BOTH perceptions in the interaction on ways to accommodate difference.*

This latest diversity issue is unique as it will affect all of us, unlike the previous Acts. Ageism is rife in organizations and affects all age groups, younger and older. It is often said that the only age it is helpful to be is between 35–40. This book's specific focus is on the effects that this has on the older person. Many of the issues raised here, however, are pertinent to every generation.

Up until now being a racist or sexist at work would more than likely cost a person their job. Offering someone early retirement to cut costs or deciding that a young person is unable to take responsibility probably would not have raised an eyebrow. This will have to change and it will not happen overnight, as ageism appears to be part of our cultural norm.

This chapter will look at ageism in the workplace and begin to explore how to manage this situation for the older worker.

The topics covered are:

1. Ageism

2. The social and economic factors of discrimination

3. The business case

4. Strategies to manage equal opportunities for the older worker.

1. AGEISM

In order to understand the issues it is necessary for us to define ageism. The definition below is the one we will use in this book:

> *Ageism is prejudging or making assumptions about people simply because of their age. It is as wrong or unacceptable as any other form of prejudice such as racism, sexism or prejudice against disabled people. Age discrimination occurs when that prejudice is institutionalized. In employment it is an action that disadvantages an individual because of their age or on the basis of assumptions, misconceptions or stereotyping about age or ability and hinders the proper consideration of an individual's talents, skills, potential and experience. Direct age discrimination occurs when an individual is treated less favourably than another, on the grounds of their age. Indirect age discrimination occurs when a requirement is applied to all but has a disproportionate effect on a particular group. Age Discrimination can be used to the detriment of people at any age and in any environment.*

Age discrimination is the act of favouring certain age groups in the workforce and sidelining others. Throughout centuries, age discrimination has evolved and developed into something that affects productivity in the workplace. Many companies appear to favour younger workers. It has become a youth driven culture with assumptions that the younger the employee, the better. It is often thought that the young achieve more, are more productive and offer creative and innovative working practices.

Some companies prefer to have older employees as they are by definition more experienced and perceived as harder workers. However, often these older workers are sidelined and feel mistreated. The collective cultural view is that younger workers are smarter and heading towards success. This brings with it a hunger and competitiveness that is seen to be good for business. Many assume that as a person grows older they become less willing, flexible and able; also that they become more unwell, take long absences and won't stay for long because they retire. The perception is that all of these factors will affect their performance which will therefore have a detrimental effect on productivity.

The above résumé may seem far-fetched and exaggerated to some of you but unfortunately it is far from the case. In a survey undertaken by Age Concern, it was reported that one person in three believes age discrimination is worse now than it was five years ago. Three-quarters of those questioned did not think age discrimination would improve over the next five years and 28 per cent thought it would get worse.

The survey reported that ageism is both legal and institutionalized: many companies have upper age limits on products such as travel and car insurance and a person at present can be sacked from their job for being too old.

As coaches we have come across numerous examples of this in our work. A female client of ours, who had all the right qualifications, applied for an editorial role on a London newspaper and was told that she was not suitable as 'there is a lot of carrying'. When the interviewer was pressed he said 'Actually we were looking for someone younger, I'm not sure you will fit in.'

Another of our clients said, 'Success only came when I lied about my age to my present employer. I knew he wouldn't employ me if he knew I was 60.'

In the research which we undertook prior to writing this book, 27 per cent reported that they had been directly discriminated against and a further 18 per cent had been indirectly discriminated against. One person reported, 'They were looking for two people in the department to promote. The role was to start new teams, which would require the wealth of knowledge gathered through years of work.' Both the older members of the team had returned to university and had postgraduate degrees. However, neither was even short-listed for the jobs. They were originally told it was because they wanted 'new blood'; two junior internal candidates were appointed.

Another client in his mid-50s was informed that as the average age in his organization was 35, 'Wasn't it time he thought about retiring?' A colleague of his had applied to do a masters degree, which was needed for promotion, but had been told that at 48 it was not worth it for the company as she wouldn't give enough years back. When she commented that many of the 29–33 year olds who did masters left within a year she was told that was different.

2. THE SOCIAL AND ECONOMIC FACTORS OF DISCRIMINATION

Age discrimination is a serious issue both for business and for society. Some wider implications include the fact that a 50+ redundant male is 50 per cent more likely to die of respiratory disease than a working male (NHS Statistics). Equally, depressive disorders are 50 per cent more likely in non-workers. This figure increases with age and with lack of qualifications. As older people are less likely to have qualifications (24 per cent of those between 50 and state pension age have no qualifications compared to 12 per cent of those between 25 and 49 [Labour Force Survey]), this is a pertinent factor.

Unemployment among older people has a dramatic impact on physical and mental health. It is estimated that it costs the UK Government £5 billion in benefits to those who might be working and that the cost of age discrimination to the economy is £31 billion in lost production.

3. THE BUSINESS CASE

In a Chartered Institute of Personnel and Development (CIPD) survey in September 2004, it was reported that HR managers have the highest resignation rate of all managerial disciplines. Ageism has been regarded as a major factor as those over 40 often choose to move into consultancy work due to a lack of promotional prospects. It may be your own experience that there is nobody in your organization who has introduced policies such as this before so instead of being able to call upon the organization's collective learning, you end up by reinventing the wheel. This lack of continuity can lead to a lack of trust and those who have been present in the organization for a period of time may complain that either there are 'too many changes' or they have 'been there before'. They therefore represent blocks to implementation rather than assets.

Already in some organizations such as the Health Service, where older people make up the largest proportion of the 'customer' base, employing older staff who are sometimes more empathic, would be an obvious strategy. This, as yet, is not a universal strategy in most organizations. However, the demographic forecast for the UK will mean that people over the age of 50 will represent a major part of everyone's customer base and it therefore makes good business sense to retain your present staff and plan your future recruitment strategy with this in mind (see Chapter 9).

In almost all occupations workers over 50 have been shown to be no less productive than people aged 25–49 – and to be loyal employees. As has been mentioned, this group are popular with customers and capable of enhancing customer relationships. Organizations need to become more aware of the general demography and recognize that a diverse workforce can cater for a diverse customer/client base.

The consequences of age discrimination are that older people are missing out on opportunities in the workplace. Equally, organizations are missing out on highly motivated, skilled and knowledgeable individuals who could move their business forward. Unless organizations begin to shift the way they think and act not only will they have problems in relation to breaking discriminatory laws, they will also not have a workforce that mirrors population distribution. Already organizations are beginning to reverse their policies of offering early retirement to skilled workers due to business needs.

4. STRATEGIES TO MANAGE EQUAL OPPORTUNITIES FOR THE OLDER WORKER

This section introduces you to some activities designed to help you assess the current situation related to age that exists within your organization.

✎ Exercise 1.1

The AgeTalks age-inclusive model

The model shown below in Figure 1.1 explains what organizations are required to do in order to create an age-inclusive organization.

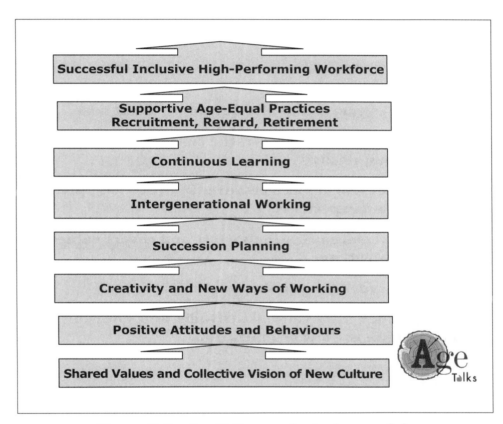

Figure 1.1   AgeTalks age-inclusive model

In our scenario, none of the organizations involved has, as yet, created an age-inclusive culture. If it had, someone like Maria would not be feeling sidelined and Salma would have no anxiety in applying for a job where she had the necessary competencies, even though she is in her mid-50s.

You may find it useful to open the debate about age discrimination by setting up small focus groups to discuss the age discrimination issues we have raised. Invite a number of the older workers to share and talk about the issues they are facing and the types of policies and procedures that would help them perform within the workplace. This could, of course, also be done with any specific groups within an organization. We will focus on intergenerational issues in Chapter 13. The two exercises in this chapter will help you get an understanding of perceptions and attitudes towards ageism in your organization.

✎ Exercise 1.2

✎ Exercise 1.3

SUMMARY AND TIPS

This chapter has given you an opportunity to consider what ageism means within your organization and to understand the necessity of changing working practices and policies to incorporate the demands of this new diversity issue. This needs to be treated as seriously as any other diversity issue such as racism, gender or disability.

The post-war baby boom, the lack of babies being born today and extended longevity have each created this new situation for organizations. This new phenomenon requires a real understanding of both the demographic situation and the law in order to effectively plan equal opportunity recruitment and retention policies.

Six tips

1. **Profile your organization and customer–client base.**

2. **Analyse skills and resources in the context of current and future business needs.**

3. **Use your older worker as a resource in order to apply their knowledge and experience.**

4. **Understand the organization's overt and covert values and attitudes towards age.**

5. **Be an ambassador for equal opportunities.**

6. **Encourage open discussion of attitudes and solutions to combat ageism in your organization.**

PROFILING YOUR ORGANIZATION'S DEMOGRAPHY

This exercise is designed to help you understand and profile your organization's demography and consider:

(a)   whether ageism may exist within your organization, and

(b)   how the demography of the organization can meet current and future business needs.

This activity must be performed by someone who is authorized to have access to personal employee files and must be kept within the bounds of the Data Protection Act and current employee law.

PROFILING YOUR ORGANIZATION'S DEMOGRAPHY

Take employee records and calculate the percentages of staff that you have within the following age brackets:

Age bracket	Percentages
16–19	%
20–29	%
30–39	%
40–49	%
50–59	%
60–65	%
65+	%

1. **Once you have a completed record of these figures you will then be able to analyse your organization's demographic profile. You will need to have answers to the following:**

Is your current age profile a reflection of the general working population?

Comments:

Does your profile mirror the general population?

Comments:

Can you understand the reason for the specific constitution of your current workforce?

Comments:

Could it reflect any sign of age discrimination, either overt or covert?

Comments:

If so, what might be the reasons for this?

Comments:

2. Consider and identify the age demography of the customer–client group on which your business relies.

Does your working population reflect that of your customers' age group?

Comments:

On first glance do you feel that the demography of your workforce meets the needs and wants of your customer–client base?

Comments:

Are your promotional and succession policies equipped for a period of time when there are more older workers and fewer younger workers available?

Comments:

What key skills and competencies are required to make your business, products or services effective?

Comments:

What skills, experience, knowledge and talent might you utilize in your older workers in order to ensure that you offer them equal opportunity and encourage them to stay within your organization?

Comments:

What do you need to put in place to ensure equal opportunity?

Comments:

Looking at the statistics you have gathered you will need to be aware of two factors:

1. With the present demographic trend there will be, over the next ten years, an increasing number of older people in the workforce.

2. Even with sufficient numbers of employees within the organization, the new Age Discrimination law will make it illegal to give older workers early retirement. It will also not be possible to exclude them from any training, promotion or other benefit that is being offered.

These factors mean that it is essential that you develop systems, strategies and policies that achieve equal opportunities for all age groups, including those who would previously have retired at 60 or earlier.

 Exercise 1.2

SETTING UP THE FOCUS GROUPS

Produce a short document that explains that the changes both in the law and demography. Also make people aware that the organization needs to change its policies and attitudes in light of these facts.

You have options with regard to whom you invite to these sessions as you know your organization best. The group could be made up either of self-selected groups or a specifically selected group. These could include:

- anyone who is interested in the subject and wants to contribute;

- those who are 'older' workers (50+);

- groups of varied age cohorts.

We suggest that the focus groups include approximately 6–8 people and, depending on the size of your organization, you may choose to run several focus groups with different age profiles so as to gain as much knowledge as possible.

It is important that the invitation makes clear that the focus groups will provide a safe environment for discussion and sharing of solutions, that it will be confidential and that no individual statement will be quoted unless by specific permission.

Ensure that each focus group has at least one flipchart or method of recording ideas and concerns. Enlist a facilitator who can maintain a safe and creative environment to capture ideas. It may be appropriate for this work to be completed by an external facilitator who will not be seen to have any internal political agenda.

Some of the questions you may choose to ask within these focus groups could include:

- Have you experienced age discrimination?

- How do you feel older people are perceived in your workplace?

- Do you consider discriminatory behaviour and attitudes to be institutionalized or confined to specific groups?

- Do you feel valued for your knowledge and experience? If so, in what way?

- Do you think or feel that you have fewer qualifications than your younger colleagues?

- Do you feel that you get adequate opportunities for training and development?

- Are you working (a) because you have to (b) because you want to, or (c) both?
- If you don't enjoy your work, what action could the organization take to support you?

If you are within ten years of retirement age do you feel at the end of your career or do you feel there are new work experiences you would like to have? If so, what is preventing you from pursuing these?

- Do you feel you are currently given enough opportunities to experience new challenges?
- How might the organization help you to move forward?

At the end of the focus groups, retain copies of the outputs and collate the key points into a brief report. Ensure all participants receive a copy. It is really important that the report is put into action. One way to achieve this would be to set up a small working party of HR and some of the focus group members to develop new policies, systems and practices that will support equal opportunities for all. A small advisory group of older workers should be involved in the development of these policies.

 Exercise 1.3

AGE BINGO

Set your colleagues in the HR department a task to monitor the use of age-discriminatory words in your organization. The first colleague to score 10, with evidence of the events, will win!

Analyse how long it took people to complete their list. The shorter the time, the more prevalent ageism is likely to be in your organization. Explore how you are going to change this language in your organization. Language colours our thinking and while we use discriminatory words we continue to think discriminatory thoughts.

AGE BINGO

Keep this piece of paper with you as you go to meetings, or walk around your organization. Tick off terms as you hear them. The first person to get 10 wins:

Terms to look out for are:

Young whippersnapper	
Old fart	
Grumpy old man	
Miserable old woman	
Dinosaur	
Brat	
Flighty young thing	
Past it	
Over the hill	
Wet behind the ears	
Childish	
Senile	
Stuck in the past	
Looks 12	
Irresponsible young thing	
Losing their marbles	
Old codger	
Bright young thing	
Old fogey	

CHAPTER 2

The Age Discrimination Regulations 2006

The UK has been a leading player in Europe in the field of discrimination law. The earliest law introduced was the Sex Discrimination Act in 1976 followed by the Race Relations Act also in 1976 and the Disability Discrimination Act in 1995. Together with Europe the UK is developing these laws further and three directives implementing these have been passed:

1. The Council Directive 2000/43 – The Race Directive, which states the principle of equal treatment between persons irrespective of racial or ethnic origin.

2. The Council Directive 2000/78 – The Framework Directive, which states that there should be no discrimination on the grounds of sexual orientation, religion or belief, disability and age in employment and occupation.

3. The Council Directive 2002/73 – Sex Discrimination, which amends the 1976 Equal Treatment Directive.

The focus of this book is age discrimination and how this will affect you as HR personnel and managers and your staff. The new law, which is part of the European Employment Directive, comes into force in October 2006 making it illegal to discriminate on the basis of age. The new employment legislation will give greater protection to everyone and will certainly have a major impact on how older people are treated in the workplace. It will be promoted and enforced by a brand new Commission for Equality and Human Rights (CEHR).

This chapter aims to put the law in context, raising the main points that will affect you in your role overseeing employment issues. The topics we shall cover in this chapter are:

1. Law questionnaire
2. Chronology and actions to date
3. The legal position
4. The international position
5. Practical implications for your organization.

1. LAW QUESTIONNAIRE

Use the following questions to help you reflect on your organization's readiness for the new Age Employment Regulations.

		Yes	No	Don't know
1.	Do you know that there is a new Age Employment Regulation being introduced in 2006?			
2.	If so, have you prepared for the introduction of the Age Employment Regulation?			
3.	Do you know the consequences of not meeting this law?			
4.	Have you defined ageism for your company?			
5.	Do you have an age-discrimination policy?			
6.	Have you age-profiled your workforce?			
7.	Does your firm encourage early retirement?			
8.	Do staff have to retire at a specific age?			
9.	Have you investigated current attitudes to age in your company?			
10.	Have you ever advertised for 'a young vibrant' member of staff?			
11.	Have you ever advertised for a 'highly experienced' member of staff?			
12.	Are jokes about age commonplace in your workplace?			

If you have answered yes between 10–12 times you know your Law and are well prepared. Move to Chapter 2!

If you have answered yes between 7–10 times you are well on your way but may benefit from a quick skim through this chapter.

If you have answered yes to fewer than 7 questions we would recommend you read this chapter in detail.

2. CHRONOLOGY AND ACTIONS TO DATE

To help you put the new law into context we have briefly outlined the steps that have been taken so far leading towards the introduction of the legislation.

In 1999, the Government produced a code of practice after consulting key employer and employee representative groups. It encouraged employers not to make employment decisions (recruitment, selection, promotion, training and development, redundancy or retirement) based on age. This code is voluntary and individuals cannot bring claims against employers who don't use the code.

A report by the Cabinet Office, *Winning the Generation Game* (April 2000) made 75 recommendations to Government on policy towards older people. It included recommendations on changing the culture and stereotypes regarding older workers, on the Government as an employer, on benefits and pensions, and on encouragement for training, work and volunteering.

New Deal 50+ was introduced in April 2000. Its aim is to help people from welfare to employment. It is open to all over-50s (up to any age) on any kind of benefit, not just the registered unemployed. This is important due to the high levels of 'hidden' unemployment in this age group. There are fewer than 200 000 over-50s registered unemployed but there are 1.5 million on sickness and other benefits. New Deal 50+ is not compulsory and includes advice sessions, work trials and training allowances.

The EU Council Directive 2000/78/EC established a general framework for equal treatment in employment and vocational training and guidance. It is commonly called the Employment Directive. It is designed to outlaw discrimination at work and training on grounds of age, sexual orientation, disability, religion or belief. It sets a framework which will ensure that there are minimum standards for combating discrimination throughout the European Union.

In November 2000, EU member states agreed to introduce legislation on age discrimination by December 2006. This long run-in period was introduced at the request of the UK Government to allow time for employers to adapt their employment working practices. It was thought that legislation on age was raised more complex issues than the other discrimination issues. The first phase of Government consultation took place in early 2002, with a second phase in July and October.

The Department of Work and Pensions Green Paper, *Simplicity, Security and Choice, Working and Saving for Retirement*, December 2002 sets out measures to promote flexible working and retirement, gradual retirement and opportunities to re-train and to work and save longer. It sets out a strategy to help people plan their retirement, with a twin approach to encourage more saving and promote longer working lives. The Green Paper suggests that those people who wish to defer claiming their state pension are given a fair deal. It also states that there will be consultation on the proposals to allow people to continue working for the sponsoring employer while drawing their occupational pension, opening flexible routes into retirement.

The Green Paper deals with the following issues and proposals:

- Providing extra back-to-work help for those aged 50 and over and piloting measures to help recipients of incapacity benefits return to work.

- Treating men and women between 60 and their State Pension age as active labour market participants .

- Managing the graded rise to 65 years in women's State Pension age which will occur between 2010–2015.

- Bringing forward more generous increases for deferring state pensions and maintaining State Pension age at 65.

- Implementing by December 2006 age legislation covering employment and vocational training, in which compulsory retirement ages are likely to be unlawful unless employers can show that they are objectively justified.

- Allowing people to continue working for the sponsoring employer while drawing their occupational pension, raising the earliest age from which a pension may be taken from age 50 to age 55 by 2010.

- Changing public service pension scheme rules, for all new members initially, to make an unreduced pension payable from 65 rather than 60.

In July 2003, the Department of Trade and Industry published its consultation document *Equality and Diversity: Age Matters,* to seek views on how to implement legislation prohibiting age discrimination. Consultations have taken place over a period of time until October 2005. The final document, the Employment Equality (Age) Regulations 2006, were eventually laid before Parliament on 9 March 2006 and, subject to approval by both Houses, they come into force on 1 October 2006.

3. THE LEGAL POSITION

The scope of these Regulations apply to employment and vocational training. They prohibit unjustified direct and indirect age discrimination, and all harrassment and victimization on grounds of age, of people of any age, young or old.

As well as applying to retirement they:

- Remove the upper age limit for unfair dismissal and redundancy rights, giving older workers the same rights to claim unfair dismissal or receive a redundancy payment as younger workers.

- Allow pay and non-pay benefits to continue which depend on length of service requirements of five years or less or which recognize and reward loyalty and experience and motivate staff.

- Remove the age limits for statutory sick pay, statutory maternity pay, statutory adoption pay and statutory paternity pay, so that the legislation for all four statutory payments applies in exactly the same way to all.

- Remove the lower and upper age limits in the statutory redundancy scheme, but leave the current age-banded system in place.

- Provide exemptions for many age-based rules in occupational pension schemes.

- Require employers who currently set their retirement age below the default age of 65 to justify or change it.

- Require employers to inform employees in writing at least six months in advance, of their intended retirement age, allowing people to plan for their retirement.

- Introduce a new duty on employers to consider an employee's request to continue working beyond retirement.

You will, of course, need to refer to the details of these Regulations in more depth when they are passed through Parliament, and also take legal advice to ensure all legal avenues are covered.

The Age Employment Regulation will revolutionize working practices unlike any of the previous anti-discrimination laws. It will affect us all during our careers. It will be based on the familiar concepts found in existing discrimination laws and will cover direct and indirect indiscrimination, harassment and victimization. It will cover everyone seeking employment, vocational training and promotion. The law refers to employment in the broadest sense possible. It includes the self-employed person, apprentices, trainees, members of the armed services and police force.

The protected group, whom we will call employees, are protected while at work, before the relationship has begun and after it has terminated. The law affects every system and procedure. In particular, the application process, promotion and training, terms and conditions and non-renewable fixed contracts. These regulations will also affect agencies that place employees.

The regulations also apply to professional bodies, trade unions and employer organizations affecting both their own employees and their members. The trustees of occupational pensions, providers of vocational summer schemes and internships and government training schemes will all also need to meet the terms of the regulations.

As stated above the law covers four different types of discrimination The following definitions come from lawyers specializing in the field of discrimination.

Direct discrimination occurs where a person is treated less favourably than another on the grounds of age, for example, a 55 year old not being recruited to do a particular job because the employer thought, reading their CV, they were too old. It would also occur if they perceived they were too old even if their age was not actually known. It would also constitute age discrimination if a person is excluded because they are too young. The European law, unlike the one in the US, affects all ages. Direct discrimination also occurs if you are seen to associate with or express views on behalf of the person being discriminated against.

Direct discrimination is difficult to prove and the law acknowledges this and has added some assistance. Firstly, once the employee has proved circumstances from which an inference of discrimination could be drawn, the employer must prove that this wasn't the case, otherwise a tribunal must find in favour of the employee. Secondly there will be a questionnaire procedure to allow the employee to find evidence. Under the new legislation, direct age discrimination will be allowed in exceptional circumstances. There will be various situations where an employer can safely justify this. For example, employing a child actor to play the part of a child in a film or play.

Indirect discrimination takes place:

If A applies a provision, criterion, or practice which he applies or would apply equally to persons not of the same age as B but:

1. which puts or would put persons of the same age as B at a particular disadvantage when compared to other persons;

2. which puts B at that disadvantage;

3. which A cannot show to be a proportionate means of achieving a legitimate aim.

To justify indirect discrimination there does not need to be a specific example. This will therefore be easier to justify than direct discrimination. An example would be: an employer not allowing a 57 year old go on a course as they may be retiring soon.

The Regulations allow pay and non-pay benefits to continue which depend on length of service requirements of five years or less or which recognize and reward loyalty and experience and motivate staff. For benefits determined by periods of service longer than five years the employer must meet a special justification test. The test is that it reasonably appears to the employer that the way that it uses length of service to award the benefit fulfils the business need.

With regard to the National Minimum War, the Regulations also contain an exemption for different rates of pay for the 21-year-old and under. This is divided into two bands – 16- and 17-year-olds and 18–21 year-olds.

Victimization, under the Regulations, occurs when an individual is treated in a way that is detrimental because:

- they have made a complaint about being discriminated against or harrassed;

- they intend to make a complaint about discrimination or harrassment;

- they have or intend to act as a witness or give evidence in support of another person(s) relating to a complaint about discrimination or harrassment.

Victimization may present itself in many ways. It may be that individuals are refused requests for time off, denied promotion or training, ignored by their manager or colleagues, criticized continually for their work, have work allocation or shift arrangements altered, and so on. If this happens and an organization does not take reasonable steps to prevent it, the organization will be liable to pay compensation. Individuals who victimize may also be ordered to pay compensation.

'Harassment' is defined as occurring where on the grounds of age:

A engages in unwanted conduct, which has the purpose or effect of violating B's dignity: or creating an intimidating, hostile, degrading, humiliating or offensive environment for B. The conduct is deemed to have the required effect if having regard to all circumstances including in particular the perception of B, it should reasonably be considered as having that effect.

It is not acceptable to make jokes about other diversity issues. At present, however, jokes about age are socially acceptable to most people. If the law is to be followed to the letter an employee will be able to make a case for age discrimination based on jokes. It is uncertain as yet how the tribunals will respond to this.

Retirement and pensions, which are very contentious issues arising out of the legislation, will be discussed in Chapter 15.

The Regulations will not mean that employers have to recruit, promote, retain, or train people who are not competent, capable, and available to perform the essential functions of the post concerned or to undergo relevant training, simply that they will have to be transparent and be able to justify their decisions.

4. THE INTERNATIONAL POSITION

The issue of age discrimination and the ageing workforce is global and some readers may find it useful to put the EU and UK position into a global context. This is particularly relevant to global organizations and those that trade internationally.

Australia

Age discrimination legislation was introduced in Australia in June 2003. It was the first country to propose a law that, in addition to employment, also covers access to goods, services, facilities, land, housing and education. The Age Discrimination Bill 2003 grants powers to the Human Rights and Equal Opportunity Commission to heighten public awareness, educate Australians about age discrimination, and handle age discrimination complaints. The introduction of the Bill is the culmination of an extensive consultation period and is a result of cross-government priorities including the National Strategy for an Ageing Australia, the issues arising from the Treasurer's Intergenerational Report, and continuing welfare reform.

United States

The Age Discrimination in Employment Act (ADEA) was passed in the US in the 1960s, prohibiting age discrimination for the over 40s. At that time, approximately half of all private job openings explicitly barred applicants over age 55, and a quarter barred those over age 45. The ADEA covers employees over 40 and specifies bans on discrimination in hiring, firing, promotion, layoff, compensation, benefits, job assignments and training. Younger workers under age 40 are not protected by the ADEA, but are sometimes protected by state law. Exempt from the law are elected officials, independent contractors, partners in a partnership, military personnel, and non-US citizens working outside the United States.

Europe

Prohibition of age discrimination in employment in Europe stems from the 2000 European Union Employment Directive on Equal Treatment prompting the development of age discrimination legislation in member states. The Directive mandates that all EU member states introduce legislation prohibiting direct and indirect age discrimination in work by 2006. The Directive sets a rather broad framework, leaving it up to each individual country to decide on the specifics of legislation such as whether to ban mandatory retirement.

Implementing age discrimination legislation will, in many ways, improve the path towards reaching the European Employment Strategy employment targets for older workers (55–64) from the current 38 per cent to 50 per cent by 2010. Following are some of the EU country developments in implementing age discrimination laws.

Belgium

A new general anti-discrimination law was adopted in Belgium in February 2003, prohibiting discrimination on many grounds, including age, and in application to various contexts, including employment, and supply of goods and services. The new law also broadens the competencies of the Centre for Equal Opportunities and the Fight against Racism. Previously, Article 3 of the Act of 13 February 1998 on Employment Promotion prohibited imposing a maximum age when recruiting employees. It is worth noting that in regard to employment, the new legislation provides protection for workers who initiate a procedure against an employer on the grounds of discrimination. The law provides, among other measures, for the reinstatement of workers unfairly dismissed in these circumstances, or compensation equivalent to six months' pay.

Finland

A new Finnish Constitution of 2000 explicitly prohibits any discrimination on the basis of racial or ethnic origin, religion or belief, age or disability. In addition, the Contracts of Employment Act revised in June 2001 and the Penal Code implemented in 1995 also provides protection against age discrimination. The scope of protection covers all employees and job seekers and covers pay, and working conditions, including those under collective agreements. Finland was one of the first countries in the EU to have actively reversed their policy on ageing workers. Via its National Programme on Ageing Workers launched in 1998, Finland sought to promote older workers' participation in the labour force, particularly improving the employment opportunities of people aged over 45. The Programme sought to reduce age discrimination and premature retirement by promoting practical learning and developing links between health, education and working life.

Ireland

Ireland is one of the few EU countries to have already implemented age discrimination legislation. The Employment Equality Act of 1998 prohibits discrimination, both direct and indirect, in relation to access to and conditions of employment and promotion. It protects all workers aged 18–65 in the public and private sectors, as well as persons receiving services of employment agencies or represented by trade unions. Defence forces, police forces and the prison service are exempted. In addition, the Equal Status Bill of 1999 covers discrimination on the grounds of age, but in a more general sense, and applies to all persons aged 18 or over. Further, the Equal Status Act introduced in February 2000 prohibits discrimination in the provision of goods, services, disposal of property and access to education, on any grounds covered by the Employment Equality Act of 1998.

The Netherlands

The Dutch Parliament passed age discrimination legislation in September 2003, and they are awaiting Senate approval. The law bans any differentiation in employment based on age, including hiring, promotion and dismissal. It also applies to vocational education and guidance, and membership in employers' and employees' organizations. The Commission on Equal Treatment will oversee the implementation of the law. Previously, prohibition of age discrimination was not included under the General Equal Treatment Act of 1994, covering discrimination on the basis of sex, race, religion, political conviction, or marital status. Since 1994, the Netherlands has utilized the National Age Discrimination Office (LBL) to help combat age discrimination.

5. PRACTICAL IMPLICATIONS FOR YOUR ORGANIZATION

The forthcoming legislation will affect all areas of employment. In this section we will touch briefly on some of the main issues. These are discussed in detail in their own chapters.

Retirement age

The default age, set at 65 or over, will be reviewed in five years. According to the proposals mandatory retirement below 65 will require objective justification. Employees will be given legal right to request work beyond 65 modeled on the existing rights of asking for flexible working. The important change comes in that employers will be required to give six months' notice and the procedure for this will be covered later in Chapter 15. Staff will be be protected by unfair dismissal and age discrimination laws if employed beyond 65. (See Chapter 15.)

Recruitment

Decisions about recruitment, selection, and promotion should not normally be based on age. Age limits in job advertisements will become a thing of the past. Employers should be able to apply an age limit to recruitment but only if they can justify doing so. There will be very few positions where there is a genuine occupational requirement relating to age.

The area of concern is not in the direct discrimination but in the indirect, for example, it will be discriminatory to ask for ten years' minimum experience as this will discriminate against the younger worker. Graduate schemes will also come under scrutiny as it will not be possible to say 'graduated within the last two years' as this may discriminate against the older worker. Similarly the 'Milk Round' as currently practised may need reviewing to include all age groups of graduates. It is also important to ensure that internships and modern apprenticeships and any other scheme which were previously directed to one age group are now open to all (see Chapter 9).

Unfair dismissal

The new provisions remove the upper age limit for unfair dismissal and redundancy rights. They also address two issues in respect of dismissal through compulsory retirement: the reason for the dismissal, and its fairness. Again this will be covered in more detail in Chapter 15.

It is proposed that the provisions relating to unfair dismissal are changed so that employees can seek redress at any age, but retirement at an employer's justifiable mandatory retirement age, or any default age set out in legislation, will be a fair reason for dismissal. There are also plans to change the way that financial compensation is calculated so that the basic award will no longer be based on the employee's age. The calculation of the award will continue to take account of the employee's length of service. The maximum length of service considered will remain 20 years. Of course, we must remember that age discrimination is not just about old people – young can also be treated badly, and exploited and abused.

Redundancy

The Statutory Redundancy Payments scheme will remain largely in its current form, using the same age bands and the same multipliers. The upper and lower age limits, 18 and 65, will be removed , as will the tapering rule for 64 year olds. The maximum amount of service that can be used for a calculation remains limited to 20 years. Entitlement would end at 65 or at the employer's normal retirement age for the job.

The Regulations contain an exemption for enhanced schemes, details of which are in the Age Regulations.

SUMMARY

This chapter has focused on the changes in the law that are due to be introduced in 2006. It has given an overview on why the law is being introduced and how it will affect employers and employees. The most salient points have been raised; and as pointed out they will be covered more fully in later chapters with further facts and exercises. The focus of this book, as stated in the Introduction is the older worker. This in no way minimalizes the issues that are affecting the younger worker and the exercises suggested throughout the book can be easily adapted for any group. It is also important to remember that the older worker does not work in isolation but in intergenerational teams where all members will be affected if there is any discrimination.

CHAPTER 3

Demographic Changes

Monika Queisser of the Organisation for Economic Co-operation and Development commented: 'The ageing workforce is the biggest economic challenge policymakers will face over the next 20 years.'

The world is facing an unprecedented situation in terms of population shifts. In stark terms we will not have enough people to run our businesses, buy our products, look after our elderly and pay the taxes necessary to cover health and pensions. Unless individuals and businesses take this seriously we could be heading for a social and economic catastrophe.

This chapter will put this situation into context and cover the following topics:

1. The demographic situation in the UK, EU and globally

2. International trends

3. Effects on the economic situation

4. Essential business response

5. Assessing business needs: What you need to do.

1. DEMOGRAPHIC TRENDS IN THE UK, EU AND GLOBALLY

By 2050 the elderly will outnumber children for the first time in history.

The greying of the 'baby boom' generation and the generation born in the years immediately after World War II, will mean that the age group of 60+ and older is growing 60 per cent faster than the overall world population. In 2003 there were approximately 700 000 (6 per cent) more children under 16 in the UK than people of state pension age (SPA). However, from 2007 the population of SPA is projected to exceed the number of children and by 2031 is projected to exceed it by approximately 4 million (36 per cent). (See Figure 3.1.)

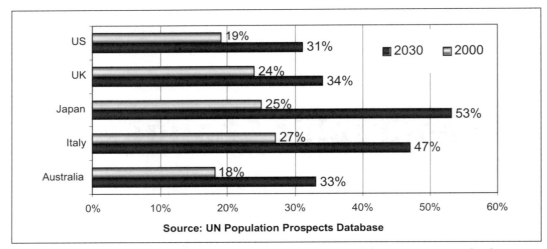

Source: UN Population Prospects Database

Figure 3.1   Ratio of retirement age to working-age population

The UK labour force will start shrinking by 2010 and this situation will worsen during the 2020s unless proactive steps are taken by organizations. By 2007 it is expected that there will be more people of pensionable age than children under 16 in the UK. (Office for National Statistics, Population Trends, 2001.)

Factors that are influencing demography

Increasing health and life expectancy, the low fertility rates, low work activity rates, and the retired and ageing population are radically altering the population.

The single most important factor in determining future population is the total fertility rate (TFR). The TFR is defined as the average number of babies born to women during their reproductive years (see Figure 3.2). A TFR of 2.1 is considered the replacement rate; once a TFR of a population reaches 2.1 the population will remain stable assuming no immigration or emigration takes place. When the TFR is greater than 2.1 a population will increase and when it is lower than 2.1 a population will eventually decrease.

Region	1990 TFR	2000 TFR	2010 TFR	2025 TFR
World	3.4	2.8	2.5	2.3
Less developed countries	4.7	3.1	2.7	2.4
More developed countries	1.9	1.6	1.7	1.7

Figure 3.2   Total fertility rate trends

With the introduction of the pill in the 1960s this generation had real choice regarding the number of progeny, for the first time in social history. According to the UN 62 per cent of women in marriage or relationships are using some form of birth control.

Other factors are also influencing the low birth rate: for example, poor public health and industrial pollution are blamed for a decreasing male sperm count in the UK, Russia and other nations.

The result has been that parents worldwide have had fewer children and birth rates are expected to fall below 'replacement' rate before 2050. This is also reflected in the fact that many young women and couples in their 20s and 30s are choosing not to have children at all, preferring instead the affluence they can enjoy without the additional burden of a family. Wealth discourages childbearing as people make decisions to put material aspirations before childbearing. 'Capitalism is the best contraception' states Wattenberg (*Newsweek* 27 September 2004).

The fact is that the demographic trend has changed dramatically in the last 50 years as a result of effective contraception, economic stability, social change and healthcare.

Trends in ageing

The trends in ageing are set out below:

- The UK has an increasing and ageing population. While the total population increased in size by 54 per cent between 1901 and 1997, the number of older people aged 50 and over more than tripled.

- The proportion of the total population which is aged 50 and over doubled in the last century from nearly 1 in 7 in 1901 to 1 in 3 in 1997.

- The population of the UK was estimated to be 59.6 million in 2003, of which around 11 million were over SPA (over 60 for women and 65 for men). This group makes up 18.5 per cent of the total UK population.

- Women accounted for 72 per cent of those aged 85 and over in 2003 and by the age of 90 women outnumber men by more than three to one, although this gap is narrowing.

- There will be 25 per cent more 85 year olds over the next five years.

2. INTERNATIONAL TRENDS

The population trends we are experiencing in the UK are set to be mirrored in most developed countries over the coming decades. The post-World-War II effect impacts many other nations. For example, by 2025 the number of people aged 15–64 is projected to dwindle by 10.4 per cent in Spain; 10.7 per cent in Germany; 14.8 per cent in Italy; 15.7 per cent in Japan. In Japan the working age population was due to decline by 0.6 per cent during 2005.

The demographic time bomb is equally dramatic in China, where there are likely to be 265 million 65 year olds by the year 2020. Companies may hope to be able to source workers from Eastern Europe but Hungary, Poland and the Czech Republic are also ageing and in East Asia countries such as South Korea, Thailand, Taiwan, Singapore and Hong Kong are experiencing the same demographic trends and are likely soon to have a median age of 40 (World Economic Forum Report).

In Italy some towns are populated with double the number of older people. There were one-third fewer children under 6 in 2004 than there were in 1971. Local schools and gyms have closed. Seniors' clubs are expanding. Italy's pension system is underfunded and there will simply not be enough money coming in to meet the need. This situation is also likely to be reflected in Germany.

For two decades countries such as Indonesia, India, Brazil, Mexico, the Philippines, Iran and Egypt may be able to provide workers although even in 2005 it is reported that Western organizations are experiencing a skills shortage in India. There is also an ethical question as to whether the rich countries should drain skills from their poorer neighbours. But even these countries will, as a result of economic progress in the twentieth century, be experiencing the same demographic slide within two decades, as a declining fertility rate and longer life spans skew the age ratio (*Business Week*, February 2005).

France is, however, making strides in boosting their population (*Sunday Times,* 19 June 2005). As a result of the generous subsidies to parents and the 35 hour week regulations of 2003–2004, France is likely to become the most populous – and possibly dominant – country in Europe, increasing from 60 million today to 75 million by 2050.

3. EFFECTS ON THE ECONOMIC SITUATION

As this generation of baby boomers came into the workforce in the West, Japan and later into Latin America and East Asia, they enabled the growth of worldwide organizations by providing the practical labour and creativity necessary to succeed.

The New World Economic Forum report on ageing, January 2004, suggested that the UK's impending workforce contraction could start having an effect on firms by 2010. These changes will impact pension provision, health and care services for the elderly, housing, employment, training, savings trends, and consumption patterns. Factors, in fact, with far-reaching consequences for business.

However, despite the fact that this demographic calculation has been available for some time, even actuaries of insurance and pension funds have failed to prepare individuals, government or organizations for the problems that will be arising from this shift.

What really has pushed ageing to the top of the global agenda are ballooning fiscal gaps in the US, Europe, Japan and elsewhere that could worsen as boomers retire. While US social security is projected to remain solvent until at least 2042, the picture is worse in Europe. The US have been proactive on this issue for some time. Not only do they have the anti-ageism law, which has encouraged older people to stay in work, it has also succeeded in persuading most citizens to have private savings plans, whereas in much of Europe up to 90 per cent of workers rely almost entirely on public pensions. Benefits are also generous. Austria guarantees 93 per cent of pay at retirement; Spain offers 94 per cent. Without radical change, pensions and elder care costs will escalate and be prohibitive for governments to manage (Washington Centre for Strategic and International Studies).

Adults with fewer children inevitably have had more disposable income to spend on goods and services in the twentieth century. The number of young ready to take their place in the workforce when this generation retires is greatly reduced. This will certainly hit both productivity and the global economy. The already inadequate pension arrangements of most countries in the world will mean that the ageing population will have less to spend on goods and services. With fewer people working and paying tax the young are likely to be taxed heavily in order to support those of pensionable age and will therefore also have less to spend.

4. ESSENTIAL BUSINESS RESPONSE

This demographic situation has a significant impact on business. The issues that are most significant for UK industry are:

- the fact that the working-age population will be much older;

- that there are fewer people in their 30s–40s to take over senior posts;

- that even with migration they will need to attract and retain sufficient people with the right skills for their business;

- that consumers may not have as much disposable income or credit as was evidenced in the twentieth century.

Organizations will also need to be proactive about ensuring that their staff have the right skills and knowledge to meet the needs of their business. Technological advances have meant that companies can look beyond their local pool of talent to workforces across the globe. Setting up abroad – as many organizations have done – answers some of the problems but as a country becomes successful they equally become aware of their value. India has already become more competitive, and Dell has moved some operations from India to the Czech Republic in 2004.

Employing people abroad and working virtually can result in huge savings in terms of salaries, manufacturing costs and also office rental, partly due to lower rates in some parts of the world and partly due to home workers. However, much of the world is still lagging behind with regard to telecommunications and several companies in the Middle East still report that they are unable to set up secure home working systems for their staff.

Beyond this there is also a cultural shift that needs to occur alongside technological development and many managers even within Europe find it difficult to manage remote workers. The question for UK-based organizations will therefore be whether to send their staff abroad, bring talent into the UK, or recruit and employ locally.

Economic inactivity

A large number of older people are economically inactive and could provide a resource (see Figure 3.3).

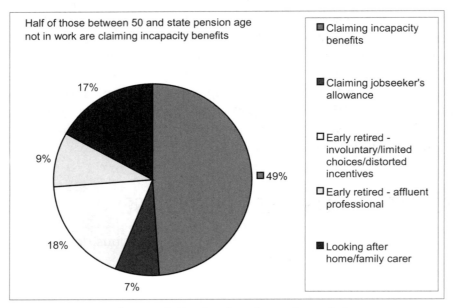

Half of those between 50 and state pension age not in work are claiming incapacity benefits

- ■ Claiming incapacity benefits
- ■ Claiming jobseeker's allowance
- □ Early retired - involuntary/limited choices/distorted incentives
- □ Early retired - affluent professional
- ■ Looking after home/family carer

Figure 3.3   Scale of work activity

Source: Labour Force Survey

This situation will only get worse without intervention. The UK will face a much greater percentage of its population being inactive due to the ageing population, reflected by an over 27 per cent increase in the total dependency ratio and a 66 per cent rise in old age dependency rates between 2000 and 2030.

Impoverished pensioners and inadequate numbers of young in the workforce are likely to have a negative impact on business as there will be less disposable income to spend on goods and services.

More needs to be done in the UK to get inactive groups into work (World Economic Forum). When judged against the top five OECD nations, the UK comes out as worst in terms of activity rates for all age and gender groups and particularly with older people. If the UK maintains the current activity rates between 2000 and 2030 the ratio of workers to retirees is expected to fall from nearly 2.8 to 1.8.

The solution for business and the economy lies in developing policies to entice workers to defer their retirement at rates similar to OECD top performers such as US, Canada and Australia. Taking this approach would mean that 'the UK could reduce its dependency burden by raising its activity rate to 2.7 workers per retiree in 2030, nearly matching its current rate' (World Economic Forum Report).

The ageing working-age population

By 2006 45–59 year olds will form the largest group in the labour force.(See Figure 3.4.)

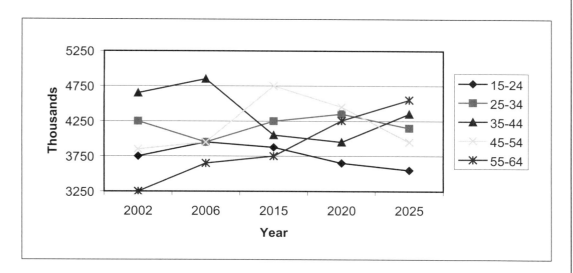

Figure 3.4   UK working-age population 2002–2020

Source: (The Employers Forum on Age (EFA), February 2005)

Sixty-eight per cent of employers seeking skilled staff are experiencing recruitment difficulties – but they may be looking in the wrong places as alongside a global pool of workers, companies have frequently ignored older people.

Companies will now need to recruit, manage and retain the talent that exists within the ageing workforce, rather than let this knowledge walk out of the door. This will mean that they will need to persuade people to work who might naturally have assumed that they were ready for retirement.

Issues such as the existence, or otherwise, of extended family links in facilitating participation in the workforce is important as well as other factors such as caring and childcare. With the feminization of the workforce the pressure of caring for ageing relatives can be complicated.

Some European countries are making progress. In Finland new government and corporate policies are boosting the average retirement age: no longer is Italian home appliance maker Indesit Co. coaxing older workers to retire early to make room for younger recruits. Instead it is teaching its over-50 staff in its seven Italian factories new skills such as factory and supply chain management. Indesit's HR Director Cesare Ranieri comments, 'so far the programme is going smoothly'.

Luxembourg-based steel-maker Arcelor which until 1991 offered early retirement at 92 per cent of pay at age 50 says it has more than doubled productivity since raising the retirement age to 60. Among other things they offered an incentive to older workers in the form of increased salaries if they were prepared to undergo extra training. They have also made it easier to

DEMOGRAPHIC
CHANGES

work part time. 'The policy proved very successful,' says Arcelor HR Manager-Director Daniel Atlan.

Unless companies explore different working practices and new ways to utilize their older workers through flexible working and staged retirement they will find that they do not have sufficient brains or brawn to maintain productivity, let alone grow.

Potential leadership gap

With fewer .people in the 35–44 age bracket there is likely to be a leadership gap, especially after 2015 when those in the 45–54 age bracket are also likely to decline. In the next ten years this will be a very real problem for companies as they simply won't have the availability of talent to replace those wishing to retire from senior posts.

There are also gender differences in managerial positions of all ages, but particularly with people in their 40s. People are marrying and having children at a later age. This generally means that there are more women of a younger age but that many women choose to leave or work part time in their 30s in order to have children.

The declining gap between the sexes of the economically active UK population is illustrated in Figure 3.5.

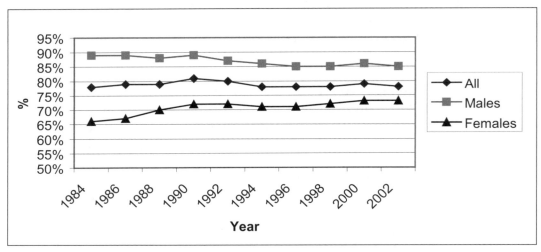

**Figure 3.5 Economic activity rates by sex
(per cent) (EFA, February 2005)**

Source: Social Trends, Office for National Statistics, 2004

In the EFA survey of February 2005 those in their 30s profiled as the least happy cohort, finding balancing work and family very stressful. As a result of this, companies are losing intellectual capital and leadership potential because working practices continue to make life so difficult for this age group. The introduction of work–life and flexible policies is helping to retain talented men and women in managerial and leadership roles.

However, the UK Department of Trade and Industry (DTI) policy that has offered flexible working options for parents of children under six years old has caused division. Some workers without children have come to resent this concession. Perhaps if they were able to understand that the global community needs to produce sufficient numbers of children to maintain productivity and adequate tax levels to support the whole population some of this resentment would be dissipated.

Flexible and part-time working packages and staged retirement procedures could enable organizations to retain adequate supplies of people of management and leadership level.

5. ASSESSING BUSINESS NEEDS

It will be up to HR and people managers to evaluate the implications of this situation on short-term and long-term productivity. It will be necessary to influence senior management to take action sooner rather than later to ensure continuing productivity and competitive edge.

It will therefore be up to HR and people managers to assess business needs and resource skilled workers. Finding the best supply of talent may be a challenge and persuading more groups of currently 'inactive' people to participate in the workforce is one solution to this problem.

Both private and public sector organizations will need to attract back the over 50s in order to leverage their skills and knowledge. This will place demands on management to provide new employment packages and practices that benefit all parties.

The UK has lower productivity than France, Australia, Italy and Germany and this will need to be addressed through training and motivation.

SUMMARY

The demographic trends have important implications for those involved with the people management requirements of any business or organization.

These challenges will not be solved overnight. It will be a continuing process of evolution and it is unlikely that any policy decided upon in 2006 will be adequate to still be relevant in 2010. It will be up to HR and line managers to review the situation frequently in order to identify and keep abreast of their productivity needs.

We hope that this chapter has helped you to understand the demographic issues that are likely to face your organization in the coming decades and begin to consider what action you may take. We shall investigate suggestions and solutions that you may be able to adopt in Section Two.

CHAPTER 4

Understanding Your Older Workforce

Your challenge in this new situation will be to retain and utilize available talent in order to provide your organization with the productivity it requires for continued and future success. To do this effectively it can be helpful to understand the pressures and aspirations of your workers in order that you can support their work performance.

One HR manager commented to us recently, 'I know what motivates our younger staff, but I am going to have a steep learning curve to find the best ways of motivating older staff.'

In order to gain the most from their staff, managers will benefit from understanding the emotional consequences for older individuals of the legal, demographic and financial changes that have occurred. This can help them to understand some of the pressures they may be under. Worries such as financial insecurity or feeling left behind can cause stress. Where there is stress there is lack of productivity. We cannot cover all factors and it is important to note that different types of people will respond in different ways to life events. However, in this chapter we shall identify some of the main issues that will be facing this generation of workers as they head towards normal retirement age only to discover that this date has been postponed by five years and also to find that their pension provision may well have been reduced by recent market trends.

The topics we shall cover include:

1. Changes in the workplace
2. The 1960s and social change
3. Male–female relationships
4. The sandwich generation
5. Physical health
6. Finance and pensions
7. Retirement
8. Job security
9. Learning new skills
10. Demotivation
11. Goals and aspirations.

1. CHANGES IN THE WORKPLACE

The workplace has changed dramatically over the last 5–10 years, with the technological changes of computers, the internet, email and mobile phones. This has introduced the global economy, with all its 24/7 demands and expectations of immediacy.

The workplace that this older generation entered was radically different. It was slower paced. A letter would arrive on a person's desk and it could frequently be four weeks later that a reply was sent (in the mail). International telephone calls had to be booked. There was a telex system until, in the 1980s, there was the introduction of the fax machine. There were secretaries and administrative staff who typed letters on typewriters and had to Tippex out mistakes and provide carbon copies.

Whether they were graduates, or started work straight from school, the expectation was that they learnt their career in the workplace and planned to stay in it for their working life. The post-war generation were raised in the 1950s where there was a predominant need for security and a desire to be certain about their future. They expected to be able to map out their life based on certain fixed points which would only go off-course if there were disasters such as a death, sickness or war. They had grown up to believe that it was their right to retire on a good pension and that if they had contributed towards a pension fund that this would be adequate for their old age.

Even in the 1970s people were formal in the workplace – you always referred to a boss as 'Mr' or 'Mrs' and organizations were more hierarchical in structure and tone. Several older people still complain when a stranger calls them by their first name on being introduced in person or over the phone, although this is now common practice. They are not necessarily being difficult or snobbish: it is just not what they were exposed to originally.

Despite today's world of fast-paced change, technology and globalization most older workers have adapted extremely well to managing computers, emails and the internet – albeit that they may have to call up a son or daughter occasionally for help to download the latest software or reprogramme the video!

2. THE 1960s AND SOCIAL CHANGE

The sixties were a time of extraordinary social change. Pop stars such as the Beatles and Rolling Stones proved that whatever your background you could become rich and successful. The youth culture challenged all aspects of authority and establishment, with the introduction of *Private Eye* magazine and the TV programme *That was the Week that Was*. People who had been treated with great respect before, such as politicians and doctors, were questioned and confronted.

The baby boomers sought to create a new world order, to make peace not war and influence culture from the perspective of the young. The introduction of the pill enabled people to enjoy sexual liberation without the fear of pregnancy and there was no threat of HIV and AIDS. The bra-burners of the 1960s and 70s promoted women's liberation.

Few people travelled abroad for holidays until the charter and package tour boom of the 1960s. Before that air travel was the domain of the rich, the diplomatic or senior corporate. Until the immigration from the Commonwealth, issues of multi-culturalism and ethnicity were seldom experienced by the average person.

The grey- (or not so grey-)haired people you have in your organization will have been through these times. They will have experienced the 1950s where family and security and the established 'norms' were instilled into their brains through television programmes and romantic movies. Then the 60s came and the world changed and opened up. What followed were increasing rates of divorce, changes in education, global opportunities, economic ups and downs and the world they had been brought into hardly existed any more.

This generation are still playing their part in breaking ground. As an older generation they are refusing to age in the way their parents did so Mick Jagger still struts his stuff, in his early sixties.

3. MALE–FEMALE RELATIONSHIPS

Expectations of relationships between the sexes both at home and at work were very different in the 1950s to today. In 1965, for example 51 per cent of women were working – mostly part time - and there were very few single parents. By 2003 73 per cent of people in the workplace were women.

Many of these women were brought up in the 1950s with messages such as 'look after your man' and 'men know best'. Women did not get property rights until the 1970s and could not take out a mortgage on their own without the signature of a man. Although the 60s brought a radical shift in thinking and in the relationships between men and women due to the women's liberation movement, the fact is that belief systems presented as fact by authority figures such as parents when you are young condition your mind and become 'the way things should be done'. Therefore it can jar when things are done differently to the way they were done when one was a child. Most of the time people can adapt to the new ways but when they are tired or something has gone wrong, or something unexpected has happened they shift back into disempowered thinking such as 'this shouldn't be happening to me'.

People in your organization may therefore seem as though they are at one with the roles they lead but there may be an underlying ambivalence. This is likely to be exhibited at times of stress, often in a way that can appear very uncharacteristic.

For example, you might have a very smart senior woman who appears to be on top of everything but whose inner belief may be that 'I should not have to be managing home and work'. This causes inner conflict, which can be tiring. Another example would be a 56-year-old man who is faced with possible redundancy whose belief is 'I have worked for this company for 25 years and they should not be treating me this way...' but may never say this to his manager.

These are the silent issues that affect how the organization, teams and individuals operate. If they are put onto the map and talked about, even in a general sense, and without focusing on an individual, it enables people to share some of their issues and reduces stress. It also enables everybody in the organization to learn about the issues of different age groups and enables people to develop empathy and work together to solve problems.

Working practices

Working practices are also in transition. Working customs and 'norms' were developed by males. The factories of the Industrial Revolution spawned the modern organization and were run by men. Thus the norms of business quite naturally tend to be male norms. Therefore female behaviour can challenge these norms as inevitably not all women act like men, although many of the early feminists adopted more male behaviour in order to be accepted. The song from My Fair Lady *'Why can't a woman be more like a man'* might well define some of the confusion that has existed in the workplace during this time! The lead group may have seen female colleagues through a lens of male perspective as to what is 'right' behaviour at work. Of course in today's world all these norms and perspectives are up for review and realignment but this is not necessarily an easy process.

As this generation of women entered the workplace most expected to work until they had children and then to work part time. Divorce was rare and so they did not expect to have to be responsible for their – and their children's – financial wellbeing for the rest of their lives. Thus they frequently made little pension provision as it was expected that both the state and their husband's pension would provide.

Most of the women who did work were in jobs such as secretaries, nurses, teachers, retail workers and very few made it to management positions. Nurses could work up the hierarchy but it was unusual to get a female doctor. Today there are a large number of female doctors.

Wives were most often at home looking after the home and if in the workplace they had a 'job' rather than a 'career'. Only 7 per cent of the 1950s' generation went to university. Figures from the Higher Education Statistics Agency reported in 2003 that since 1994 the number of male students has risen on average by less than 1 per cent per year whereas in the same period, women student numbers have risen by 42 per cent. Women now make up 59 per cent of university entrants.

The expectation was that men would provide the bulk of the pay and even today women generally earn less and still hold fewer of the senior positions. As women are frequently in more menial roles one can still occasionally experience an older male asking an executive woman to 'make the coffee'. This can, of course, be offensive and irritating and yet one also has to understand that this is the world of work into which the older male entered. In 2005 many women are finally making it to senior posts. Indeed there are those now who are earning more than their husbands; so the trend for women being breadwinners and men househusbands is growing. This in itself can cause conflict for those men brought up to feel that it was their responsibility to provide and protect, and also takes some adjustment for women.

The generation of women of 50–65 are sandwiched between women of retirement age who never expected to work once they were married and the generation who were brought up to expect that women would work full time and achieve equal success to men as well as have a family. This middle group has benefited from the stimulation and economic prosperity that is brought about by the opportunities that have presented themselves for women in the workplace. However, many women of 50+ are struggling to manage home and work, sometimes alone, sometimes with the additional responsibilities of stepchildren and several lots of ageing parents. This group has been lead to expect the reward of a secure retirement at 60 but if they took time out to have children they are facing an impoverished old age on a low pension as they will not have paid the necessary National Insurance to merit a full pension. Those who divorced before pension provision was taken into account may watch ex-husbands enjoy a much more affluent old age to their own.

Divorce

The number of divorces in the UK increased by 3.7 per cent between 2002 and 2003. This leaves more men and women living alone, which is not what they were conditioned to expect. Many of your older workers may have experienced two or three marriages. This results in children spanning a large age group.

This can mean that a 60 year old can still have children of school age, and stepchildren and parents/step-parents/parents-in-law to manage. This has financial as well as emotional implications.

The over-50s' divorce rate is also soaring. From 2000–2005 the divorce rate among the over-50s has risen by 8.7 per cent. Men, on average, now get divorced at 42 compared with 39 a decade ago. Women are typically 39 compared to 36 a decade ago.

Experts attribute this trend to the rise of financially independent women leaving when their children have left home – a consequence of the 'empty nest syndrome'. Over-50s' marriages are generally more stable than those of younger couples but they are not immune to problems. One in seven people aged 50–64 is now divorced, compared to one in eight of those aged between 35–49. There is also evidence that more older people are divorcing for a second time. As a Relate counsellor commented, 'People are living longer and healthier lives, and have more choices than ever. Someone in their 50s who is in an unhappy relationship could face a further 30–40 years.'

Seventy per cent of older men live as part of a couple but only 40 per cent of older women do. Half of all women over 65 now live by themselves, which can mean that they have little or no emotional or practical support in their personal lives. Bereavement is also an issue. Men and women may be looking forward to a lonely old age, with fears about health and financial security.

4. THE SANDWICH GENERATION

People are marrying later and having children later. The average age of a woman having a first child is projected to increase to over 29 years for women born in the late 1970s onwards. This is much later than it was previously and this means that there will be a proportion of women in the workplace of 45+ with very young children.

Another significant change concerns life expectancy. Between 1981 and 2002 life expectancy at age 50 increased by four-and-a-half years for men and three years for women. By 2002 women who were aged 65 could expect to live to 84, and men to 81. Projections suggest that life expectancies at these older ages will increase by a further three years by 2020. Therefore many people of 50+ still have elderly parents who may need support, care and attention and are sandwiched between these two demands.

The children of this age group are also frequently struggling. The price of housing in the UK is so high that they often stay at home until well into their 20s or if they leave home then return because they have run up debts, are finding it difficult to get into the job market and have returned to their parents for help. These are the 'boomerang generation' who are finding it difficult to manage economically on their own. It is an unsatisfactory situation for all concerned – parents are having to subsidize accommodation and graduates who have to rely on their parents because they either can't find a job or are on a very low income feel frustrated and inadequate that they are unable to become independent.

These issues were not such a problem for the men who developed the original culture of the workplace as they generally had wives at home who dealt with family matters. It is thus often still not seen to be acceptable within the workplace to have these external demands on an employee's time. Several 50+ men, in particular, have reported high levels of stress at being the only child available to look after an ageing parent but feeling unable to draw attention to their plight to their manager, fearing that it will look as if they are 'uncommitted' to their work.

In the past when women worked there was often an extended family to help look after home and children. Today people frequently live a long way from their original home and support network. Women who are grandparents can still be working out of financial necessity and cannot meet the demands of their children and grandchildren. This can trigger guilt and anxiety, distracting their mind from their work. A male insurance worker in his 50s commented to us:

> *Neighbours called to say that my mother was ill and I needed to go and take her to hospital. I was in the middle of a meeting and had to explain that I was unlikely to return that day. My mother had the early stages of*

Alzheimer's and I knew I was in for a long haul. Managing work and life since that time has been exhausting.

People therefore juggle 'How do I meet my responsibilities?' – such as how to take their parent to the hospital, going to a school play or parents meeting – with meeting their business targets.

These issues are increasingly going to be a problem in organizations as the population ages, unless managers and HR departments start to recognize these and to introduce new ways of working.

5. PHYSICAL HEALTH

Although ageing does not necessarily physically drain you – and this generation is physically younger and fitter than their predecessors – physical changes inevitably take place with age. There will be a proportion of the older workforce who will experience physical fatigue. One of the frequent issues raised is the increasing drain of energy experienced by those older workers who have a long commute. They can be leaving home very early, experiencing extended periods of travel time, working long days and may be returning to an empty house where they then have to manage home and sustenance. Equally they may be returning to a home full of young children demanding attention!

In a situation where a person is resentful at having to continue to work for a longer period than they expected this stress can lead to illness and to sabotage behaviours.

People also find the ageing body difficult to deal with. It is a truth that people frequently feel the same inside and yet when they look in the mirror they see an image they don't recognize – or don't wish to recognize.

Women particularly can suffer from what is regarded as the 'invisibility factor' once they reach a certain age. The female manager of a restaurant commented to us recently that she could not see how she could employ a waitress over the age of 30 because 'pretty young waitresses draw men into my restaurant and keep them happy'. Of course she won't be able to do this once the Age Employment Regulations come into force but it is certainly a reflection of how older women can be treated.

Bel Mooney, a columnist of *The Times*, commented, 'I didn't plan it this way – I wasn't supposed to get old.'

The celebrity- and youth-obsessed culture that has been created by Hollywood, media and the advertising companies has done little for the average older woman. Appearance seems ever more important and 90 per cent of those having cosmetic surgery are women. Even younger women are reportedly having liposuction before they return to work after maternity leave. Hopefully the Age Discrimination Regulations will place the focus on skills and competencies rather than age or appearance.

6. FINANCE AND PENSIONS

Many older workers who believed that by the time they were in their 50s and certainly 60s they would have paid for their homes and be picking up a pension based on final salary are finding that things have changed. As a result of divorce and maintenance payments many people are still paying for mortgages or renting property for themselves and ex-spouses, that they did not expect to be doing at this stage of their lives.

The consequence of divorce impacts both men and women. Whichever partner had the highest pension settlement would be required to give a proportion to the other partner if they divorced after 1999. Those who divorced before this time had no proportional sum for a retirement and, as we have mentioned before, there will be a substantial number of people – mainly women – who have nothing but their state pension or their work pension.

Alongside this, pension funds are depleted as a result of the fall in the stock market and people's welfare is very dependent on the global economy and the housing market. There is a group of people who have the majority of their equity in their home but very low income. And others who have very little equity in their homes and risk losing them but equally must continue to work to pay off mortgages and debt.

Educational demands for children have changed and from 2006 universities will be charging up to £3000 per annum for fees as well as the cost of living, which will put more financial pressure on older people with younger children. Where parents cannot find the funds to give financial support to children and are aware that their children will have to take substantial loans this can also cause guilt.

There is a shortage of care homes for those who have elderly parents and even in state care homes the rates are means tested and can be expensive. People may therefore find themselves paying large sums for residential care. This may equally deny them their inheritance. With the amount of inheritance left after tax, the opportunity to pay off a mortgage from a legacy becomes less likely.

People certainly worry about their finances in old age and increasingly will feel that they must stay in work as long as they can in order to save money for what they generally expect will be a long period of retirement. Most do not want to be a burden on their children.

The parents of the 50–60s' generation did not expect to live until they were 80 but many have done so. Today's 50 year olds know that it is likely that the majority – but obviously not all – will live until 80 or 90.

This group is generally aware that they have to do something to provide for their old age. As this was not the expectation when people joined the workforce and started pension plans they did not take adequate cover to cover this extended life. Even the actuaries of the pension companies did not forecast the impact of demography to adequately cover people's extended longevity. (For example, this trend was directly responsible in the downfall of the Equitable Life insurance company. Rentokil Initial faces a similar problem. Hence, most final salary pension schemes are being phased out for lack of funds.)

General savings in shares, ISAs and PEPs have reduced as well, leaving people who thought they had made adequate provision with a shortfall of funds.

Impact of pension policies on retirement

The normal retirement age is increasing and may, within five years, disappear altogether. The impact of this is that, having believed for the 30–40 years of their working life that retirement would come at 60 for women and 65 for men, – and that one's old age would be taken care of by the state – the older worker is faced with a reality that is very different from the expectation. The deal has changed and the rug has been pulled out from their feet. People who have contributed 5–15 per cent of their annual salary for years to a company pension scheme can now end up facing an impoverished old age because the scheme has failed. They feel literally robbed of money that they feel is their entitlement. Problems with endowment policies have compounded this situation.

> *I paid 14 per cent of my salary into the Public Service Pension Fund for 30 years and I am now told I do not have a pension as there is insufficient money in the fund. I feel robbed.*

Others who have retired are returning to work in order to make ends meet. The Office of National Statistics has reported a rise of 30 per cent from 1998–2005 of women working over pension age, with a figure of some 650 000 women now working over 60. There are 2.59 million aged 50–59 in work, up nearly a quarter on 1997. Older women's personal income is only 57 per cent of older men's (National Statistics). Women are nearly twice as likely as men to work past retirement age, mainly because they lack a private pension or full entitlement to a state pension. 'The Government treats pensioners like second-class citizens and female pensioners like third-class citizens. What is needed is a citizen's pension that doesn't discriminate against women,' Paul Holmes, spokesman for the Liberal Democrats comments in February 2005 (*Daily Mail*, 17 February 2005).

A banker who retired at 55, told of how he has had to return to work at 61 in order to survive. The stock market fall and pension problems had removed the financial security he had anticipated to be able to rely upon. Those who are self-employed have seldom made enough money to be able to contribute in any realistic way to their pensions. We spoke to a 68-year-old self-employed builder who continued his work – still lifting heavy equipment – because he could not afford to give up.

Managing this 'expectations' gap is one of the hardest challenges that an individual has to undertake and often this can only be managed by discussion and support. If it is not dealt with, people become disgruntled, feel victimized and exhibit stressful behaviours, which detract from good communication and performance. The anger and irritation triggered by a situation they feel is 'unfair' can lead people to become truculent observers of 'rights' and they would be likely to feel a heightened sense of a grievance if they feel that, on top of their other worries, there is any discrimination against them in the workplace.

Although the Age Employment Regulation is intended to help and support the older worker, the fact that companies will have to adhere to its clauses even after an employee is 65 may well, unfortunately, put organizations off employing them for fear of costly litigation.

7. RETIREMENT

The grass can be greener on the other side in the imagination but is not always so in real life. People can long for retirement but then find it lonely and difficult. Others dread retirement and do not plan for it.

HR professionals can help people accept and plan for retirement and also stagger the journey towards this stage of life so that a person is well prepared. Many companies are offering pre-retirement courses and phased retirement programmes to help people during this adjustment phase.

Equally there may be employees who have retired or been retired who are not enjoying their retirement and might welcome a return to part-time working. You may be able to utilize their knowledge and skills within your organization. People frequently comment that they have a preconception of what it is to be 70 and imagine themselves to be old before their time. As George Thomas, the former Speaker of the House of Commons who continued to be energetic well into his 80s stated, 'I thought my mother was old at 70. I now know better!'

8. JOB SECURITY

Discrimination, as we have discussed in Chapter 1 on age discrimination and diversity, is a reality of working life. Although it affects young and old this book is specifically looking at the issues of the older workforce. With recent trends of downsizing and mergers and acquisitions older people were frequently given 'early retirement' packages during the 1990s. This had led to a general fear in the older worker that they would be the first on the list to be 'let go' and given early retirement or redundancy. Many employees of 50+, for all the above reasons, believe that they are nearing retirement age and are too old to start something new, to learn new skills, to start new jobs, or to move into higher roles.

When people feel under threat and defensive they can tend to resist change, fearing for their security. This can lead to a blockage of knowledge flow and productivity. They fear they are seen as past it and not taken seriously.

This can result in 'fight or flight' behaviour – either hiding in the shadows and not putting their head above the parapet to be counted or becoming aggressively vociferous about the 'way it was done in my day'! Obviously this is a worst-case scenario but in our experience both these situations arise quite frequently.

If someone has lost their job or been made redundant, a common experience for those having to seek new jobs at this stage of life is to believe (and be told overtly or covertly) 'you're too old for this post'.

A 54-year-old woman who was made redundant has found it impossible to find a job of the same calibre as her qualifications: 'I assumed I would be working again within two months.' The older worker can frequently feel relegated to the 'scrap heap' once their company has got what they needed from them.

HR Departments will, under the new legislation, need to review their redundancy process, and ensure that it does not look like an 'early retirement' system. They also need to identify how to motivate staff during the possible disengagement stage leading to retirement.

9. LEARNING NEW SKILLS

It was less common for people to go to university when they left school in the 60s and 70s. Therefore older workers, even senior managers, are less likely to have the same standard of professional or academic qualifications as some of their younger colleagues.

Older people also often fear that they are unable to learn as effectively as young people. Worries about 'losing their memory' can mean that they lack self-confidence in their ability to learn new information and skills, particularly when having to do so within a group of younger people. This is particularly true of managers and senior managers.

This lack of confidence can undermine their performance and their ability to ask for help. We have personally known of senior managers who have asked for management development coaching where the coach was asked to enter by the back door so that their staff did not see that they needed help. Companies often promote the ideal of 'continuous learning' but those closest to the top may not be demonstrating this themselves, either through fear or complacency.

It has been common practice that a 50+ employee is seen to be too old to receive training or development and that, because of their age, they have reached a 'grey' ceiling. With nearly one million people already working beyond the age when they are entitled to a state pension and with more and more people of pensionable age in employment – a figure which will inevitably increase over the next few years – organizations will benefit from ensuring that their employees have the adequate skills and knowledge for their job.

The legislation offers them some hope. Companies will now have to offer training equally to everyone within the organization bar the odd exception. The tight labour market and almost full employment have resulted in growing numbers of companies wanting their older workers to stay on and if they are to do so they will need the ability to continue to learn.

10. DEMOTIVATION

If your older staff do not feel valued for their knowledge, skills and wisdom then they are likely to become demotivated. The demotivated older worker can be troublesome. They may have experienced 'too many' change initiatives; they may have witnessed the failures of projects, changes of senior management, a succession of mergers; broken promises, and senior managers who say one thing and do another. One event after the other can slowly nail the lid of hope and optimism firmly down so that the person simply stays on 'waiting for retirement'.

The problem with this is that they can spread a web of disillusion around them and infect other people with their negativity. These people frequently do not realize that they have choices with regard to how they manage this situation and we shall suggest some ways of supporting them in later chapters. Of course demotivation is not just a problem for the older worker as people get demotivated at all ages but with a larger proportion of older workers than previously it will be necessary to engender a culture whereby employees take responsibility for their own attitude and motivation, alongside the reasonable expectation of support from their organization.

The opposite case can also exist, where people want to continue to work because they are enjoying the stimulation of the workplace: 'I want to work until I am forced to retire.'; 'I would like to work as long as I am fit.' And yet these people do not always feel 'heard' or able to express their enthusiasm and feel discriminated against. A frequent comment we hear is:

> I was pushed to the 'exit' due to my birth date, and not due to my competencies, health and energy or my willingness to work. People were not interested in listening to my ideas about what I could contribute.

The disillusion and anger of those who have been given early retirement packages against their will is reflected in comments such as:

> I was forced out of employment because I had turned 50. I had worked 36 years in the company and they showed me no respect. I was a number, but I still had a lot to give; I knew the business well and had plenty of ideas.

This is as true in the public sector as it is in the private sector. As one client told us, 'The Civil Service seemed to have covert but collective perceptions that constitute a 'grey ceiling' blocking promotion. Impossible to prove, of course!'

11. GOALS AND ASPIRATIONS

It is easy for people to assume that older people do not have goals and aspirations, that they have achieved all or most of what they set out to achieve and closed the door to new aspirations. With life expectancy into the 80s there is still plenty of time for people to forge new ventures. Many people are now studying for degrees later in life, taking professional qualifications they never thought they would achieve, learning languages and musical instruments, exploring new depths of personal and professional development.

It can be of great benefit to a business to encourage these goals. Studying is a very rejuvenating process and brings confidence and a resurgence of new energy and ideas. Equally new challenges at work can help the older worker to feel useful and that they are still contributing.

At the same time it may also be a time when people have to adjust to the fact that they are never going to achieve the goals they may have harboured earlier in their lives – never become the chief executive, the concert pianist, the millionaire; and this can also require some support.

Whereas some workers will have managed to reach senior level posts other 'greying' workers will be having to accept that they may now never do so. This can be a disillusioning moment and an HR professional or line manager can help such a person come to terms with this situation, or help them to seek another challenge that might fulfil some of their ambitions in a different way.

SUMMARY

This chapter has raised a number of the issues that are affecting some of the 50+ people in the workplace in order to help you understand your workforce. Organizations do not have to take responsibility for the ills or imbalances of society, but if they want to get the best out of their staff it can help them to be aware of the pressures they may be under so that they can support them.

Although we have pointed out the challenges facing the older worker we would like to emphasize that many of this group feel young and fit and willing to contribute. Inevitably these people are less likely to present a problem – other than demanding that you utilize their knowledge and energy to the benefit of themselves and others.

In Section Two these topics will be expanded upon with specific exercises and strategies as to how to change views, beliefs, behaviours and culture in your organization.

Managing and Motivating the Older Worker

CHAPTER 5

Changing Attitudes and Stereotypes

XYZ has started to introduce cross-departmental project teams as a new way of working. This was an idea that came directly from the heads of department so they are determined to ensure that the first project group works really effectively. Bill, Chris, Mary and Ahmed, the four department heads in the division, are having a meeting to discuss whom it would be best to invite into the project team.

'It is really important that we ensure that we have a good skill mix and that we choose the people who are able to do specific functions to take this project forward,' says Mary.

Bill says, 'That is absolutely right and this is an opportunity to let people who may find the routine work difficult star at their particular expertise.'

'So,' said Ahmed, 'Let's make a list of people and their specific skills.'

They start to do this and Chris says, 'Simon in your team, Bill, is quite good at financial analysis, isn't he?'

Bill groans and says, 'Oh no, we can't have him. He is such an old misery, always putting down any idea, always saying, "We've done it before a hundred times".'

'What about Jim from your team Mary?' Ahmed suggested.

Mary says, 'Oh no, he is one of the dinosaurs too! I don't think we can have anyone from that group.' They all laugh.

Ahmed comments, 'We can't dismiss all of them because after all Jim is best at doing that work.' Bill says, 'That's all very well Ahmed but it seems to me that most of the over 50s are just sitting here waiting for their pension. They complain if you ask them to do anything new and then when they finally agree ...'

Mary continues his sentence, '... take for ever to learn a new skill.'

Possible outcome

They shoot themselves in the foot, as, based on their assumptions that all older workers are dull, they don't create the best project team; and the Managing Director (MD) stops this new way of project working.

Our scenario shows clearly the stereotypical thinking held by some of the department heads about older people. This is not an uncommon view but is one that will not be useful in the light of the demographic changes that are occurring; furthermore, actions based on these assumptions will be illegal when the Age Discrimination Regulations become law in 2006.

Beliefs and assumptions affect our thinking, behaviours and communication. This chapter focuses on understanding beliefs and attitudes and how to help people to create alternative views and ways of thinking. The topics covered are:

1. The business case

2. Stereotypes

3. Beliefs and habits

4. The Power of Intention

5. Beliefs to Expectations

6. Strategies and exercises to challenge stereotypes.

1. THE BUSINESS CASE

In our work we are often in dialogue with highly skilled and motivated older workers who have been discriminated against because of their age. We also meet others who have heard about discriminatory experiences and assume that 'there is no point applying for a job' as they believe they will be turned away at the first post once their age is known. The consequence is that organizations miss out on talent and wisdom.

> *My manager seemed to see me as expendable (when several people in their 20s joined the team) and started a campaign of put-downs and negative, bullying behaviour. Despite attempts on my part to assert myself and ride it out I eventually took time off because of stress and finally left due to a kind of constructive dismissal (Social worker).*

An MD of a small management consultancy who is nearing seventy told us that she never discloses her age and if she is asked to send a CV with a proposal she always takes ten years off her real age. She says that she has to spend a lot of time trying to make herself look younger. She is not alone; recent research statistics on attitudes to age show that:

- 50 per cent of people over 50 said that they had been discriminated against on the grounds of age.
- 44 per cent of a sample of 1648 managers interviewed by the Institute of Management said that they had experienced age discrimination.
- 55 per cent of the sample of managers said that they had used age as a criterion in recruitment.

As we explored in Chapter 3, Demographic Changes, the demographics will have an effect not just on the organization's staff but also the organization's customer base.

One very good business reason to alter stereotypical attitudes is demonstrated by some recent research on consumer spending. Independent research by www.fiftyon.co.uk, a new employment website for the over 50s, reports that:

- 'Grey' consumers, who typically have greater purchasing power than younger people, appear particularly keen to deal with people closer to their own age rather than less experienced people who are often currently employers' first choices.

- The over 50s have a collective pot of £175 billion, possess 80 per cent of all private wealth, and their disposable income is 30 per cent higher than the under 50s.

- Over eight times as many people prefer to get advice on their finances from someone aged 45–59 than someone younger than 30.

- A third of the people over 45 like to be served by someone aged 45–59 when buying things for their home, for example furniture and DIY equipment.

As the demographic profile of customers and clients will continue to reflect an ageing population it makes good business sense to employ and retain older people in your workforce in order to service their needs.

2. STEREOTYPES

Stereotypes are shaped by our beliefs, expectations and cultural experiences. The human brain stores information that we use frequently into the sub-conscious, thus releasing the conscious mind to deal with whatever situation is presenting itself currently. The brain is designed to categorize things into boxes, as this helps it to manage the enormous quantity of information that enters the brain every day.

However, what people tend to do with this stored information is see it as facts, as reality, instead of analysing each piece of information on its own merits. For example we hear an American accent and we create a picture of a stereotypical American, often to be surprised that they do not fit our model. This is hardly surprising when every age, shape, size and nationality can be found on that continent.

We will all have a stereotypical view of an old or older person. What do we mean when we call someone old? When does old age begin?

> *When I was young I was called a rugged individualist. When I was in my 50s I was considered eccentric. Here I am doing and saying the same things I did then and I am labelled senile,* George Burns.

Some 60 year olds are extremely fit and well, both physically and mentally. Some 40 year olds can act as if they were 70! Some, contrary to popular belief, can use a computer. A survey commissioned by Age Concern and

Microsoft reveals that a quarter of the over 50s use a computer in their spare time – spending more time in front of their PC (on average nine hours a week) than watching TV . The majority of older users (64 per cent) believe that using a computer has made a positive difference to their lives. More than half of these older users (59 per cent) email friends and families and 48 per cent surf the Internet. The stereotype of older people being intimidated by computer technology couldn't be further from the truth – a staggering 81 per cent of users found it easy to use a computer, with just 19 per cent saying they experienced some difficulty at first.

Equally, stereotypical thinking can alter through time. When the baby boomers were young their parents expected to be treated with respect, and treated younger people as 'callow youth' who knew very little about anything. However, much of this was transformed in the 1960s when youth took centre stage. This group of baby boomers have gone on trying to hold centre stage for the last 40 years. Many are now in their 50s and early 60s and they don't for one minute see themselves as an old person – Jane Fonda being one!

It is important to help people not to make generalizations but to form their views and language around specific cases.

Stereotypical views about the older person are already changing. The soap brand Dove is tackling the conventional view of beauty. They have produced large billboard adverts showing a picture of a 96-year-old great grandmother. They ask if she is 'wrinkled' or 'wonderful' as part of its mission to 'widen the definition of beauty'. Other women in the campaign include a grey-haired 45 year old, whose poster asks if she is grey or gorgeous, and a 22 year old whose ad ponders if her freckled face is flawed or flawless. 'The advertising endeavours to spark a debate by challenging people's perceptions about what constitutes beauty,' said Lever Fabergé, the company that owns the beauty brand.

With the change in legislation the 50+ are also not seen as old in the eyes of the EU and other government bodies. Your challenge is how to change these stereotypes and work effectively and possibly in new ways with this group. Some organizations are already doing this successfully.

3. BELIEFS AND HABITS

What is happening in a person's 'inner' world of thinking will impact on their behaviour and communication. What we see is their behaviour and not the thinking inside. If one is going to truly communicate with people and enable them to change it is necessary to understand what lies behind the words. Without this, misunderstandings occur that can lead to sabotage-type behaviour and conflict.

The more we understand why others respond in the way they do, the easier it is to communicate with them. When we communicate with individuals all we see is the external behaviour and activity. However, this is driven by internal mechanisms such as thinking, emotions, beliefs and expectations.

The model below 'Beliefs to actions' demonstrates a process from which beliefs and personal values lead to thoughts and expectations, which, in turn, have associated emotions. How a person is feeling emotionally will influence their behaviour – for example, if a person is feeling anxious they will communicate or make a decision very differently to the way they would if they were feeling confident. Ultimately, therefore, this process drives the action a person will take.

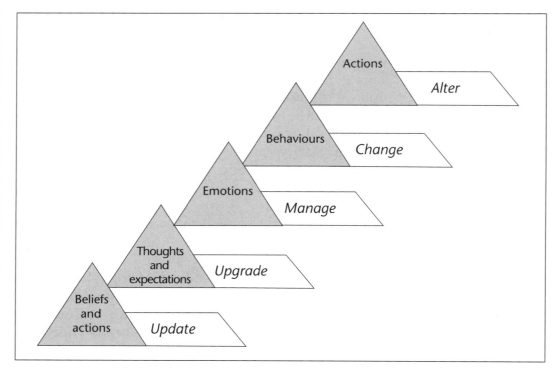

Figure 5.1   Beliefs to actions

In managing an older worker it is helpful to understand that their beliefs were influenced and inspired by their parents and the world they grew up in. It was very different to today's world, as we discussed in Chapter 4 Understanding Your Older Workforce.

Some people find it easy to update beliefs and to upgrade expectations to meet today's situation and manage associated emotions; others are simply set in a state of fixed perspectives and may need help to let go of these and accept the circumstances they are facing today.

Everyone has their own set of values and beliefs. From day one each person will have had a vast number of experiences, learnt many lessons, and heard opinions given as facts from parents, teachers, bosses and other significant individuals. All this information is stored in the brain and called upon when needed. As children we are taught ways of responding and these become automatic and are often used without conscious intent.

For example, if as a child you learnt that being late is a sign of disrespect, your immediate response whenever someone is late for a meeting is to be instinctively irritated and dismissive rather than finding out the reasons. The values that are instilled into people as children are different in different generations. Unless these are talked about and understood there can be constant misunderstandings.

The brain builds habits of thinking and behaviour. Understanding the way that the brain is programmed to build habits of thought and behaviour may shed some insight into the behaviours of people you may perceive to be 'stuck'. The fact is that from the moment of birth the brain evolves to build neural habits of thought. When a person learns a new skill, or thinks a thought frequently the brain takes this information and programmes it into its unconscious so that it becomes 'automatic'. This tends to result in the person believing that this is the 'right' way to do something; or that their way of looking at a situation is the 'right' way of doing so; or that a statement they believe in or have heard from childhood is the 'truth' although in fact it may simply be a learned opinion.

The series of diagrams below demonstrate how the brain is designed to build habits of thinking and behaviour.

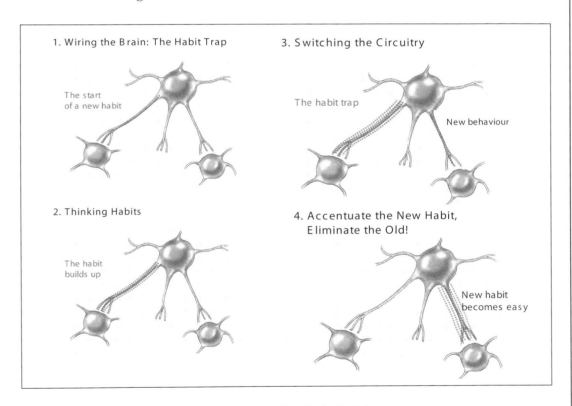

Figure 5.2   The brain's habit trap

You will see from this that if you wish people to change you need to reinforce the new habits regularly or the brain will draw people unconsciously back to the old and comfortable way of thinking or behaving.

In introducing the Age Discrimination Regulations you will want to help people to change attitudes, emotions, thoughts, behaviours and actions in many different people and it may help you to bear in mind that repetition and reinforcement of your key messages will be necessary if you are to do this successfully.

4. THE POWER OF INTENTION

As Adelaide Stephenson said: 'We judge ourselves by our intentions and others by their behaviours'. If one is truly going to communicate with people and enable them to change it is necessary to understand what lies behind the words. It is precisely these misunderstandings that lead to sabotage behaviours and conflicts. In order for there to be good communication, both parties need to seek to understand what is going on in the other person's inner world.

Trying to understand the intentions beneath the behaviours is not always easy but it is usually worthwhile. The following diagrams show how differently individuals can view a situation. These thoughts affect how they react and the outcome.

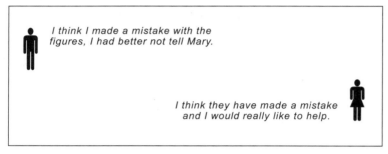

I think I made a mistake with the figures, I had better not tell Mary.

I think they have made a mistake and I would really like to help.

Figure 5.3   Inner thoughts

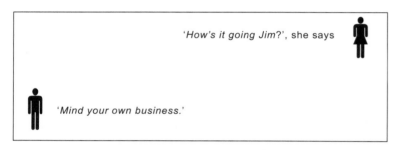

'How's it going Jim?', she says

'Mind your own business.'

Figure 5.4   Conversation

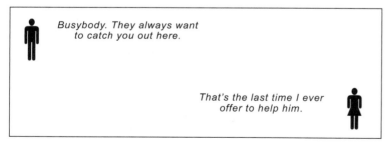

Busybody. They always want to catch you out here.

That's the last time I ever offer to help him.

Figure 5.5   More inner thoughts

The result is that Jim is not supported and doesn't feel able to ask for help. Mary becomes defensive and unwilling to help and firms up her belief that the older worker can't learn new tasks. Both of them think the other is rather difficult and avoid spending time together even though they are in the same team and working closely together would improve productivity. Mary's question comes from a positive intention to offer Jim some help and feedback on how he is doing. However, their assumptions lead to misunderstandings.

5. BELIEFS TO EXPECTATIONS

Beliefs lead to expectations of oneself, other people or situations in general. For example an expectation of yourself might be:

I should be able to achieve a distinction in my professional certificate and if I don't I have not come up to my own expectation of myself and I shall not think so highly of myself.

Your expectation of someone else might be:

My boss should have given me a bonus because I worked really hard last year and it is unfair that this was not recognized.

Your expectation of a situation might be:

People should wear ties to work and if they don't they are unprofessional.

Equally, if your mother was good at mathematics your expectation of yourself might have been, 'I should be able to do maths'. Her expectation of you may also have been, 'My children should be able to do maths because I can do it.' If your father was a banker he may well have expected that you also become a banker. You may then have felt guilty if you did not do what he expected – leading to an expectation of yourself such as, 'I should have become a banker but I really wanted to go into design.'

Of course every single person in the world has their own very unique set of beliefs and expectations and, as you are no doubt aware, conflict arises when two people with differing expectations are trying to work together and do not give respect for their different viewpoints. Some people are absolutely rigid in some belief systems seeing their belief/way of looking at things as *the* right and only way to manage a situation. These people can tend to become judgemental and critical of others.

Fixed expectations can be the problem …

'*I* think this is the right way to do it so they *should* do it this way too.'

What are YOU expecting of:
1. *Yourself?*
2. *Other people?*
3. *The situation itself?*

Alternative:
'I would prefer it if they behaved this way … but I can manage it if they don't!'

Figure 5.6 Fixed expectations

6. STRATEGIES AND EXERCISES TO CHALLENGE STEREOTYPES

As has been explained, all opinions are formed through the combination of external experience, messages received from others and your own personal response. These become both individual and cultural beliefs rather than reality. It is important that you challenge stereotypes and help people to change their attitudes and perspectives. Unless this occurs true change will not happen.

The information and exercises in this chapter are designed to help you to challenge and change attitudes within your organization.

SUMMARY AND TIPS

This chapter has highlighted the necessity for changing organizational attitudes and beliefs about the older worker. It will be essential to treat all workers, whatever their age, equally within every business activity. However, more than that, the effects of feeling ignored, sidelined and less able will affect individual performance and will leave you with a large part of your workforce not working at full capacity. In the light of the demographics, as previously discussed, businesses will, over the next 10 years, find themselves with a large percentage of people previously perceived as 'old'; the over 50s. In order to maximise business productivity, this attitudinal work needs to be done at an early stage as it will take time to embed.

Changing beliefs and challenging stereotypes is the foundation stone for any change. We take actions and make decisions 'on automatic ' due to our beliefs. Our beliefs drive us and negative beliefs will lead us to negative situations. If you, as the person responsible for the change in working practices, are able to help your colleagues to change their beliefs you will put your organization into a strong position to manage the future. See more on this subject in Chapter 6 on People Management.

Six tips

1. **Identify the stereotypes and assumptions that exist in your business.**

2. **Analyse how frequently age is a factor within problem situations.**

3. **Ensure everyone knows that stereotypical assumptions about age will become illegal with the new Regulations.**

4. **Identify specific business benefits to your organization of changing assumptions around age.**

5. **Include change-belief work and stereotyping in management training.**

6. **Broadcast the added value brought by your older workers.**

CONSIDER THE CULTURE IN YOUR ORGANIZATION

One of the first things you will need to do to develop an age-neutral culture is identify what stereotypical thinking exists within your organization around age. The following questionnaire will help you consider this. You can give this to individuals or groups within your organization:

Reproduced from *Age Matters* by Keren Smedley and Helen Whitten, Gower Publishing, 2006.

73

CONSIDER THE CULTURE OF YOUR ORGANIZATION

Questionnaire

To what extent do the following statements reflect stereotypical attitudes within your organization?

Ring one of the answers either: True, False, or Don't Know for each question

Older people:

are more reliable at work	True	False	Don't know
are difficult to teach new tricks	True	False	Don't know
don't like changing	True	False	Don't know
are experiencing memory loss	True	False	Don't know
stay in the same job for years	True	False	Don't know
think they have 'seen it all before'	True	False	Don't know
don't like being managed by a younger person	True	False	Don't know
expect to be listened to just because of their age	True	False	Don't know
dismiss younger people's ideas	True	False	Don't know
are stubborn	True	False	Don't know
think they 'know it all'	True	False	Don't know
think they should be able to retire at 60	True	False	Don't know
take more sickness leave	True	False	Don't know

The following questions help you to identify these more specifically:

How are stereotypes exhibited within your organization?

What are the myths existing in your organization?

How are older workers talked about?

What are the taboos?

What action might you need to take to address any of these?

Develop an action plan to challenge the stereotypical thinking.

Questionnaire interpretation

If you have marked any as true, there are stereotypical attitudes in you company.

DRAWING – STEREOTYPING

This exercise can be carried out individually or in a group in order to identify people's initial stereotypical thinking on age.

 Handout 5.2

STEREOTYPING

a) Draw a picture of an older person in the space below.

b) When the picture has been drawn, if working in a group, divide into pairs and consider the following:

- Does the picture depict somebody real?

- In the workplace or outside the workplace?

- Efficient or inefficient?

- With a good or a bad memory?

- Somebody fit or stooped?

- Lively or boring?

- Why did you draw that picture?

- When did you first form images of an older person?

- How true are they of today's older person?

c) Come back to the whole group and share the answers from part (b) and discuss the following questions.

- Is holding this stereotype helpful for you both in the workplace and outside?

- What do you need to do in order to change this image?

- Can you identify 2–3 older people who do not fit your stereotypical picture?

- What role models can you think of as a substitute?

d) Create a plan of action based on your answers.

 Exercise 5.3

CHALLENGING BELIEFS

Step One
This type of exercise will be very useful to you when you are changing attitudes towards the older worker within your organization. People of all ages can experience 'stuck' beliefs that are limiting and negative. For example, a young worker may assume that their manager who is over 50 will be difficult and like their parents, and an older worker may assume the same about a younger worker.

CHALLENGING BELIEFS

Step One

Think of a time when you had a belief, such as 'Father Christmas was real' or 'Girls aren't as clever as boys' and then it changed.

What helped you to change your belief? Was it another person's comments; was it something you read; was it something you saw; something you heard; something that you noticed; something that just intuitively didn't feel right any more, or did you believe it because your parents believed it had to be true? It may have been a number of these.

Step Two

Now think of a 'stuck' belief you have that is no longer doing you any good, for example 'you will always be achy after 50' or 'my memory will go downhill when I am 40', or 'younger managers aren't supportive of the older worker'. Think of what you would like to believe.

For example, 'I will be fit and energetic after I'm 50.'

'My memory will stay at full capacity as I age.'

'My age makes no difference to the support I get.'

Step Three

Now think of the strategy that you used to change the belief in Step One and see whether you can apply the same strategy to the 'stuck' belief you have in Step Two. This is likely to require you to go into the same mental, physical, emotional state that you were in previously, to help you open more doors of perception. In order to create this state think of the situation as if it was happening now. Associate into it and feel the feelings right now, it can help when thinking about the situation to use present verbs rather than past. For example, I see, I feel, I hear. For example take yourself back to when you saw your mother/grandmother win Scrabble and you knew she was as clever as your father and say to yourself: I see my mother at the board making a 30-word score. I feel proud and I hear my Dad saying 'you are clever'.

Step Four

Now apply this strategy to your stuck belief. As you do this you will find that the belief shifts and the new belief takes its place.

VALUES AND ATTITUDES EXERCISE

This is an exercise that can be done with a group of mixed ages and could be used very productively with a team, where there are issues amongst team members that may well be age-related.

Allocate a room with plenty of clear space. Label each corner of the room with a poster: one says 'Agree'; one 'Disagree'; one 'Strongly Agree'; one 'Strongly Disagree'.

Ask all the participants to stand up in the middle of the room. Explain that you, as a facilitator, are going to call out a statement and they should move to whichever corner of the room reflects their opinion of the statement.

After they have moved to the corner ask them to have a brief chat with the person standing next to them as to what has brought them to that corner.

Ask them to move to somebody in a different corner and discuss briefly with them why they are where they are.

At the end of the round ask them to get back into the middle and repeat until you have completed the exercise with all the statements you have chosen to include.

At the end of the session bring the group together for a plenary session to discuss what they have discovered about values and attitudes concerning these statements.

Follow this up by recording ideas of what the group think needs to be done (a) within the team (b) individually (c) within the organization to address any issues that may have arisen.

Statements can include:

1. 50 year olds are past it and too old to train.
2. 50 year olds nowadays are cooler and younger than they were.
3. Young people learn more quickly than older people.
4. Most older people are technophobes.
5. You have to be under 40 to be ambitious.
6. Training is more widely available to anyone under 45.
7. It is difficult to get promotion once you are over 45.
8. Nobody wants to employ anyone over 55.
9. There is an unspoken grey ceiling within this organization.
10. It is difficult to get on in this organization because old people never leave and hog the jobs.
11. Most people are desperate to retire as early as possible.
12. It is difficult for older and younger workers to work together.

CHAPTER 6

People Management

Bill and Mary, two senior managers, have asked for a meeting with Sally from HR. Bill and Mary are at a loss. They both have male workers in their late 50s whom they believe are only there for the money, have no interest in anything related to their business other than creating trouble through negative gossip. They know that they can no longer suggest early retirement but unfortunately their performance is not quite bad enough to start disciplinary proceedings. However, the present situation is untenable. Bill and Mary believe that they have done everything they can to motivate these two people and are coming to Sally to see if she can help find a legal way to encourage these two people to leave the company. Sally listens to their story and acknowledges their feelings and frustrations. She says to them, 'I am glad you have come to talk to me about this because this is my job. People are my business. I couldn't begin to do the stuff that you do – it is really important that we share our knowledge.'

She realizes that they believe that they have covered every avenue of performance management but, based on her own expertise, she is certain that there are other things that can be done to get these two back on board. Sally explains that, 'Getting good performance out of a human being is similar to getting the most out of a highly tuned racing car. If you want a racing car to go the distance at speed you wouldn't think twice about spending time and money in keeping it at its peak. That means the right support team, the best fuel and tuning and a highly trained driver who understands their machine. A human being is far more subtle and complicated than a machine. However, as we all know, people do need fuel. Have you ever,' she asks them, 'found yourself without time for lunch and by 3-o'clock being tired and grumpy and unable to think straight?'

Bill laughs, 'Do you know I do that about three times a week and then I have to apologize for being snappy!'

'Well, your two workers are no different to you Bill. They may appear to be different but they will have the same basic needs. Our job is to find out how you can get those needs met and find out whether they are emotional, physical or practical.'

'That makes sense Sally,' says Mary, 'but how do we do that because I really am stuck?'

Sally replies, 'Well that is where I and the training team come in. We can really help you with these skills.'

Bill says 'I'm on for that as well, with the agreement that we give it six months and if things haven't begun to change, we talk again.'

Possible outcomes

If Bill and Mary had not gone to see Sally the likelihood is that relationships between managers and staff would become increasingly strained. One of them may well have gone off sick and grievances or disciplinary action may have been taken. Having talked to Sally, who has studied people management, it is quite probable that the situation will change and relationships will improve. Very often all that is needed is a new approach to the problem and seeing the situation from the other person's perspective. If things don't work at first everybody will have a greater understanding of one another so as to work more cohesively towards finding a solution that benefits all.

Having looked at the law, demographic change and the social issues facing the older worker this chapter will focus on how you can maximize the potential of this group through understanding how they operate.

There are some straightforward and well tried and tested models that can help managers to understand and empathize with their colleagues and direct reports in order to make a useful relationship, work effectively together and get the most from their staff. Without this building block of knowledge, policies will fail. If the Age Employment Regulations are to be implemented successfully it will be helpful to take some time to read this section to understand how to integrate policy and behaviour.

This chapter gives you the essential building blocks in an easy-to-use pack as applied specifically to managing the older worker. Many of the techniques talked about can also be used with any of your workforce. The focus of this book is on the older workforce.

The topics covered in this chapter includes:

1. Self-knowledge
    –   Herrmann Thinking Preference model
    –   Motivation
    –   Transactional analysis.

2. Self-management
    –   Emotional intelligence
    –   Positive thinking.

3. Interpersonal skills
    –   Non-verbal communication
    –   Listening
    –   Empathy
    –   Questions
    –   Negotiation.

1. SELF-KNOWLEDGE

Self-knowledge is key to success. A person needs to understand what makes them tick, and how their own behaviour impacts other people. It is very easy to assume, when we are having difficulties communicating or managing someone, that it is 'all their fault'. It takes two to tango! Therefore the more a manager can understand themselves and others the better they are likely to manage.

It is important for you, in your HR role, to recognize that many of your older managers and staff will not have been brought up in a world where understanding psychology was commonplace. The explosion of self-help and psychological books has occurred since the mid-1980s, so many of your older workers will not have been brought up on these. You may therefore find that they are resistant to this way of thinking and consider it irrelevant to business, or 'psycho babble'. If this is the case, it is important to consider the individual's needs and styles, and explain any of the psychological models in a format that demonstrates either personal or business benefit. This section will offer you some ways of developing self-knowledge in an easy but practical format.

Herrmann Thinking Preference model

The Herrmann Thinking Preference model is a metaphoric model of how the brain operates. It is based on neuroscience and physiology. This model focuses on the brain's thinking functions although the whole brain is, of course, more complex.

The model was designed specifically to help individuals appreciate difference within teams and is a very easy and effective system for self-analysis. Once understood it will really help you to very quickly pick out individual styles and drivers of behaviour, so that you can understand their motivators and communicate more effectively with them. It is important for you to do these exercises yourself first, so that you understand the concepts and purpose of this model.

✎ Exercise 6.1

Your role as an HR person is to create an environment where successful communication can take place. This means that it will often be up to you to educate and enlighten people on these topics. You may need to mediate between a manager and a member of staff who are finding it difficult to understand each other. Using the Herrmann model and enabling them to understand where the other is coming from can be essential to a positive outcome.

The questionnaire in Exercise 6.1 looks at your preferences. You need to do this now. It does not look at your capabilities. We are all capable of working in each of the quadrants at different times. What it does mean is that for most of us when we are stressed and finding life difficult we revert to our more automatic way of behaviour, which is normally in our preferred thinking quadrant.

This can cause problems when you are working with someone who thinks differently from you and you are seeking a way to understand what they are saying. In these situations it is really useful to use this model to step back and think about how one person's thinking style may miscommunicate with another's. You can use the questionnaire to explore and explain how people can learn to respect and value different perspectives and approaches.

In our scenario, one of the reasons that Mary and Bill may be finding it difficult to achieve common ground with their staff is that they are coming at it from a very different direction. Let us imagine that Bill is a dominant D-type thinker and focuses on the big picture, conceptual ideas and has continually changing visions; and his direct report is a B-quadrant thinker who thinks ideas through carefully, plans, knows the set procedures and never starts something that they won't be able to complete. These different approaches can lead to difficulties and misunderstandings as they appear to have completely different aspirations and motivational drives.

Once they understand each other they can find a common language and also realize that the behaviour is not necessarily being done intentionally to wind the other person up but is simply their preferred style. Through this they can really learn to value each other's difference, and use each other's strengths.

Motivation

The Herrmann model can also help you to look at and understand different people's motivators.

Take a moment now to think for yourself of a piece of work that you have completed recently that you really enjoyed doing and were keen to work on.

- What gave you satisfaction?

Now think of a piece of work that you did because you had to but did not enjoy it:

- What made you dissatisfied?

When people are in a position of motivating others, it is easy to assume that what motivates them will motivate others. Therefore they offer that incentive to the other person, rather than finding out what motivates the other person. It is like when somebody buys you a birthday present that is absolutely their taste but clearly if they had thought for five minutes it is not yours!

For example, there is no point giving someone share options if what really gives them a buzz is a harmonious working environment. Nor in giving someone routine repetitive work if they are a person who enjoys change and challenge.

In our scenario Bill clearly does not understand what motivates his member of staff. If he were to become aware that the reason why the staff member is doing the minimum is because of Bill's habit of continually introducing new initiatives he would have the option to change his behaviour to meet his needs. His direct report is a B Quadrant thinker and wants to work in a planned, procedural way towards getting results (Figure 6.1). Bill's behaviour results in him having three uncompleted pieces of work in his 'To Do' tray, and this completely demotivates him. Bill's preference for innovation has left the staff member grumbling about 'what is the point of doing anything around here if we can't have time to finish it?' Neither party is understanding the other.

If Bill can be helped to see that his own preferred style of working is demotivating his colleague and that when he introduces new solutions he needs to spend some time explaining why it is operationally beneficial, how it will enhance results, acknowledge how irritating it must be to change course, he will begin to find a way to manage this difference successfully. The MindMap below gives some pointers towards the different types of motivators that will help a manager to get the most out of their staff, whatever their age.

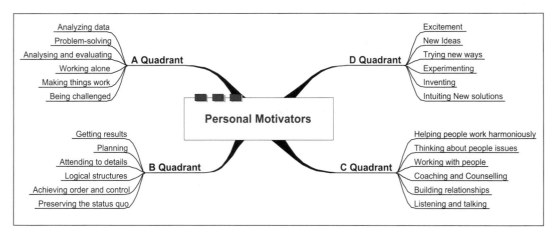

Figure 6.1   Personal motivators

For example a coachee of ours, who was a C Quadrant Managing Director nearly left her job because she felt that the relationship with her boss had deteriorated. She felt undervalued and although she still enjoyed the practical work, she was on the point of leaving until the HR Department suggested coaching. It turned out that her boss was an A quadrant thinker who had been totally unaware of her problems and was less interested than her in maintaining the harmonious relationship. Once he understood her needs he adapted his behaviour and made a point of coming into her office every so often to ensure that she felt valued and supported by him.

In another case a D Quadrant thinker was going to leave because his job had become too routine and although he was an expert in his field he was seeking new challenges. Fortunately his manager recognized this and was able to give him a new project that enabled him to innovate and develop new ways of servicing clients. In both these instances the organization managed to retain demotivated staff through applying the Herrmann profile to performance problems.

The Herrmann model is a practical tool that most people find easy to understand and can be enlightening to any manager trying to understand a member of staff. Whilst the model can be explored in greater detail, the information above, and referred to at different points of this book, should give individuals and managers sufficient information to begin to understand some of these subtleties of communication and how these can be applied to really make a difference to performance.

Transactional analysis

In managing an intergenerational workforce people's chronological age does not necessarily equate to the position they have in the organization. This can lead to difficulties in relationships. Situations can occur where the young person sees their older manager as a parental figure and the manager sees the young person as a child.

Equally in situations where the manager is years younger than their direct report, there can be difficulties in reconciling this with the natural order of life where the older person is generally in charge for example, teacher and pupil. For example in a large construction company we have worked with, the new graduate recruits, who are mainly young, all start at a managerial level. The majority of the staff they manage are twenty plus years their senior. Many of these young managers expressed concern, during an appraisal training, about performance managing an older more experienced person. Most thought, 'How can I discuss a performance issue with someone like my Mum?' They will think, 'What a nerve for that young whippersnapper telling me how I should do this: I have done it for 25 years!' Chapter 13 Intergenerational Working discusses this in more detail.

The responses above can be understood using a psychological model created by Eric Berne called Transactional Analysis (TA). It suggests that within each one of us we have a parent part, an adult part and a child part whether we are 2 or 102. These are known as ego states. Each ego state has specific behaviours that are associated with it. Each one of us has parts of our personality which surface and affect our behaviour according to different circumstances.

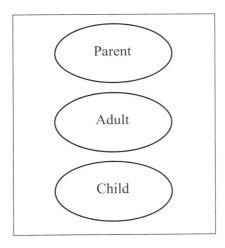

Figure 6.2   Ego states

The parent

The parent is our ingrained voice of authority, absorbed conditioning, learning and attitudes from when we were young. We are conditioned by our real parents, teachers, older people, next door neighbours, aunts and uncles, who teach us our beliefs and values. Our parent is formed by all the external events and influences upon us as we grew up. The parent has two parts that can both be subdivided into the positive part and the not so positive part:

Caring – nurturing and spoiling

Controlling – structuring and critical

The adult

The adult is our ability to think and determine action for ourselves, based on received data. The adult is straight forward and non-emotional unlike the parent and child. It draws on the resources of both the other ego states to help us make informed decisions.

The child

The child is our internal reaction and feelings to external events. This is the seeing, hearing, feeling, and emotional body of data within each of us. When anger or despair dominates reason, the child is in control.

The child has several parts to it; the adapted part that is co-operative and wants to please; the rebellious resistant part that is not so positive; the free spontaneous part that can have fun and enjoy and be creative; and the immature part that can't see reason.

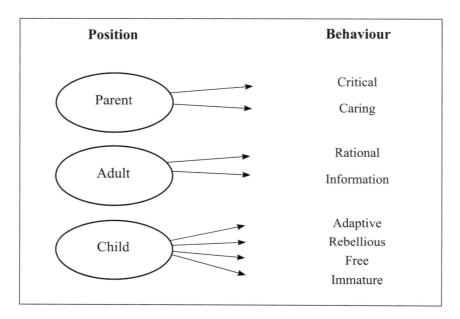

Figure 6.3   Behavioural aspects of TA

In summary:

*   Parent is our 'taught' concept of life.

*   Adult is our 'thought' concept of life.

*   Child is our 'felt' concept of life.

We communicate from one of our ego states, our Parent, Adult or Child. Our feelings at the time determine which one we use, and at any time something can trigger a shift both from one state to another and from one part of the state to another. When we respond, we are also doing this from one of the three states.

When communicating, one person can be communicating from their parent part whilst the other person can be communicating from their child part.

This can lead to miscommunication. As with thinking styles we each tend to operate from a preferred state, especially when stressed and also within different environments and contexts, these may not always serve us well.

For most of us our intention on a daily basis is to behave in an adult manner and to be rational and logical. However these other states can be triggered unconsciously by something that is said or a particular stance that another person takes. The response then becomes automatic and the person can be unaware that they have choices in how they behave. If people are going to change this, it is essential that one or other party in the communication moves into the adult position, this will draw the other into the adult state as well. If the response is 'it's not fair, why should I do it?' remind yourself who normally says 'it's not fair' – the under fives!

In the work environment the only people physically present are adults although not all of them will be operating from their adult state all of the time. We are going to take a look at the effect this can have in the workplace.

As has been discussed parents can be critical and also can be caring. There are times when it is absolutely appropriate to respond in one of these ways but sometimes through habit people fall into this position when it is totally inappropriate. For example, this can happen when a colleague does something that you don't understand. 'Telling them off' as a critical parent might create a negative response. Children respond to parents and so it is likely that their child position will be triggered and they will respond either as an 'adapted' child who wants to please and make amends with the parent or authority figure; or, as the rebellious child who tells you to get lost!

Parents often fall into the trap of assuming that they know it all and that children don't have any sensible ideas. All of us know that there are times when young people intuitively make very wise statements and others when their innocent vision creates innovative ideas. It is important to open the minds of some of your older workers to the fact that young people have equally good ideas themselves.

Unless something out of the ordinary happens, such as somebody falls down the stairs where it is appropriate to move into parental 'caring' state and look after them, the appropriate state for people in the workplace needs to be adult-to-adult. Even if people look and are 20 years younger than you or older than you they are still adults at work.

The adult position, as explained earlier, is non-emotional and non-judgemental. It is objective and rational, without being cold. Adults assess the situation in the present rather than being pulled into old and stuck ways of responding. Behaviour from this ego state is referred to as assertive behaviour.

The OK Corral

Another useful model from transactional analysis theory. This is known as the OK Corral. When we are born, unless there has been a specific birth trauma, we arrive in this world at peace with others and ourselves. We are likely to perceive the world from the perspective of I am OK and you are

OK. We then all start experiencing the world and trying to make sense of it. Children have limited resources for managing difficult situations and will move into different quadrants of the corral to protect themselves. For example, if someone was treated punitively, talked down to, and not made to feel secure as a child they may begin to believe 'I am not OK and you are OK'. This might be the only sense they can make of their experiences. If however they were picked on and bullied as a child they may have learnt that the only way to survive was to bully others. This may have made them feel stronger and in control, and they may believe 'I am OK and you are not OK'.

Others may have had the experience where they know the other person is being unpleasant, but they don't believe in themselves, and are lacking in self-confidence. They are likely to believe, 'I'm not OK and nor are you'.

These positions are perceptions of the world. The reality is 'I just am' and 'You just are', therefore how I view others and myself are just 'views' not facts. However, many of us behave as though they are facts. Feeling OK is having respect, confidence and self-belief. Feeling not OK is the absence of respect, confidence and self-belief. The chart below sets out the possible patterns of communication.

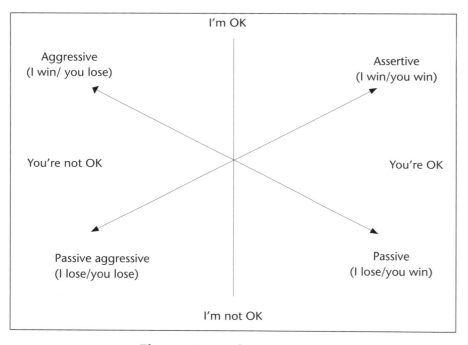

Figure 6.4   The OK Corral

As we have seen earlier, the effectiveness of our communication depends on which ego state we are in. Adult interactions produce adult responses and the basis of good adult communication is from a stance of 'I'm OK, you're OK'.

It can be particularly difficult for older workers to stay in the adult mode when they are chronologically older than many of their colleagues and some of their managers. This situation goes against the natural order of family life and therefore needs particular care and attention.

As the HR manager, enabling staff and managers to understand this model can, in our experience, make an enormous difference. Often one of the best ways to alleviate the tension is for people to acknowledge that these transactions do exist in everyday life and even to make jokes about it. For example, 'I know you think I'm too old to have a bright idea but I've got a really good idea about how to move this department forward.' Or, when an older worker is faced with a younger manager, to listen to the idea rather than believe that they are too young to have an opinion.

2. SELF-MANAGEMENT

All of us need to learn to manage ourselves in different situations. These skills are seldom taught in school but when mastered enhance quality of life, communication and performance. Here we explore two aspects of self-management: emotional intelligence and positive thinking.

Emotional intelligence

The success of your organization lies in the emotional intelligence you manage to generate in your staff. Our definition of emotional intelligence is to:

- know what you feel;

- know why you feel it;

- acknowledge the emotion and know how to manage it;

- know how to motivate yourself and make yourself feel better;

- recognize the emotions of other people and develop empathy;

- express your feelings appropriately and manage relationships.

Emotional Intelligence is a life skill that takes a lifetime to learn! Starting people off on this journey can transform their lives. Some people have a greater intuitive understanding of how emotions affect people than others do – for example C Quadrant Herrmann thinkers.

The scientific and technical revolutions of the last century tended to overshadow emotions in favour of facts. However, the majority of today's organizations rely not upon physical strength but upon the creativity and effective thinking of their staff members for success. Every business depends on the emotional input of its staff if good relationships are to develop. They also need to build emotional relationships with customers and partners. Gaining the emotional buy-in of a customer is essential within the sales process; losing the emotional buy-in of members of staff can equally result in demotivation and sabotage behaviours. As emotions are directly influenced by thinking and as thinking is directly influenced by emotions it goes without saying that service industries in particular would benefit from an emotionally intelligent workforce. Recent research studies by Daniel Goleman and Martin Seligman have shown that emotional intelligence is actually as important as IQ for business success. For example, there are many cases in the business world of partnerships and business deals that have not succeeded because there has been no regard taken of emotions. One instance where we were involved was two small high-street solicitors who merged. On the day of the smaller group moving into the bigger company's offices, the latter chose to go out for a 'final get-together', leaving only a junior receptionist to welcome the whole of the other firm. This led to such difficult relationships that it began to affect the business and we were called in.

It is therefore worthwhile running awareness sessions and training for all members of staff, and managers in particular, on the concepts of Emotional Intelligence as well as the strategies they can learn in order to develop these skills.

Developing emotional intelligence

Encouraging your staff to develop emotional intelligence can be helpful within any age group. Although the concepts of emotional intelligence may be unfamiliar to the older workers in your organization they may well find the principles of great benefit to them as they face the inevitable changes of ageing both at home and in the workplace.

In the older workforce people are more likely to have been brought up not to show emotion or ask for help, particularly from younger people. Within the workforce there are many occasions when managers are considerably younger than some of their team and this may inhibit an older person expressing their troubles, feeling that a young person would expect them to have their problems and emotions in order by this stage of their life.

Emotions are triggered, as we explained in Chapter 5 Changing Attitudes and Stereotypes, by thoughts and expectations. Basically the emotional part of us is developed during the early part of our childhood and is linked to our ability to survive. Emotions of fear or anger give us strong messages about dangerous situations, for example. They are therefore linked to the child part that we mentioned in the previous section on Transactional Analysis.

As children we grow up wanting things to be the way we expect them to be and if they aren't we get upset. Watch any small child who does not get what they want and you will notice that they either cry or get angry. However, as they grow up they learn to control these emotions in order to be accepted within their particular community.

As adults, we still maintain this desire for life to go the way we want it to go and get upset when things don't work out that way. For this reason it is enormously important to see that expectations play a vital role in emotional response – for example, if a person expects to get a promotion because of length of service but someone younger gets the job then it is likely that the older person might feel upset. 'I SHOULD have got this promotion because I have been in the organization for a longer period.' Some people learn flexibility early in life; others continue to get unsettled when things do not turn out the way they wish them to, which results in displays of anger, tears or disappointment. Where the emotions are not managed this can result in 'emotional hijack'.

Emotional hijack

The centre of our emotional response lies within a small almond shaped area of the brain called the amygdala. This is linked to our survival mechanism and when emotions are heightened it has the ability to 'hijack' our rational thinking processes. This can lead to incidents such as 'road rage'. Emotions are essential information to a human being in terms of what they like or dislike, fear or seek, and help a person make decisions.

The situations that trigger emotional responses have changed over the generations. It is no longer likely to be a snake but more likely an irate boss, a difficult customer, a delayed train. Because the memory stores emotional experiences people can occasionally have a disproportionate response to a situation because it reminds them of something in childhood, or a situation they have experienced before. Associations can be triggered and anger released before the person has consciously considered the consequences of their actions.

Part of developing emotional intelligence is therefore to help people to become aware of their emotions, to acknowledge them and learn to understand what thoughts and expectations are triggering them.

✏ Exercise 6.2

✏ Exercise 6.3

✏ Exercise 6.4

Helping people realize that they can manage their emotions and can choose their emotional state within situations through the focus of their mind empowers people and gives them choices they may not realize they had.

Applying the ABCDE model for managing emotions

This model is based on enabling people to use their thinking skills to manage their emotions.

This is a well-recognized and tested model that enables people to manage their emotion through changing their thought or expectation.

A   Identify the situation which is triggering the emotion.

B   Identify the belief , thought or expectation that they hold about themselves, other people or the situation in general.

C   Notice the emotion – for example, stress, anger, distress.

D   Disputing the belief, thought or expectation to ensure that it is helping the person to manage the situation and support their ability to achieve their goals within the situation.

E   Exchanging a negative or unconstructive thought for a more constructive thought.

For example:

A   The situation: An older person has been notified that they will be moved to another department where they will be managed by a younger person.

B   The belief, thought or expectation that this person holds about the situation – for example, 'This is unfair; this should not be happening; I am old enough to be their father; I can't manage this situation.'

C   The emotion – for example, anger.

D   Disputing the belief, thought or expectation – for example, by three forms of questioning.

         1.   Is this belief helping you to manage this situation?

         2.   Would everyone respond in this way in this situation?

         3.   Is it logical to respond this way?

E   Exchanging the belief for a more constructive thought – for example, 'I may feel uncomfortable at first being managed by a younger person but I am sure I can work well with them step by step.'

Emotions are infectious

How one person is feeling immediately impacts those around them. If someone is depressed it tends to bring other people down; if someone is angry it can cause fear in others. One short explosion can irreparably change a relationship. Bullying and harassment have been shown to cause untold emotional damage in other people and ruin lives. Therefore helping your staff to develop empathy and understanding about the emotions of others is important. See the section 3 in this chapter on Interpersonal Skills.

To understand another person's emotions takes observation. In order to get the most out of people it helps for you to explain to managers the important role that emotions play in performance. It is also helpful to give them an understanding that if something difficult is going on in a person's life this can build up to a disproportionate response should they have to give that person critical feedback, for example. Timing is everything, as is acknowledgement of their position. This does not mean that you should not give them critical feedback, but you might consider how you might (a) express understanding and empathy for their position and (b) agree a time that would suit you both to discuss business issues.

Positive thinking

There can sometimes be an assumption that as older people generally become more grumpy and negative. This is absolutely not the case but you may occasionally have to manage an older person who has become somewhat tired with life, perhaps a little cynical and has got into a habit of negative thinking.

Positive thinking models can help individuals change their focus, ditch pessimistic ways of thinking and become more positive and optimistic.

You can enable a person to think more positively by helping them avoid generalizations such as 'everything always goes wrong' or 'we tried that before so it will never work'.

Examples of negative thinking

Generalizations such as: 'Never, Nothing, Everything, No-one, Always' can lead people to make assumptions and negative generalizations about people and situations. 'That person will never amount to anything'; 'The marketing department always send us idiotic ideas'. (See Figure 6.5.)

NEGATIVE THINKING

'Everything I do goes wrong!'

'No-one appreciates what I do.'

'*I* must have done something wrong.'

'I give up: I will never get it right.'

Figure 6.5   Negative thinking habits

Reframing negatives to positives

You can also help people to focus on the positive by asking them questions that help them to notice and observe what is going right.

What can help is to challenge negative thinkers and ask them to check how rational their viewpoint is. For example: 'What is your evidence that just because it went wrong the first time it will always go wrong?' or 'For what specific reason will this never work?' or 'Just because it didn't work then does this necessarily mean that it won't succeed now?'

PEOPLE
MANAGEMENT

Reframing language is also important. Bring people's attention to the words: 'should', 'ought to' and 'must', tend to be judgemental, subjective, critical and stressful. For example, when an older manager might give feedback to a younger colleague who has completed a task saying 'but you must carry out this task this way. This is the way it ought to be done'. Although the older person may be demonstrating a method of completing a task, they could also be seen as implicitly criticizing the way the younger person is doing the task. They are also viewing the task subjectively from their own perspective of what they consider to be the right way to do the task. This situation is very common in business and limits creativity as well as demotivating younger staff who feel they have their own way of completing tasks.

A useful model to help managers to respond in these circumstances is: 'I would prefer it if they carried out the task my way but I can manage it if they don't and we can learn from the experience. It is the outcome that matters, not the way that it is done.' This enables the person to remain confident that they can manage the situation; and to learn to focus on the agreed outcome.

Helping others to develop the ability to observe themselves, their thoughts and their language will help them to manage themselves in different situations. It is important to focus on specifics so that they realize that just because they are feeling negative it is not rational to take one situation and deduce that all other situations will be the same. See Figure 6.6.

Exercise 6.5

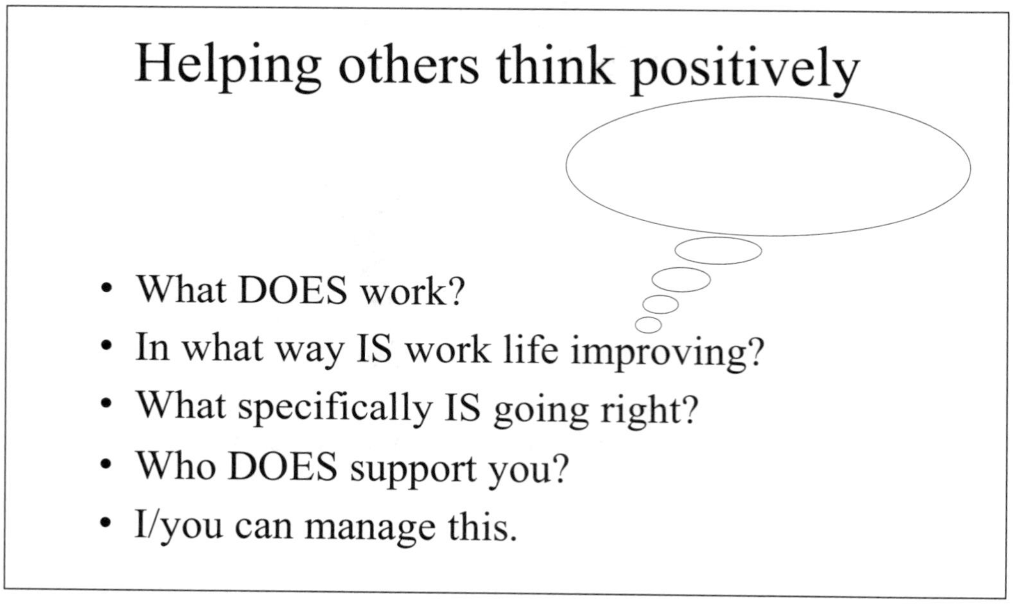

Helping others think positively

- What DOES work?
- In what way IS work life improving?
- What specifically IS going right?
- Who DOES support you?
- I/you can manage this.

Figure 6.6   Positive thinking

3. INTERPERSONAL SKILLS

Understanding yourself and the older worker is essential, as has been seen in the first two sections of this chapter. The key trick that makes all the difference is being able to communicate well so that the person you are talking to is able to feel really valued and understood. Whole books are written on this subject and if it is of interest to you they should be explored. (See the reference list at the end of the book.) The focus of this section is how can these skills help you to relate and motivate the older workers in your organization to ensure business goals are met.

Taking the scenario at the start of the chapter, in order for Bill to talk to Simon (the older worker he is having problems working with) he needs to listen to Simon and hear his viewpoint, understand what is behind the problems and then problem solve with Simon to find a solution which is good for both of them.

Non-verbal communication

When communicating, as well as communicating verbally, people communicate non-verbally. In fact the majority of the message conveyed comes through non-verbal communication such as body language and voice tone.

- Only 7 per cent of meaning is in the words spoken.

- 38 per cent of meaning is tone of voice.

- 55 per cent is in facial expression (*Source*: Albert Mehrabian).

Let's imagine Simon has agreed to come and talk to Bill about the situation.

As Simon comes in Bill watches Simon while greeting him. Bill can learn a lot about Simon's mood from his stance, tone of voice, whether there is eye contact or not, and how he greets him.

Think of a time when someone has said something and their body language did not match it. For example, you give a present to a friend and they say 'Lovely!' while they screw up their nose! You then respond with 'If you don't like it I can change it,' and they respond 'No, it is lovely.' Both of you know that this is not the case and an uncomfortable impasse is created.

Situations can arise when due to assumptions, as discussed in Chapter 5, individuals are treated non-verbally as if they are 'old'. Some of the examples we have heard are 'my manager always talks slowly and loudly to me as if I must be hard of hearing'; 'Whenever a box needs moving in the office as I go to move it some of the younger members of the team fall over themselves to stop me. They don't say anything but the message is, "You are too old to do that".'

Many of the managers we have worked with say that one of the most difficult areas to deal with is when working with someone who always tells them they will do the work, but whose body says they won't. Younger managers often report that it is the older worker who is most likely to do this. Most of us are very skilled at reading others; we are however not very skilled at talking to one another about this. The more we understand about non-verbal communication the easier it is to challenge it and to explore the real message.

PEOPLE MANAGEMENT

If, in the case of Simon, he believes that he will not be listened to, he may well think that the easiest thing to do is to agree verbally with Bill, although internally he doesn't. If Bill is tuned to more than just the words, he will be aware that there is more to it than meets the ear!

Below is a table that can help you to understand the non-verbal behaviour of others.

	Voice	Gestures	Facial expression and eye contact	Environment	Other
HINDERS	Quiet. Monotonous.	Hands in front of mouth.	Constant frowning.	Distractions – noise, visual, interruptions.	Communication that lasts too long.
	Lack of pauses. Speaking too quickly.	Dismissive gestures for example, sweeping hand.	Too much or too little eye contact.	Physical barriers.	No breaks.
	Hesitation.	Shutting out gestures for example, folding arms, crossed legs.	Constant smiling.	Too hot/cold.	Distracting clothes.
	Verbal mannerisms. Voice tailing off.		Expressions that are out of line with the words.	Chairs at different heights.	
HELPS	Clear easy to follow emphasis of key words.	Open gestures for example, palms up.	Expressions that are in step with the words.	Seating layout in line with the communication.	Short communication.
	Pauses between sentences.	Matching gestures.	Steady eye contact – not flitting, fixing or avoiding.	Free of distractions. A table for working but not as a barrier.	Frequent breaks.

Figure 6.7   Non-verbal communication

As we have said, your older workers grew up in an era where psychological theories were for the professionals and little was disseminated. Ideas about communication were neither taught nor discussed. Equally expressing emotions was generally discouraged when they were young. In fact, it was often seen as a weakness, especially for men. Many may not find it easy to express their feelings or say exactly what they mean and how they feel. They will need to be encouraged to open up without feeling they are letting themselves down.

✎ Exercise 6.6

Listening

If managers and direct reports are going to communicate with each other and make the necessary changes to improve working relationships, it is essential that they truly listen to each other. As has already been said, this involves being aware of an individual's body language.

Listening is both a skill and an approach to dealing with others. It involves being able to put yourself in the other person's shoes in order to 'hear' and intuit both what they are saying and what they are not saying. Effective listening means being able to understand what the other person is saying in the way they want it to be understood. In order to do this you have to want to understand the other person's point of view, situation and issues.

Exercise 6.7

Exercise 6.8

This can be particularly difficult when relationships are strained and the last thing you want to do as a manager is listen to the complaints or excuses from your direct reports. At times like this you have to consciously put on your listening hat and use all your skills. If someone has to say something more than twice or they repeat an action that you thought you had agreed would change, then they either haven't heard you or understood you. In both instances you need to go back to the drawing board.

Business success depends on your ability to communicate with others. Communication is a two-way process and therefore depends not only on your ability to get your point across but also on your ability to grasp the other person's point too. In fact you may often find that if you listen carefully enough the other person will end up making your point for you.

What has been said about listening is logical and should be easy though no doubt you realize that for many it is very hard. In our scenario it would be helpful for Sally to do a listening exercise with Mary and Bill so they learn how to truly listen to their staff.

If Sally is to take action to help Mary and Bill she would do well to now run through a few of the areas that may cause difficulty for them when talking to their staff. It is worth helping them to explore for themselves what might prevent them from listening effectively. Below are some examples of things that may distract and block us

- we think we know what the speaker is going to say;

- we start to evaluate or judge what the speaker is saying;

- our minds wander onto a different topic;

- we think ahead to the implications of what is being said;

- we don't like the speaker;

- we are distracted by other things going on at the same time or by the speaker's appearance or mannerisms;

- we aren't interested in either the speaker or what they are saying.

Empathy

In our scenario it is clear that neither Mary nor Bill are looking at the situation from the older worker's perspective. This is essential if you are to truly understand and develop solutions to the problem. Empathy is a very important skill in communication; it is the ability to put oneself in another's shoes, it is the understanding of the music behind the words.

Exercice 6.9

The exercise in this section enables you to experience and practise some of the feelings associated with being empathetic.

Managers can also use these communication exercises in their teams. It is a very helpful way to begin to learn about team members' body language and what really matters to them. For some members of the team this kind of team exercise can be an easier way to express their feelings than being asked directly.

Questions

If Bill and Mary are going to find out what the issues are for their staff they are going to have to ask questions. It is important to gather the right information and this means asking the right questions. It is very easy to ask questions that are not useful when we are keen to gather information or are feeling concerned about the subject. It is also important, as has been discussed earlier, to be in your adult state. A key skill lies in your ability to avoid closed questions and ask only those which open up or stretch understanding.

Some questions close down or lead the person to the questioner's conclusions. These are known as closed questions, they will not give you the necessary useful information to help the individual to find a more effective way forward. Others open up the conversation and illuminate. These are known as open questions. Questions which are open will indicate to the person being questioned that you are listening and following, rather than trying to lead them to your own conclusions.

For example: If you ask a disgruntled older worker: 'Are you OK?' or 'Are you finding your work OK?' You will get a yes or no answer. This is a closed question and generally gets a one-word response of yes or no. It is often the case that the person says yes, as they are not keen to get into a dialogue, there is little you can do, except know you have not got to the bottom of it!

If, however, you ask 'How are you finding work?' or 'What are your views/ feelings about your work?' these are open questions because the person is encouraged to answer and, even if brief, will give you more than yes or no. This gives you information which enables you to move the conversation on.

Exercice 6.10

The exercise in this section will help clarify the differences between open and closed questions and show the importance of focusing on the other person.

Negotiations

Many situations require compromise on the part of both the manager and the worker. Let us imagine that one of the reasons an older staff member is not working to full capacity is because they have an elderly ill mother for whom they are trying to arrange care. They have asked if they can come in two hours late and leave an hour early each day to manage this. This is not company policy and although it can be agreed for a short period, it is not going to be a long-term solution. The member of staff is adamant this is what she wants and should be given. In order to find a way to solve a situation such as this, good negotiating skills will be needed. Negotiating means finding a win/win solution that suits you both.

If they are going to find a solution they need to follow these steps:

1. Agree joint aims and make sure that both parties want to find a solution. If one party is not interested then different procedures will have to come into play.

2. The individuals must have mutual respect for the principle of the other having a different view, and seek to understand, as much as to be understood.

3. Agree common ground and agree they want to agree.

4. Both make concessions as trade-offs.

5. Be open and clear and not defensive and evasive when stating plans, intentions and motivations.

6. Avoid being negative and displaying feelings deliberately that they know will cause difficulty.

7. Move towards adopting the other person's terminology and viewpoints.

A possible solution to the situation outlined would be that the staff member took the time needed, whilst the situation was in crisis and a plan was made to enable them to go on managing the situation whilst doing a full day's work. For example, if they started half an hour late they could deal with any issue that had arisen overnight and make it up by taking only a half an hour lunch break.

One of the reasons many negotiations do not work is because people approach it from their child or parent state and not from their adult state. The handout provides a list of questions, which are useful to use as preparation to ensure you are in the adult position.

SUMMARY AND TIPS

This chapter has explored a number of different people management issues. All of the ideas discussed are important if you are going to understand and master working effectively with an intergenerational workforce.

Our focus has been on strategies that will help you to work with the older workers in your organizations. This group are more likely to be having difficulties because of all the issues outlined and are less likely to have been exposed to the psychological theories outlined or to have learnt the appropriate skills. It is often helpful to teach staff about these theories before a situation arises so they have the necessary skills to overcome these difficulties without intervention from either HR or their manager.

If everyone is talking a common language you are halfway to solving the problem.

Six tips

1. **Make sure you understand the psychological models discussed in this chapter.**

2. **Practise the exercises with some colleagues so you are really familiar with these.**

3. **Create some training material and handouts that can be used by you or the managers.**

4. **Set up some management training sessions for your managers and teach them these skills.**

5. **Set up training groups for some of your older workers.**

6. **Evaluate if learning these skills helps communication. If it does add these into your induction programme for new staff so you are all talking the same language.**

 Exercise 6.1

THINKING PREFERENCES

This exercise will help you to introduce the concept of thinking preference to the target groups within your organization. The activity enables people to start to identify their own thinking preference and to consider how it influences personal motivation, communication and network performance. For further information on the Herrmann Brain Dominance Instrument (HBDI) Profile see the next page.

THINKING PREFERENCES

Look at the lists of words below and circle the SUBJECTS that most interest you. Circle 5 if it is most like you, 1 if it is least like you.

If you are working with a group ask the participants to discuss their results with one another after you have explained the theory. If working alone, the coach will discuss this with the individual.

A		D	
Mathematical	1 2 3 4 5	Adaptable	1 2 3 4 5
Accurate	1 2 3 4 5	Vision	1 2 3 4 5
Competition	1 2 3 4 5	Change	1 2 3 4 5
Invest	1 2 3 4 5	Conceptual	1 2 3 4 5
Technical	1 2 3 4 5	Dynamic	1 2 3 4 5
Financial	1 2 3 4 5	Enterprise	1 2 3 4 5
Detailed	1 2 3 4 5	Big picture	1 2 3 4 5
Rational	1 2 3 4 5	New ideas	1 2 3 4 5
Critical	1 2 3 4 5	Innovation	1 2 3 4 5
Analytical	1 2 3 4 5	Entrepreneurial	1 2 3 4 5
Engineering	1 2 3 4 5	Creative	1 2 3 4 5
Sciences	1 2 3 4 5	Sales	1 2 3 4 5
Pricing	1 2 3 4 5	Breaking rules	1 2 3 4 5
Reality	1 2 3 4 5	Future-oriented	1 2 3 4 5
Reward	1 2 3 4 5	Design	1 2 3 4 5
B		C	
Integrity	1 2 3 4 5	Coaching	1 2 3 4 5
Bureaucracy	1 2 3 4 5	Harmonious	1 2 3 4 5
Boundaries	1 2 3 4 5	Communicating	1 2 3 4 5
Prudent	1 2 3 4 5	Teambuilding	1 2 3 4 5
Controlled	1 2 3 4 5	Relationships	1 2 3 4 5
Procedures	1 2 3 4 5	Expressing	1 2 3 4 5
Meticulous	1 2 3 4 5	Teaching	1 2 3 4 5
Organizing	1 2 3 4 5	Mentoring	1 2 3 4 5
Writing	1 2 3 4 5	Encouraging	1 2 3 4 5
Tenacious	1 2 3 4 5	Cooperating	1 2 3 4 5
Quality standards	1 2 3 4 5	Feeling	1 2 3 4 5
Results	1 2 3 4 5	Caring	1 2 3 4 5
Systems	1 2 3 4 5	Values	1 2 3 4 5
Planning	1 2 3 4 5	Understanding	1 2 3 4 5
Dominant	1 2 3 4 5	Belonging	1 2 3 4 5

Total the numbers in each quadrant and see whether you have a dominance in one particular area of thinking. Plot your score on the scoring table.

In the diagram on the next page you will see how this model is based on the human brain. You can see how each quadrant has specific strengths.

A: Rational/Analytical	D: Creative/Speculative
1 2 3 4 5 6 7 8 9 10 11 12 13 14 15	1 2 3 4 5 6 7 8 9 10 11 12 13 14 15
B:Organized/Procedural	C: Expressive/Social
1 2 3 4 5 6 7 8 9 10 11 12 13 14 15	1 2 3 4 5 6 7 8 9 10 11 12 13 14 15

Thinking preferences scoring table

LEFT BRAIN	Thinking Preferences		RIGHT BRAIN
A Quadrant Rational/Analytical		**D** Quadrant Creative/Speculative	
Analyses		Infers	
Quantifies		Imagines	
Is logical		Speculates	
Is critical		Takes risks	
Is realistic		Is impetuous	
Likes numbers		Breaks rules	
Knows about money		Likes surprises	
Knows how things work		Is curious/plays	
B Quadrant Organizational/Procedural		**C** Quadrant Expressive/Social	
Takes preventive action		Is sensitive to others	
Establishes		Likes to teach	
Procedures		Touches a lot	
Gets things done		Is supportive	
Is reliable		Is expressive	
Organizes		Is emotional	
Is neat		Talks a lot	
Timely		Feels	
Plans			

Based on Herrmann Brain Dominance Instrument originated by Ned Herrmann

ANALYSING WHY YOU FEEL AN EMOTION

This exercise can be done either with a group or in a coaching setting.

This exercise provides a six-step process to enable an individual to identify the thoughts and expectations that trigger their emotions. Explain that thoughts and expectations stimulate emotions and that they can use this model to develop supportive thoughts whenever they experience difficult emotions in the future. Suggest that they identify a difficult situation and reflect upon the underlying thoughts and expectations they were experiencing at the time. Finally they will be asked to replace any unhelpful or irrational thoughts with constructive ones.

Taking time to reflect and evaluate on the personal process of your emotional experience can help people to realize that there are choices and options in how they respond. To avoid emotional hijack a person needs to become aware of the fact that they may lose control of their emotions if they are not aware of building constructive and calming thoughts and expectations. They also need to learn how to choose not to get hooked into the negative emotions and demanding expectations that are likely to stimulate these situations.

ANALYSING WHY YOU FEEL AN EMOTION

1. Think of a situation in which you experienced a difficult emotional response:

Situation: ....

2. Identify the emotion you experienced:

....

3. Identify whether there was a secondary emotion (for example, did you feel angry at feeling frightened?)

....

4. Consider what you were trying to achieve in this situation: what was your goal?

....

5. Write down in sentences what you were thinking and what your expectation was:

of yourself? ....
....

of other people? ....
....

of the situation in general? ....
....

6. Were your thinking and expectations helping you to manage your emotions and achieve your goal?

If not, write down what thoughts, expectations and emotions would be more rational and helpful if you were faced with this situation again in the future:

....
....

 Exercise 6.3

BREATHING ACTION TO DELAY EMOTIONAL RESPONSE

A person faced by anger can learn to pace themselves and ensure that they only respond when they feel ready to do so. Breathe in slowly counting to three and breathe out counting to six. Focus on feeling calm and confident during this process despite other people's anger or whatever the other person's emotions are. If necessary repeat this process several times until able to express themselves in a confident way.

CHOOSING POSITIVE EMOTIONS

The following process can help people to manage their emotions within any situation. You can do this on a one-to-one basis or in a group. Ask them to consider the following questions about a difficult situation they may be facing (work on future situations, not past):

- How would I prefer to think and feel?

- When did I feel like that? I can choose to feel like that now.

- Remember and visualize this experience.

- Create new thoughts, breathe, and control physiology.

- Create a mental video and imagine yourself feeling good.

- Notice intuitive signals about situations.

- Be in the moment: only worry about what is essential now.

Developing a culture where people discuss emotions and concerns and ask for support is likely to be healthier than an environment where people hide them. Communication and assertiveness skills can enable people to express their needs and seek ways of successfully working through their problems with others, without being critical or judgemental. If someone allows emotions to build up this can result in 'emotional hijack' where a person displays an outburst of emotion that they may later regret.

Reproduced from *Age Matters* by Keren Smedley and Helen Whitten, Gower Publishing, 2006.

PEOPLE
MANAGEMENT

ANCHORING A POSITIVE STATE OF MIND

When people have developed habits of negative thinking they can sometimes forget how to be positive. One way you can help them is to enable them to use the power of memory to create a positive state of mind at any time they choose.

1. Ask the person to remember a time when they had a positive state of mind. This can be at any time of their life and in any situation as the mental and physical state they feel will be the same in different environments.

2. Ask them to identify what thoughts, sounds, emotional and physical feelings they experience when they are in a positive state of mind. Ask them to describe these to you – very often as people do this they become positive. This helps them to see that the state of being positive does not have to depend upon a particular situation but can be conjured up through their memory and imagination at any time or place in their lives.

3. Now ask them to stand up and imagine that they were back in the situation they have described to you where they felt positive. Ask them to remember the situation as if they were in it today so that they relive all aspects of the internal experience of being positive. Remind them to fully associate with the event, as discussed in the Beliefs section. Ask them to identify a word that will remind them of this positive state so that they can focus on feeling positive whenever they choose.

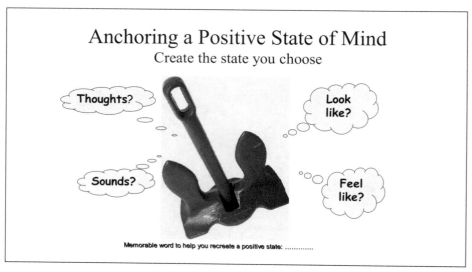

Anchoring a positive state of mind

NON-VERBAL COMMUNICATION

The following is a quick, fun exercise. Write down the words for a number of feelings on different postcards/Post-it® notes, for example, happy, grumpy, sad, content, argumentative, interested, bored.

Put the pile of cards down on a table. Ask a member of the group to pick a card and to express this emotion without words. The others have to guess the emotion. Once they have guessed ask another to pick a card. It is OK to have more than one card with the feeling on as we all express ourselves differently.

Once all the cards have been used have a discussion about non-verbal communication. How easy or difficult is it to interpret? Agree some ways to talk to people about their expressed but not spoken feelings, so that they are out in the open.

LISTENING

If you are to do this with more than two people ask the participants to get into pairs and sit opposite each other.

Ask them to label themselves A or B.

Ask A to talk about something for four minutes that interests them – if they are stuck, offer a subject such as holidays, heat waves, public transport. Tell B just to listen and say nothing.

When the four minutes are up ask B to paraphrase what A said.

Then swap roles.

Discuss with them how easy/difficult it was to retain the information and ways they could improve this.

LISTENING AND RESPONDING

This is also a pair exercise. Again ask them to label themselves A or B.

Ask the As to think of something they want to talk about and ask the Bs to come into a side room or corridor with you.

Tell the Bs that you are going to ask A to talk to them. B's role is to respond in a number of different ways.

  a) No response, that is, they are to show no interest for example, look at someone else!

  b) Look at A but make no other response.

  c) Look at A and make non-verbal responses, for example, smile, nod but no words.

  d) Respond with interest both verbally and non-verbally.

Tell B that you will call time each time they should change their behaviour.

Then swap the groups round and B now talks and A responds.

When they have both had a turn, discuss the exercise in the whole group.

Ask B if knowing that A was going to respond in a certain way stopped it affecting them. It is unlikely it has any effect. Our feelings are often triggered unconsciously, and not directly related to the present event.

LISTENING

In order to improve listening the following tips need to be followed:

- Avoid distractions. Concentrate on the speaker; watch their expressions and movements, stop phone calls, put previous or current work out of view.

- Don't assume. You'll never really understand what the speaker is saying if you make assumptions – you'll only know what you knew already. As someone once said, 'Don't assume: it makes an ASS of U and ME.'

- Don't interrupt unless they have had more than a fair hearing. Then if you must, do so diplomatically by either relating to what they have just said or even better by testing your understanding of what they have said so far, for example, 'Do you mean...?'.

- Stop talking! Nature gave you two ears and one tongue. Take the hint.

- Listen to the music. Listen to the words and the way they are being said. Are there any emotional overtones? Is there any hesitation? This is just as important as the content. Check them out.

- Ask questions. The only way you can check your understanding is by asking questions.

- Choose the venue for meetings carefully. Don't meet them in a place where they're likely to feel uncomfortable. For example if you are their boss, not in your office.

- It is important to have adult to adult conversations and neutral territory helps establish equality of communication.

- Summarize throughout the conversation. This acts as feedback to the speaker and allows them the opportunity to correct any misunderstandings.

- Remember that it is the manager's responsibility to listen and help the other person to do the same. The manager must take the initiative.

EMPATHY

This exercise is useful when helping people to learn how to be empathetic. It is helpful to have at least a group of four when doing this.

- Ask the participants to get into a group of four and give themselves a number.

- Ask each person to think about something they feel strongly about: it can be work related but it does not need to be.

- Each individual is then asked in turn to talk about the issue for five minutes, and the other three listen. As each person stops speaking they all (including the speaker) write down the feelings they have observed in the speaker.

- Take it in turns to speak, each time writing down the feelings of the speaker, until everyone has spoken.

- They then return to the first speaker and each of them in turn tells the feelings they picked up when that person was speaking. Then the first speaker one tells the group the feelings they had whilst speaking.

- After that person has spoken they discuss briefly whether the group picked up the correct feelings.

- They then do the same thing for each participant so all their feelings have been discussed.

A discussion can then take place on how easy/difficult it is to pick up these feelings and the importance of doing so when communicating.

Reproduced from *Age Matters* by Keren Smedley and Helen Whitten, Gower Publishing, 2006.

QUESTIONS

This execise is undertaken in group of four or more.

1. Divide the group into pairs.

2. Ask one person in the group to give the other a £5 or £10 note.

3. Ask them to then leave the room.

4. Tell the people in the room that they are to hide the money. Their partner will be asked to find the whereabouts of the money by asking open questions. They are not to answer any closed questions.

5. When they answer, they are to be as vague as they can. For example when they are asked, 'Where is my money?' this could be responded to by 'In the universe.' This will encourage the questioner to ask more specific questions until they can find the money without moving from their chair.

A useful refinement of this exercise is based on the fact that many of us withhold information when we are asked a question because we do not want to give the information. This is usually because we don't believe there is anything in it for us. We often, when we use this exercise, tell the 'hider' that if the seeker changes the focus from themselves and their money to the 'hider' and shows interest in what the 'hider' needs in order to return the money, the 'hider' now should answer in a clear useful manner.

Use HOW, WHEN, WHAT, WHERE, WHO, WHY, WHICH when asking opening questions.

 Handout 6.10

TIPS FOR QUESTIONS

Open Communication	Closed Communication
Questions that lead to the exploration of feelings and facts	Questions that can be answered 'Yes'
Questions of 'who', 'where', 'what', 'when'?	Questions that start with 'why' usually invite defensive responses.
Questions of 'how' help with description rather than explanation	Questions that speculate or invite speculation
Questions that focus on one point at a time	Questions that press for specific data
Rhetorical questions: 'Don't you think that?'	Leading questions
Questions that neither of you know the answer to before you ask it	
Questions that help imagination of new behaviour, new self-image	

NEGOTIATIONS

Sample preparatory questions to ensure that you are in the adult position.

1. What do I ideally wish to gain from this negotiation and investment of time?

2. What does the other party most likely wish to gain – ideally?

3. What must I come out with at all costs?

4. In which areas can I be flexible?

5. What does the other party most likely feel they must gain?

6. In which areas can I realistically expect the other party to be flexible?

7. What can I offer that will be valuable for me and easy for them to give?

8. What can I request that will be valuable for me and easy for them to give?

9. How is their attitude likely to be initially? How can I influence their attitude constructively in the initial stages?

10. What is my own attitude towards the other party? How can I constructively influence my own attitude in advance of the meeting?

11. If no agreement is achieved, what alternative outcome can I envisage that will pave the way for a future 'win/win'?

12. How can I prepare myself now for the worst possible outcome?

CHAPTER 7

Managing Continuous Change

Jim, a long-serving employee at XYZ Organization, is working at his desk when Heidi comes in and says to Mary, his manager, 'I've just completed the audit on the department and it seems totally clear to me that the MD's idea of moving my department to Asia, where it will run at a quarter of the cost, is the only way forward. Once I have passed this by the MD I will tell the team. I can't see there will be any problem as it is so obvious that this is what has to happen to maintain profits.'

Mary responds, 'How exciting: a whole new life! I wonder if I can be transferred.'

Moments later Jim, who has overheard this conversation, stomps into Raj's office: 'You're always the man of reason but even you will be horrified by this! This company has changed so much since we started. We now work with people who are situated halfway across the world, whom we don't even know, and I have to consider them in my thinking. And now, not happy with that, those money-grabbing bosses have decided to move Heidi's department to the Far East. What effect is that going to have on our friend Maria?'

Raj sighs, 'Yes, I can see that this could be a problem for Maria, if that really is the case. But the world has changed and we have to accept that we can now work using modern technology, anywhere and with anyone. We have to keep up with competition Jim.'

'Well, that's another thing,' says Jim. 'Do you know you can't even go to the toilet without someone phoning you on the mobile asking why you hadn't answered an email that came 3.5 minutes earlier! It's ridiculous – and it's just not possible for a man of my age.'

Overhearing this conversation is Myra, who is 10–15 years younger than Jim and Raj. She pipes in, 'This technology and speed of response and the increased intensity of work is no joke for me either. If it goes on like this I can't imagine how I'll cope – I'm already doing the work of three people. Those early retirement packages that were meant to 'slim down' the workforce and increase profitability in the world of technology have just left the likes of us working 100 times harder.'

'I know that's true Myra,' says Raj. 'However, there are lots of things that have really improved in life. Do you remember those days, Jim, when everything was done with carbon paper?'

'Yes' says Jim 'and do you remember those days when somebody did my typing?'

Maria walks down the corridor and pops her head in. 'Well you two don't seem to be doing much work – what's the goss?'

'Haven't you heard?' says Jim in a very serious voice, 'Your department's being moved East.'

'East where – east of town?'

'No,' says Jim, 'South East Asia.'

'How can I work in South East Asia for goodness sake?'

Jim says 'I don't expect it will be any of you working in South East Asia.'

'Oh no, I'll be made redundant – they'll redeploy some but they won't redeploy me. I haven't been here that long and I'm too old. I'll never get a job. How on earth am I going to put the kids through university? And it's not just me – how are any of the others going to manage. We are all at such different stages of life. We'll need to support each other through this. Oh, this is terrible'. She bursts into tears.

'I have to admit,' says Jim, 'that these kinds of changes just leave me feeling so drained and insecure. We all know that when there are fewer jobs it won't be us they choose.'

'That may not be the case Jim,' says Raj, 'because experience does count and we have certainly all got that!' and laughs.

'Yeah, you may be right,' Jim says, 'but nothing stays the same for more than a week – it's always one new initiative after another and I'm exhausted.'

Possible outcome

Maria becomes severely stressed and anxious. This leads to less creativity, lower productivity, negative behaviours that affect both her work colleagues and her home and customer relationships. Jim is a saboteur, winding others up against management decisions and generally creating stress and negativity around him. He is unable to listen to any of the positive arguments for the change and continues to be demotivated and demotivate others. Raj struggles with keeping positive and feels as though he is being placed in the position of being the agony aunt, which in itself is exhausting.

Over the last 20 years organizational and business life has changed beyond all recognition and this has intensified dramatically since the turn of the twenty-first century as advances in technology have impacted working practices exponentially. Things began to really change in the early 1990s with the advent of desktop computers and fax machines. Many people believed that their working life would be revolutionized and made easier by these innovations. Most organizations responded to this by slimming down their workforce. This was compounded by the recession of the early 1990s when large numbers of people were laid off.

With the advent now of mobile technology, organizations are setting themselves up to be available 24/7 and to be able to respond to customer demands within an instant. This is resulting in people working harder and longer hours with expectations of a speed of response that is unsustainable for many individuals, whatever their age. However, for the older worker this is likely to be even more difficult and could well impact their performance.

The topics covered in this section are:

1. Change in the context of the older worker

2. Understanding change

3. The Change Preference model

4. Leading change

5. Strategies to support the individual through change

6. Managing intergenerational teams through change.

1. CHANGE IN THE CONTEXT OF THE OLDER WORKER

Our scenario raises a number of issues that specifically affect the older worker. Jim raises a point about work insecurity. This is not something that this group of workers ever expected to face – particularly if they made certain career choices that were regarded as 'safe'. People often came into a job for life and expected to stay in the same company, moving up the ranks if appropriate, until retirement. However, they now have to deal with unexpected situations such as the possibility of redundancy and redeployment, often without the necessary support.

In the scenario we see Raj becoming the supporter of his colleagues when potential difficulties arise. In our opinion, although peer support is very useful, many workers need independent support which could be offered by the HR Department, or by a coach or mentor. Some organizations also offer, if an individual is highly stressed, external support in the form of Employee Assistance Programmes. However, if these issues are raised early and people given skills and strategies to manage difficult situations, the need to call upon these programmes would be reduced.

One of the most destructive elements in any business is the disgruntled, disappointed worker. In our scenario we see this through Jim, who is eager to be the bearer of bad news and who is likely to spread his complaints far beyond just Raj and Maria. This type of individual can have devastating effects on the workforce, leading to lack of motivation and productivity.

When people are disgruntled they are much more likely to behave in an unpleasant manner and often their anger and disappointment is displaced onto other colleagues. Nobody likes a difficult atmosphere and this can result in staff leaving just to avoid such a situation. Organizations are often aware that they can lose the very people they need for their business.

2. UNDERSTANDING CHANGE

This next section will give you some suggestions as to how to support older workers through continuous change.

The way people respond to change will be a pattern that they have developed over the years and for many older workers they will have been doing it this way for 30+ years. It is really essential that no-one's pattern is dismissed or denigrated but that you work with individuals to help them to see that there are other ways of operating. For most of us consultation about change reduces anxiety and allows people to understand other people's views and open up to them.

In order to help people manage change it is important to properly understand their concerns, aspirations and expectations. It is all too easy to judge 'difficult' characters such as Jim through one's own filters and write them off as 'grumpy old men'. However, this does not address the real issues or remedy the situation.

Many of these people will not have had the privilege of training courses that explain different styles and so one cannot make assumptions that they realize that there are different types of approach that are valid. Equally, even if they have had training in psychometrics or the ways people think it is quite possible that they will, when under pressure, forget it all and just 'react'.

It is important to understand your own reactions to change. Be aware that you personally will have your own filter which will affect how you respond to change. If you are going to be a true influencer within this situation you need to practise looking at change from all the viewpoints so that you can offer an integrated and holistic approach. This also enables you to understand better people's concerns and drivers so that you can support continued performance throughout the change period. If the specific change affects you personally make sure that you are able to be objective and, if not, seek another colleague to support your initiatives.

3. THE CHANGE PREFERENCE MODEL

Different people manage change in different ways. One of the fundamental points to remember is that in order to help someone you need to get into their shoes and understand how they change. You need to understand how they manage change and offer help using their preference rather than your own preferences.

If a proposed change causes a person stress they revert to their preferred mode of behaviour and they often find it difficult to be helped out of that approach in order to engage with the change process.

You will therefore need to encourage managers and individuals to understand themselves.

✎ Exercise 7.1

Figure 7.1 sets out the four change preferences and Figure 7.2 explains the model, based on Ned Herrmann's divisions of the brain (see section 1 of Chapter 6) and shows what the initials stand for. The first point to make is that, apart from one or two exceptional people, we operate in different modes at different times when experiencing change. However, we may have a strong preference for a particular mode, in which case we are likely to rely on that approach most of the time.

Analyse and evaluate	**Explore and discover**
Resist and stay in control	**Accept and help others**

Figure 7.1   The four change preferences

Before you interpret your profile as a whole, it is important to understand how each mode operates. Let us first look at each mode, and consider how this affects an individual's approach.

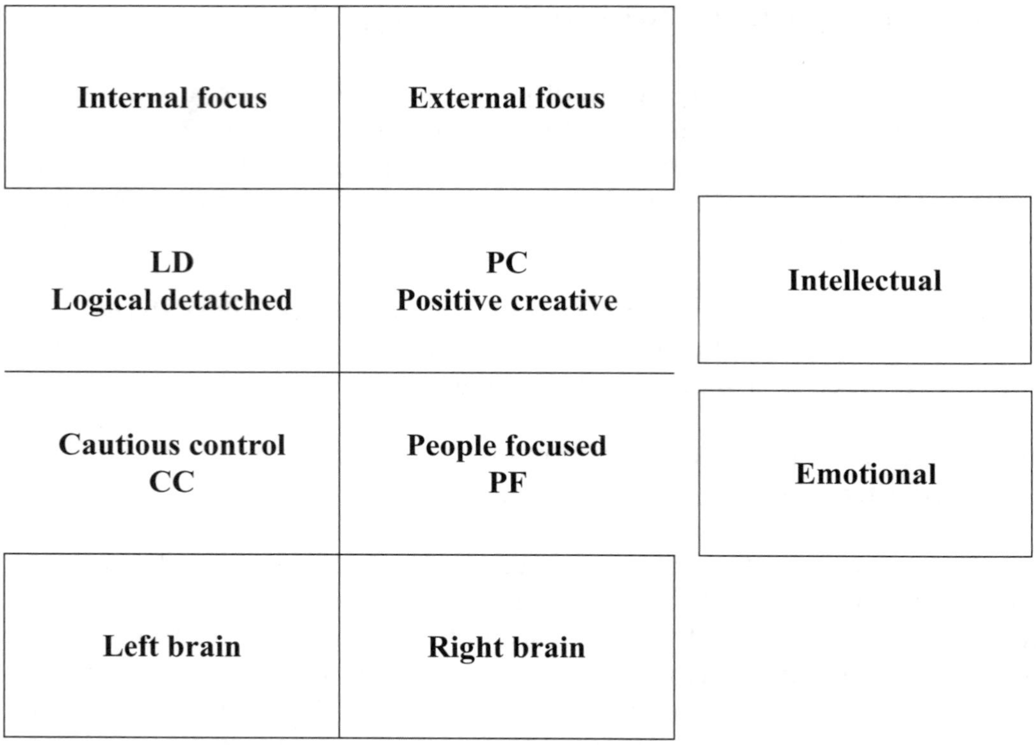

Internal focus	**External focus**	
LD **Logical detatched**	**PC** **Positive creative**	**Intellectual**
Cautious control **CC**	**People focused** **PF**	**Emotional**
Left brain	**Right brain**	

Figure 7.2   Ned Herrmann's divisions of the brain

Application of change preference

Logical Detached (LD)

In the scenario given at the beginning of this chapter the possible change that is happening in the organization is the relocation of one department to the Far East. Depending on an individual's preferences they will respond differently to this change. Heidi's preference is LD, Logical Detached, which is A Quadrant. She has an unemotional and rational perspective on the change. She is interested in the facts of the matter and the implications. She is unlikely to challenge the nature and dimension of the change or consider the emotional impact on herself or others but will focus on the analysis, and what that means in relation to the bottom line.

The positive side of an A Quadrant person is that careful, meticulous, logical, analytical work will have been done so that the facts behind decisions will be correct. This is essential to keep any organization or business on track. They also will be able to plot the effect of change during the process and have the necessary information to make appropriate amendments. Once they have been convinced that a change is a logical decision they will be eager to ensure that every step continues to be analysed and evaluated, and modified if it deviates from the original targets.

The kinds of questions that A Quadrant people would be asking are:

> *How will the new department be structured?*

What percentage of the present workforce would be offered relocation packages?

Would preference for relocation be offered to people in her department or other people in the company?

How many people do we have to let go and how much is that going to cost us?

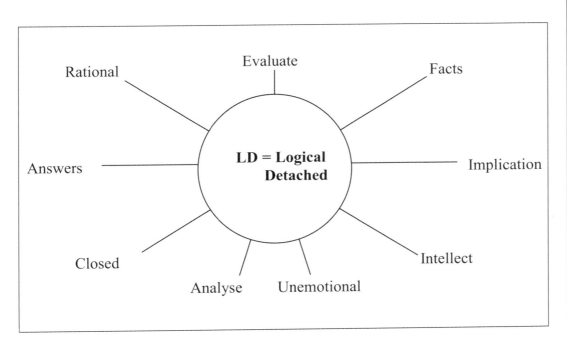

Figure 7.3   The Logical Detached approach to change

Cautious Control (CC)

Jim fits perfectly into this quadrant. His modus vivendi appears to be keeping the status quo and he is particularly interested in how it affects him, and those that he identifies with. His general stance is negative and he is willing to express his view and argue his case with any argument that comes into his mind. This sometimes appear to others to be illogical and emotional. A person acting from this quadrant does not see themselves like this and this in itself can cause difficulty in communication.

The positive side of this is that they are, in their resistance to change, cautious and are often able to help other more impetuous people to reconsider before making mistakes. Once they are either convinced of the advantages of the change or realize that the change is going to happen whatever they do, they can use their organizational and practical skills to ensure that the change occurs in a planned, timely and efficient manner.

The kind of questions they may ask is:

How does this really fit into the organization's business plan?

How will this affect our customer service?

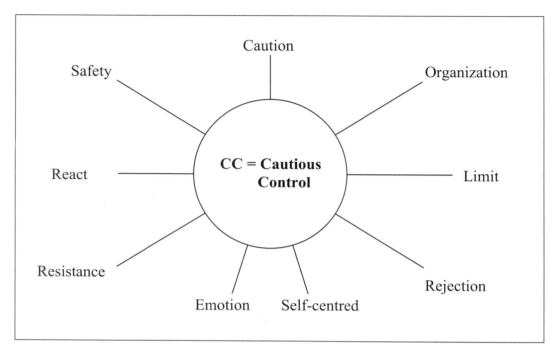

Figure 7.4   The Cautious Control approach to change

Have you considered how this fits into our Health and Safety Policy, our Risk Strategy and our Employment systems?

What is your timing on this? I think it needs to be approached really slowly and carefully if it is to be any use.

People Focused (PF)

Maria and Raj both fall into this category and exhibit the behaviours slightly differently. The reason for this is that Raj is a C/D individual and Maria is a C/B individual. Both of them have just accepted the change and don't appear to be planning to challenge this. Their reaction, as seen with Maria, is emotional, both for herself and her colleagues. Raj, who is not directly affected, exhibits concern, empathy and other ways of looking at the situation. Maria instinctively suggests that they need to act as a group on this and share the experience so as to support one another.

Many people in the C quadrant get stuck with the feelings, whether it is misery, happiness or anger and find it difficult to see beyond this. The positive side of this is that this group flag up the emotions that are probably being felt by many but not being understood or expressed. If feelings are not discussed, they will find other ways of expressing themselves and this can be destructive.

The sorts of questions a C Quadrant person will ask are:

How is this going to affect our lives and our families?

Will the team that we have been building be split up now?

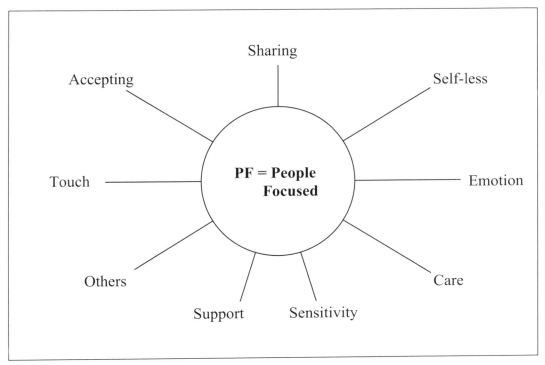

Figure 7.5   The People-Focused approach to change

What are you going to do to help us with this?

How are we going to get the same level jobs and be financially secure?

Positive Creative (PC)

In our scenario Mary is a clear Positive Creative, or D Quadrant, and Raj has some D characteristics. Mary expressed excitement and quite clearly wanted to be part of the move, and to manage the challenges that it would bring. Raj has demonstrated his D-Quadrant thinking throughout our scenarios by always looking on the bright side of life and at other viewpoints. Mary gets her energy from taking risks and having new adventures. She, like Heidi, does not focus on the emotional impact of the situation for herself or others. Once Mary has an idea she can become single-minded and can become very pushy and demanding in order to meet her goals, with little tolerance of other views.

The positive aspects of the D Quadrant Positive Creative is that they are very future-oriented, big-picture, imaginative thinkers who see multiple possibilities within any situation. They thrive on change rather than being scared of it.

The sorts of questions they will ask are:

What new systems do we need to introduce to make this work?

Is there going to be any red-tape that holds us back getting going?

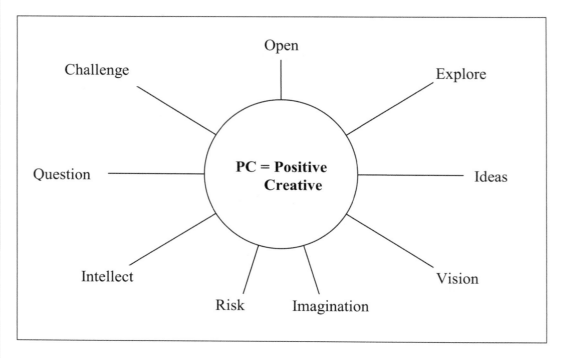

Figure 7.6 The Positive Creative approach to change

Have you considered the new proposal I made last week as a way of doing this?

What will success look like when we've got there?

4. LEADING CHANGE

The leader of the change initiative may or may not have an understanding of difference and needs to be given the information in this chapter before they propose any change. Those who lead teams also need to be aware of how team members may react so that they can approach the team with new initiatives in a way that can be heard and taken on board by all. The leader needs to be able to understand the strengths of each different approach so they can utilize these in moving forward. When approaching their team they need to ensure that they articulate this to cover the needs of each quadrant as is described in the following figure:

A Explain the facts and figures	D Outline the vision Highlight the new development
B Clearly lay out the proposed plan in detail, step by step, with the rationale explained	C Acknowledge the feelings that team members may be having

Figure 7.7 Leading change

Allow everyone in the team to express their views, feelings, concerns and opinions and don't curtail this process too quickly. It is really important that people experience a sense of involvement and ownership in the change process, so ideally include the team in on any possible developments as early as is feasible. An older member of staff will probably really want to have the benefit of their experience taken into account. It is too easy to ignore past learning and just assume they are negative comments whereas actually it is important to analyse and listen to see how you can utilize the arguments put forward for the benefit of all.

The leader should not only talk about the change once: they need to reinforce key messages and actions on a regular basis and allow others to offer opinions about each step. It is important that the leader should not expect total harmony and agreement at the start of the process: it is perfectly likely that people will be resistant to change and take time to accept their proposals.

Your own role in being responsible for the people aspects of the business is crucial at these times. You can really help a leader understand some of the subtleties and emotional consequences of change initiatives. The way a leader communicates these messages is key because it will affect the outcome.

For example, in a recent merger situation the leader stood up and read his prepared speech from a piece of paper stating that there was to be a restructure and redundancies in the company to the assembled employees. He then left without taking any questions, leaving a stunned auditorium. This had a much more devastating effect on morale and cohesion than if he had stayed in the room to allow people to express concerns and ask questions. He also missed out on the knowledge and experience that existed within his workforce that could have allowed him to consider other options.

5. STRATEGIES TO SUPPORT THE INDIVIDUAL THROUGH CHANGE

We have given you some indicators as to the kind of responses you may experience. The likelihood is that you, as an HR person, will be seeing the individuals who are finding managing change the most difficult, and who already know that their manager is finding them a problem. It is important for you to remember that there will be different pressures and concerns for older workers than on their younger colleagues and these need to be understood and addressed. For some, as has previously been discussed, there will be a mismatch between the reality of today's business environment and their expectations. This can lead to both disappointment and disillusionment. These factors will affect an individual's response to change. See Chapter 4, Understanding Your Older Workforce.

'Old dogs' rarely have real difficulty learning new tricks, they more often have difficulty convincing themselves that it is worth the 'effort', (Schaie and Giewitz, 1982). It is really essential that you work with individuals to identify their way of dealing with change by exploring the changes they have undergone during their working life, how they managed them and what helped them to manage them. By gathering this information you will be able to help them to use these strategies in the new situation. People often forget that they have successfully managed change many times in the past both in work and home life.

It is very easy to assume that an older person is stuck in the mud and very easy for the older person to assume that this is what you are thinking. This needs to be explored honestly if you are going to be able to move forward with them. Giving people the benefit of the doubt that they will manage successfully can bolster their own confidence in their ability to do so.

In some instances the change may trigger more radical responses that are greater than those you yourself can deal with. It is important to offer people coaching, training or Employee Assistance Programmes in order to enable them to embrace the change and carry on working effectively.

6. MANAGING INTERGENERATIONAL TEAMS THROUGH CHANGE

By now you will realize that different team members will react differently through periods of change. The key to successful team management is to help each type of thinker to feel positive and not threatened by other people's different approach. Our stereotypical view of older people is that they will be resistant to change and many of their younger colleagues may take that view. However, unless life events or personal development have changed somebody's intrinsic preference then once an optimistic person such as a D Quadrant, they nearly always stay an optimistic person. We authors know plenty of 70+ D quadrants who continue to start new business ventures.

It is often difficult for older workers to be heard because nobody expects them to have new innovative ideas. This can cause enormous frustration as well as a loss of possible potential new ways of doing business. A common theme from both men and women of 50+ in our own research was that they now feel 'invisible' and one of the key messages was that they really wanted people to listen to their experience and their ideas, without necessarily feeling that they have to take them on.

A B-person, who is most likely to be resistant to the change and cause difficulty within the team, is often scared they will be marginalized. For all the reasons outlined above, they believe they have reason to be scared. It is therefore essential, in the light of the Age Discrimination Regulations, that you make it clear that age will no longer be a factor in deciding who is made redundant as that would be illegal. This may reduce the anxieties that can fuel what is seen as negative behaviour.

Within any team within your organization you are likely to see examples of all the different Quadrant responses change. You can assist team leaders and individuals to help them work together and to focus on the positives that each quadrant brings to the whole rather than resent the differences. The strength of any team lies in this difference but very often the difference becomes the hindrance. For example a D thinker who decides that they have a bright new idea and is determined to action it can ride roughshod over a B person who is still trying to get their head around the last but one idea. The C person, seeing the B person distressed, puts their energy into supporting the B person rather than listening to the positives of the D's ideas. The A person quietly scribbles on a piece of paper, working out whether D's idea is a sensible rational idea based on facts rather than a mad cuckoo-land idea as they so often regard D's work.

One of the ways that really helps teams to get through this is humour. If people's differences are seen warmly and not aggressively you can help them to laugh at their own and each other's quirks, and help them gently to take on different people's perspectives. For change to be successful you need all four factors:

A	D
• Evaluate facts and figures • Develop spreadsheets • Prepare technological solutions • Critical assessment and analysis of the pitfalls	• Scope the vision • Explore possible options • Break through old rules and routines • Have amazing new ideas • Inspire others with entrepreneurial spirit
B	C
• Prepare plans and steps • Assess risk • Maintain standards and quality control • Ensure practical procedures to ensure results • Keep organized records • Check systems to ensure compliance	• Understand and empathize with feelings • Support individuals through the change process • Know what it takes to build team morale • Ensure open communication • Take time to listen

Figure 7.8 Managing change as a diverse team

SUMMARY AND TIPS

In this section we have explored some of the factors that affect change in organizations and their likely impact on the older worker. This group of staff have already been through an enormous amount of change during their working lives and may appear as though they feel weary of it. The information in this chapter will have given you new ways to work with individuals, leaders and teams in order to ensure the change process works successfully.

This has always been important and is now crucial, as a larger percentage of your workforce will increasingly be over 50. Greater understanding and appreciation of different viewpoints and experiences within an intergenerational workforce leads to creative performance.

As the people champions in your organization, you are central to the success of this process and to the efficiency and profitability of your organization. The ideas discussed in this chapter are the foundation and building blocks of many of the topics discussed in Section Three.

Six tips

1. **Do the change profile on yourself, the leader and any relevant individuals.**

2. **Don't make assumptions about why people are responding in particular ways.**

3. **Help change agents within the organization to plan the way they introduce new initiatives.**

4. **Set up some training in understanding change before the event so that people have learnt the skills to manage change.**

5. **Support those who are particularly anxious or stressed and ensure they have resource phone numbers and web links.**

6. **Listen to your older workers and use their experiences as a resource rather than a hindrance.**

CHANGE PREFERENCE QUESTIONNAIRE

The following questionnaire, devised by Rupert Eales-White, enables people to understand their change preference. This questionnaire is based on the Herrmann Thinking Preference Model that you saw in Chapter 6. If you haven't read this yet, it would be useful for you to read this section before completing the change questionnaire. As with all exercises, we suggest that you do the questionnaire yourself before you share it with others.

CHANGE PREFERENCE QUESTIONNAIRE

For each of the areas covered, please choose the word with which you identify most. Give that preference 4 marks. In each category, there are four choices, and so you need to allocate 3 marks to your next choice, then 2, and finally 1 mark for the item with which you least identify.

Please complete the form.

1. Jobs

	Marks
Researcher	A
Administrator	B
Writer	C
Social Worker	D

2. Words

	Marks
Harmony	A
Beauty	B
Intellect	C
Efficiency	D

3. Words

	Marks
Keep	A
Evaluate	B
Share	C
Change	D

4. Words

	Marks
Idea	A
Feeling	B
Organization	C
Fact	D

5. Phrases

	Marks
The right answer	A
Safety first	B
Go for it	C
Sixth sense	D

6. Sayings

	Marks
Smile and the whole world smiles with you	A
Nothing ventured, nothing gained	B
The facts speak for themselves	C
Look before you leap	D

7. How someone who did not like you might describe you

	Marks
Being stuck in the mud	A
Being as dry as dust	B
Wearing your heart on you sleeve	C
Having your head in the clouds	D

8. Attitude to risk

Do you prefer to:

	Marks
Take risks	A
Share risks	B
Avoid risks	C
Analyse risks	D

9. Attitude to change

Do you prefer to:

	Marks
Analyse and evaluate ideas	A
Implement ideas that are practical	B
Generate ideas	C
Look to see how ideas will affect others	D

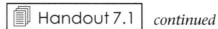

10. Actions you take

	Marks
Do you prefer to:	
Make a new friend	A
Change your approach	B
Have a debate	C
Control a situation	D

11. How you would describe yourself

	Marks
Practical	A
Rational	B
Friendly	C
Imaginative	D

12. How someone who did not like you might describe you

	Marks
Rebellious	A
Weak	B
Over-cautious	C
Cold	D

SCORING SHEET

Score yourself on the scoring sheet below. Transfer each mark into the appropriate place. With our example the C-mark would go into the PC column; the A mark into the LD column; the B mark into the CC column and the D mark goes into the PF column. When you have completed the form add up your totals and fill in the Profile Score.

Question number	LD	CC	PF	PC
1	A	B	D	C
2	C	D	A	B
3	B	A	C	D
4	D	C	B	A
5	A	B	D	C
6	C	D	A	B
7	B	A	C	D
8	D	C	B	A
9	A	B	D	C
10	C	D	A	B
11	B	A	C	D
12	D	C	B	A

TOTALS   +   +   +   **= 120**

Your profile

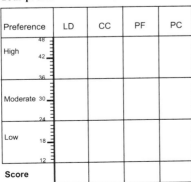

Example

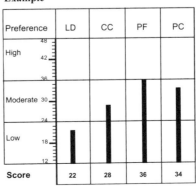

Reproduced from *Age Matters* by Keren Smedley and Helen Whitten, Gower Publishing, 2006.

MANAGING
CONTINUOUS
CHANGE

Health and Wellbeing

Simon comes into the office cock-a-hoop. He has completed the London Marathon after months of training. Maria claps her hands and Jim says, 'I never imagined you'd do it! I thought we were too old for that kind of thing!'

Maria says, 'Don't let Heidi or Bill hear you say that Jim. They certainly think we are too old. I have just received a memo sent from Sally offering anyone over 50 a health check. One minute they want us to work hard and say we are the same as everyone else and the next minute they are checking us because they think we are falling apart.'

Simon retorts, 'That is something that she won't be able to do when that new Law comes in. If the law can keep me at work it can accept that I am healthy. Anyway, look at me!'

Audrey, a colleague, says, 'Yes it is all well and good. We are the same but there are differences. I certainly don't see the body of a 25 year old when I look in the mirror and I am aware that I do have different aches and pains than when I was younger. I don't think anyone should be asking to test us because of our age but I do think realistically that there are things that change – I have just been prescribed reading glasses! I have been squinting for weeks because I didn't want to look like an old woman.'

Raj walks by, still with his coat on, and Simon says 'Half day Raj?'

'No. I have been to the doctor,' Raj replies. 'It was hard enough getting today off. I don't think there is anything seriously wrong but the doctor wants me back for tests which means I will need to take more time off work. I wish they made it easier for us to do this. I end up by leaving it so late before I go to the doctor that I cause myself more problems.'

Possible outcome

Raj takes sick leave rather than taking short periods off to go to the doctor. The medical tests show that his illness has progressed and he takes long-term sick leave. The doctor made it clear that this could have been prevented had he addressed his illness earlier. Staff hide their physical ailments for fear of being judged as 'old'.

'You're as young as you feel' is a phrase that has been repeated over generations of history. In the aftermath of the 2005 General Election it was interesting to observe that Michael Howard decided that 63 was 'too old' to lead a political party whereas the 64-year-old Ken Clarke felt up to the challenge. Only a few months later, in 2006 Sir Menzies Campbell was elected leader of the Liberal Democrats in his 65th year. Then, at the other end of the scale, David Cameron became leader of the Conservative Party at 39 – an age some considered too young! This just demonstrates how confused people are on the subject of age.

Most people in their 80s and 90s report that they feel 18 inside. Some of them are still extraordinarily fit as well – we probably all know an 80-plus person who is still participating in Scottish dancing, or swimming in the sea every morning, walking five miles a day, running, cycling or participating in yoga classes or martial arts. Older people frequently participate in sponsored walks and even marathons.

As your workforce is likely, with the demographic trends, to be populated by a higher proportion of older people then one thing you will want to focus on is helping people to 'feel young' both mentally and physically.

This chapter will give you some strategies and information designed to help maintain the physical and mental energy of your older workforce because there are some very real and practical steps that you can take to support this. The topics will include:

1. Dispelling myths

2. Sickness absence

3. Mental faculties

4. Physical health

5. Promoting good health in your organization

6. Managing stress

7. Healthy environment, creative culture

8. Physical testing.

1. DISPELLING MYTHS

There are many myths about ageing that, as we have mentioned before, probably date from the last century, where average longevity was 60–65, rather than the current 80 years old. Beliefs and urban myths abound around dotty aunts or aged great grandparents but the reality is that many old people are perfectly fit and healthy. When people do become ill it tends, on average, to be only for the last two years of their lives. It is therefore important to challenge the language and myths that exist within your own corporate culture to open people's minds up to the fact that existing beliefs and ideas about health and age are probably outdated.

2. SICKNESS ABSENCE

There is some evidence that absence rates are higher in older workers than in younger workers. However, younger workers take sickness absence too, and in fact most older people are remarkably healthy, particularly when supported and encouraged to partake in healthy lifestyles. Rates of disability are steadily declining, even amongst the very old. In 1994 73 per cent of adults 78–84 years of age reported *no* disabling conditions and even amongst those over 85, 40 per cent had no functional disabilities (Manton, Stallard and Corder, 1995. *Directory of Positive Psychology 2003*).

✎ Exercise 8.1

Although inevitably there are cellular changes with age and physiological systems can slow down and become less efficient (Birren and Birren, 1990) older adults tend to make gradual lifestyle changes to accommodate diminishing physical abilities (Williamson and Dooley, 2001).

3. MENTAL FACULTIES

The 'use it or lose it' adage applies to most aspects of the physiology of human beings. If you have your leg in a splint for a few weeks at any age the muscles start to deteriorate within 48 hours. The concept of memory deteriorating with age is dealt with in Chapter 11 on Lifelong Learning and it is important to help your workforce to be aware that continuous use and practice will usually help to keep both their minds and bodies shipshape.

The myth that memory gradually deteriorates from 30 onwards, and especially from 60, again probably harks back to a time when old people put on their carpet slippers for the final years of their lives and did not continue to use their minds. In previous eras many people would die almost as soon as they retired; in today's world people continue to remain active mentally and physically for longer. Many achieve academic and professional qualifications late in life. Recent research by Benjamin F. Jones for the National Bureau of Economic Research (NBER) argues that great achievements in knowledge are produced by older innovators today than they were a century ago. Jones has used data on Nobel Prize winners and great inventors and has discovered that the age at which noted innovations are produced has increased by approximately six years over the twentieth century (Benjamin F. Jones, NBER Working Paper No. 11359, Issued in May 2005 NBER Program(s)).

Therefore, provided the brain is not damaged through a stroke, Alzheimer's or other degenerative brain disease, older adults in cognitively challenging environments show minimal decline in thinking and learning abilities. So challenge the 'I am getting old so my memory is going' remarks you may hear around your organization and publicize statistics on the mental achievements of older people.

4. PHYSICAL HEALTH

We often hear people say to us: 'I'm 50 now so I wake up with aches every morning'. Biological age frequently has nothing to do with chronological age. Just because one person suffered aches it does not mean that every person when they reach 50 will suffer from aches. Limiting beliefs need to be challenged because they may have adverse consequences. For example, in some cases if a person expects to have more aches and pains as they age they will not necessarily go to the doctor to seek help. Equally a person experiencing pain may well be more pessimistically focused on their problems than those who do not hold these beliefs. There is a body of research that demonstrates that pessimism itself has negative effects on the immune system.

Professor Robert Weale of the Institute of Gerontology at King's College London researches biological age and has devised some tests. He has discovered that some people can be as much as ten years younger biologically than one might expect chronologically.

5. PROMOTING GOOD HEALTH IN YOUR ORGANIZATION

Information

It is important to offer information and research that dispels the ageing myths so as to ensure that the older worker is treated on equal terms to those who are younger. Publicize statistics and case studies of the physical and mental achievements of older people.

Offer resources, directories, phone numbers and weblinks to those bodies who can provide support and information regarding specific illnesses or conditions about which people may be anxious.

Dispel fears: fear produces stress and stress depletes the immune system. People may well be anxious about genetic predisposition to certain illness: for example, if breast cancer is in someone's family then they may benefit from information on the genetic or causal links to this condition. There is also research demonstrating that the fact that one's mother has experienced breast cancer does not necessarily signify that a daughter will do so. The death rates from breast cancer have, in any case, reduced by over 20 per cent in recent years.

Encourage people to become aware of recent research because so many myths date from previous generations and not their own. Recent research is generally more positive and optimistic, as medical practices have improved and, without war and deprivation, health has improved alongside it.

Twenty practical steps you can take

1. Ensure that there is an adequate supply of water. Drinking 1–2 litres of water per day maintains the body's fluid levels and supports mental and physical function.

2. If possible, provide the services of an occupational health consultant so that problems can be identified and managed early.

3. Make it easy for people to visit a doctor. Hours of GP surgeries do not make this easy. It is well documented that it is difficult to get men, particularly, to go to seek advice early enough in their sickness, and this can lead to more major problems. Make sure that your organizational culture values good health and makes it possible for people to ask for time out.

4. Where possible provide health checks and advice in-house or at a nearby medical centre.

5. Arrange for discount membership rates at a local health club so that people can maintain a healthy lifestyle by visiting the club on their way in, at lunchtime or at the end of the day. Many companies have encouraged people to take a rota for gym visits so that one person covers another person's desk in order to allow each person adequate time for exercise. Exercise equals strength and stamina. If people are chained (through general work culture or habit) to their desk at all hours of the day they are unlikely to take adequate exercise during a day. Strong bodies equal strong minds and also strong bones.

6. The brain takes 25 per cent of the body's energy resources and does not function well if not given regular breaks so encourage visits to the local park or a trip to the gym during a lunch hour as healthy body supports a healthy mind.

7. Lunch at the desk does not encourage knowledge sharing or the ability for the brain to stop and assimilate the information gained during the morning. Legally all employees should take at least a half-hour lunch break. Enlist managers' help in enforcing this.

8. Encourage people to leave the office at a reasonable hour.

9. Some companies are providing break-out rooms where people can take time away from the desk, relax and refresh their mind and body. This is particularly beneficial for roles such as helpdesks or where an individual is under a great deal of pressure.

10. With more women in the workforce of menopausal age it is important to encourage them to take weight-bearing exercise in order to ward off osteoporosis.

11. Arrange screening for osteoporosis, breast and prostate cancer, diabetes, blood pressure, cholesterol, and so on.

12. Encourage people to eat lunch away from their desks. This is good for concentration and creativity.

13. Arrange yoga or tai-chi or pilates courses in the lunch break. Gentle stretching improves strength and flexibility.

14. Introduce massage sessions. Several consultants do in-house visits and can offer both full massage and at-the-desk neck and shoulder massage. This relieves tension and releases stress toxins that build up in muscle tissue. The power of touch is healing and therapeutic.

15. Provide a canteen where healthy food is available. Protein lunches will maintain mental and physical energy levels throughout the afternoon more than carbohydrate meals.

16. Ensure the drinks dispenser provides hot water for herbal teas as well as coffee.

17. Provide fresh fruit and vegetables and salads as these increase health and immunity.

18. Engage an Employee Assistance Programme to offer counselling, legal and other advice lines.

19. Provide coaches and training to help people maintain their wellbeing.

20. Set up network groups where people can discuss issues and generate ideas for healthy living. Many more people are living alone in the 21st century and social support is a well-documented factor that supports good health and emotional wellbeing. In these forums people can share concerns and develop solutions to daily problems that might affect wellbeing.

6. MANAGING STRESS

✎ Exercise 8.2

A common saboteur of health, effective work performance and communication is stress. As you will be aware from Chapter 4 on Understanding Your Older Workforce, this group of employees may be experiencing pressures beyond the workplace that may impact their emotional equilibrium. This will affect their performance and health. Stress renders people stupid – and sick! In the next section we shall outline some information that may help managers to support workers through difficult situations so as to maintain health and productivity.

Recognizing stress

Older people frequently do not have in-depth knowledge about stress as there was less information on this issue when they were younger. In our experience one of the most frequently asked questions by managers of all ages is 'How do I recognize stress in my staff?' Most of your staff who are under pressure will endeavour to disguise their problems as it is often regarded as a weakness in many corporate cultures. The post-war 'stiff upper lip' concept tends to live on. Detection on the part of the manager can therefore be through small behavioural changes and reduction in effective working. (See Figures 8.1 and 8.2.)

As stress depletes the immune system early detection is important. Continual anxiety can lead to depression and burn-out.

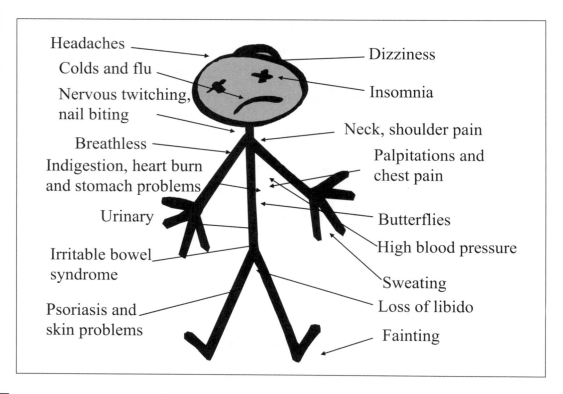

Figure 8.1 Symptoms of stress

🖉 Exercise 8.3

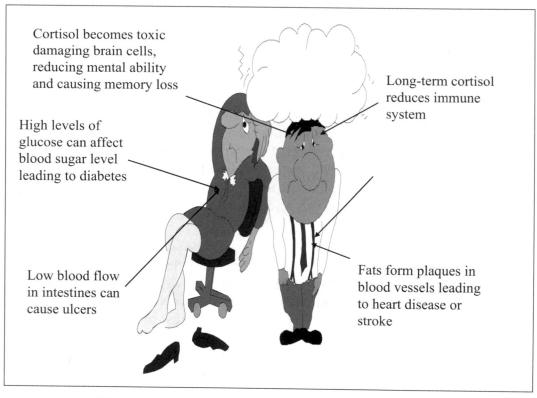

Figure 8.2 Long-term health effects of stress

Stress impacts longevity. The chemistry of stress can lead to heart disease, high blood pressure and diabetes. As female longevity is no longer as great a differential to male longevity as it used to be, it can be argued that work factors are likely to influence health and age of death. Studies have shown that those who are competitive and aggressive, with a tendency to anger, are likely to die ten years earlier than those who are more relaxed. It will benefit people to learn ways of managing stress and emotions so as to be able to retain both health and also clarity of thinking and communication (Dr Michael Babyuk, *Sunday Times, 26* January 1997).

Stress impairs mental performance

Stress inhibits the cerebral area of the brain and energy is directed to survival; to 'fight or flight mode' where the natural process of the body generates physical strength and/or speed (see Figure 8.3). In survival mode people do not have access to complex thinking and creativity, which is what most organizations require today. This leads to an inability to perform normal duties.

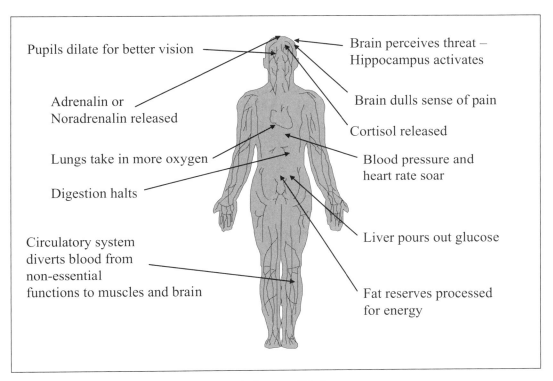

Figure 8.3   Fight or flight response

Stress can also lead to tiredness and exhaustion, which slows productivity. Behaviours also change and stressed employees have a tendency towards impatience and intolerance. This will affect both team performance and the interface with clients and customers. Cooperation deteriorates as people move into fight or flight mode, with some becoming aggressive and others uncommunicative.

When people become overwhelmed by tasks and thoughts they no longer manage their time effectively. This can be observed through them being late for work, late for meetings, coming into work too early, leaving work late. Boundaries become blurred and they lose the ability to think clearly and focus their energy and time into what matters most. Instead they fill their time with small, less relevant activities.

Managers need to be observant of their staff and look out for tendencies such as procrastination, being rushed, and making careless mistakes and bad decisions. They may also notice some visual signs which are unusual and demonstrate lack of self-care and haste such as non-matching shoes, socks, suit, being unshaven, unwashed hair, or, for a woman who normally makes up, being unmade up.

In the older workforce people are more likely to have been brought up not to show emotion or ask for help, particularly from younger people. Within the workforce there are many occasions when managers are considerably younger than some of their team and this may inhibit an older person expressing their troubles. They may feel that a young person would expect them to have their problems and emotions in order by this stage of their life. The 'flight' response can lead to people retreating into their offices, hiding their emotions and being buttoned up and unsociable. As with all stress, recognizing these symptoms early and talking about them can prevent further problems.

The figures below show the process of events from a pressure point to the feeling of being overwhelmed which many people are experiencing today with regard to their workload. It is important to realize that negative thinking leads to a stress response so make sure that your thinking is positive and helps you manage the situation calmly and with confidence.

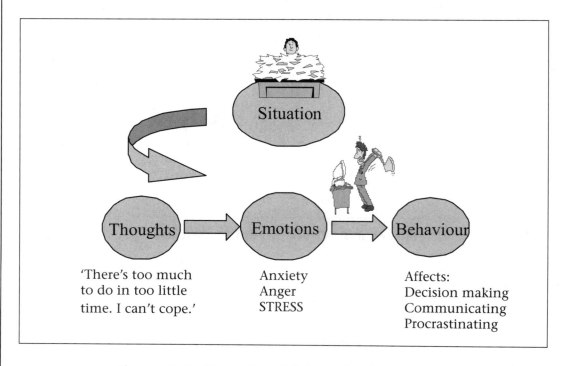

Figure 8.4   Negative thinking leads to stress

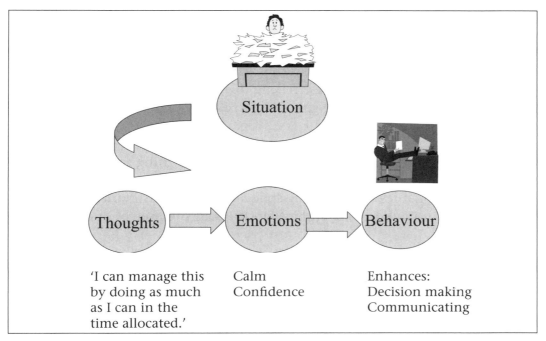

Figure 8.5   Positive thinking promotes confidence and wellbeing

7. HEALTHY ENVIRONMENT, CREATIVE CULTURE

The environment has now been proven to impact health. Hospitals such as the Chelsea and Westminster in London find that uplifting pictures, plants and colour reduce the number of painkillers their patients require by enhancing the immune system.

While you are not dealing with sick people in the workplace, environment will also have a part to play in preventing sickness and maintaining wellbeing. Pictures and plants can make an immediate difference to people's frame of mind, encouraging a calmer workspace and inspiring a more creative exchange of ideas. Natural daylight raises people's energy. If you are unable to provide windows then ensure that the lighting is as natural as possible. Recognize that creativity and the vision of a better future seldom come from long days of fire-fighting in basement offices with no natural daylight. People require time and space for reflection and inspiration. The physical environment of the office can enhance this feeling of wellbeing, so create an office that is uncluttered and makes doing business easy.

8. PHYSICAL TESTING

Under the Age Discrimination Regulations it will, of course, be important for you to provide facilities for all age groups. A person's age should never be used to make judgements about their physical or cognitive abilities or their fitness. When a judgement is required about a person's health, an occupational health or medical practitioner should be consulted. For example if you have previously given people a physical test. It will also be necessary to prove that their physical abilities are necessary for their job. This is important information should you be taken to an industrial tribunal.

It is useful for you and line managers to be aware of the physiological needs of your older workers and also to support them through emotional concerns that are the result of ageing. For example, worries about aches and pains, or specific conditions; worries about their changing and ageing bodies. Maintaining flexible joints and exercising to counteract the natural changes in metabolism that result in weight gain can also help people to feel good.

Many women report feeling invisible and vulnerable as older women and this can impact their ability to feel confident about running presentations or taking a stand in front of other people, particularly if they are experiencing hot flushes. Companies are providing style and image consultants who can help a person continue to look and feel good about themselves into older age.

Conversely there are, of course, plenty of examples of baby boomers, male and female, who are still looking and feeling great. Helping people to feel good will benefit your company as when people feel good about themselves they are healthier, more confident and more creative.

The exercises that follow enable you to audit the health of your organization.

SUMMARY AND TIPS

We hope that this chapter has helped you to realize that the ageing process does not necessarily have to lead to incapacity or illness. Preventive action can really make a difference. You can play your part in helping a person reduce their stress by providing training or coaching in stress management and stress prevention techniques. The information on emotional intelligence and positive thinking in Chapter 6 People Management will help you give individuals specific models that might help them to manage and move on from stressful events.

We firmly believe that if you take some of the actions suggested in this chapter you will help your workforce to retain health, energy and emotional wellbeing for longer, for the benefit of all.

Six tips

1. **Publicize positive information regarding health and old age.**

2. **Provide support, counselling and information to help people take control of their health.**

3. **Encourage time away from the desk at lunchtime for exercise and to enjoy fresh healthy food.**

4. **Set up support systems where people can discuss experiences and concerns regarding health and fitness.**

5. **Set up exercise classes and massage in the lunch hour.**

6. **Challenge myths about ageing and develop a culture and language that views older people as healthy, fit and energized.**

 Exercise 8.1

SICKNESS ABSENCE EVALUATION

- To evaluate the situation in your own organization investigate the sickness figures by age.

- Calculate whether there are any specific trends – are there seasonal differences?

- How do older people's sickness rates compare to those of younger people? How might you address the underlying issues these demonstrate?

ADDRESSING THE CAUSES OF STRESS: CULTURAL AUDIT

What stresses one person may well not stress another. However, there are likely to be some common themes with regard to causes of stress within your organization and it is certainly worth carrying out a stress audit to identify what these might be. If you can tackle the direct cause of stress – such as job role ambiguity or job design – then you can remove those situations that cause stress.

There are companies who can run a stress audit for you. Alternatively use the questionnaire below to gauge individual responses. Run focus groups to discuss the findings, and identify major organizational and cultural causes of stress. Finally brainstorm solutions and actions that can be taken to remedy these.

STRESS FACTORS AT WORK

Listed below are various kinds of problems that may arise in your work. Indicate to what extent you find each of them to be a problem, concern or obstacle in carrying out your job duties and responsibilities. Circle your answers

	This factor is a problem ...	Never	Seldom	Sometimes	Usually	Always
	Conflict and uncertainty					
1.	Not knowing just what the people you work with expect of you	1	2	3	4	5
2.	Feeling that you have to do things on the job that are against your better judgement	1	2	3	4	5
3.	Thinking that you will not be able to satisfy the conflicting demands of various people over you	1	2	3	4	5
	Job pressure					
4.	Feeling that you have too heavy a workload; one that you can't possibly finish during an ordinary day	1	2	3	4	5
5.	Not having enough time to do the work properly	1	2	3	4	5
6.	Having the requirements of the job conflict/impose upon your personal life	1	2	3	4	5
	Job scope					
7.	Being unclear about just what the scope and responsibilities of your job are	1	2	3	4	5
8.	Feeling that you have too little authority to carry out the responsibilities assigned to you	1	2	3	4	5
9.	Not being able to get the information you need to carry out your job	1	2	3	4	5
	Rapport with management					
10.	Not knowing what your manager or supervisor thinks of you – how he or she evaluates your performance	1	2	3	4	5
11.	Not being able to predict the reactions of people above you	1	2	3	4	5
12.	Having ideas considerably different from those of your managers	1	2	3	4	5

(Centre for Stress Management)

If you have scored 45–60 it would indicate that there are areas of work that you find difficult, and could benefit from some training, coaching or support to help you manage.

If you have scored 35–45 pressures could be building up and you would do well to observe which work factors cause you most difficulty.

If you have scored 25–35 some factors of your work environment may cause you stress.

If you have scored under 25 then your work environment would not appear to be causing you stress.

ADDRESSING INDIVIDUAL CAUSES OF STRESS

At other times it may be a particular individual's viewpoint of situations that might be causing them stress so it can help to ask employees to identify their personal causes of stress, particularly focusing on age-related pressure where you might be able to take action to support or alter situations.

Once individuals have identified their major pressure points you can work with them to take action to manage them. Stress factors are, in the main, problems to be solved. The information in the People Management section (Chapter 6) can give people specific models to maintain emotional wellbeing.

INDIVIDUAL AGE-RELATED SOURCES OF STRESS

Listed below are various kinds of problems that may arise in your work. Indicate to what extent you find each of them to be a problem, concern or obstacle in carrying out your job duties and responsibilities. Circle your answers.

	This factor is a problem ...	Never	Seldom		Usually	Always
	Role related					
1.	Fear of redundancy or being offered early retirement	1	2	3	4	5
2.	Feeling that you are being 'pushed out' of major activities	1	2	3	4	5
3.	Feeling less able to influence people now you are older	1	2	3	4	5
	Health and wellbeing					
4.	Feeling tired during the working day	1	2	3	4	5
5.	Not having the opportunity to exercise	1	2	3	4	5
6.	Not having access to fresh and healthy food	1	2	3	4	5
	Family factors					
7.	Being sandwiched between the demands of older parents and young children	1	2	3	4	5
8.	Worried about your financial situation for the future	1	2	3	4	5
9.	Anxious about taking time out of work to deal with family or health issues	1	2	3	4	5
	Technology and change					
10.	Feeling tired by continuous change	1	2	3	4	5
11.	Not being confident to manage the latest technology	1	2	3	4	5
12.	Finding life has changed too fast for you to be able to manage	1	2	3	4	5

(Centre for Stress Management)

If you have scored 45–60 it would indicate that you are finding life difficult now you are older, and could benefit from some training, coaching or support to help you manage.

If you have scored 35–45 pressure of life could be building up and you would do well to observe your mental, emotional and physical responses to situations over the next few weeks.

If you have scored 25–35 you are likely to be managing life quite well but may find some situations harder than others.

If you have scored under 25 then you seem to be managing life well.

Practical Steps to Achieving an Age-Inclusive Culture

Recruiting and Selecting Older Workers

Sally has called a meeting with Bill and Mary, who are both looking for new members of staff to join their team. They are due to discuss the short-listing of potential candidates. Sally opens the meeting by saying, 'I wanted to discuss your shortlist because I am wondering what criteria you chose people on. I can see that some obviously did not meet your specification, and I understand about those but there are three or four that we need to discuss in more detail.'

Mary says, 'Well, as far as I'm concerned, anybody over 50 is going to cause me trouble. Why would people leave their job at that age? They are either no good or they are difficult.'

Bill says, 'The last thing I need is another Simon'.

Sally jumps in, 'I thought we'd had this conversation. Ageism is an important diversity issue and we cannot discriminate against people because of their age.'

Bill adds, 'They all look as though they have done masses but how am I to know that they can do it well?'

Sally says, 'You won't know that unless you interview them. I think we need to go back over anybody who is 50+ that was placed in the 'discard' pile and look at their competencies and abilities.'

Possible outcome

You miss really excellent candidates who have everything you need and you set yourself up for litigation.

By 2011, 35 per cent of the population will be aged over 55 and 18 per cent will be aged between 45 and 55. Almost 40 per cent of the UK labour force will be aged 45 or over – and 16–17 year olds will make up only 17 per cent of the workforce. There are currently 20 million people aged 50 and over in the UK. By 2030 this figure is expected to reach 27 million – an increase of 37 per cent. A worker is commonly perceived as 'older' at the age of 50 and even younger.

Increased life expectancy, combined with shortfalls in pension provision, will mean that employees will retire later. Employers will have older workers to recruit and manage, and fewer younger workers – the balance will change.

Age discrimination is a luxury that companies can no longer afford. Under the proposals set out in the Age Discrimination Regulations 2006 decisions on recruitment and selection based on age will be unlawful. It is only lawful to discriminate at the recruitment stage against job applicants:

1.   whose age is higher than the employer's Normal Retirement Age or, if there is no NRA, higher than 65.

2.   who will reach the NRA or age 65 within six months of making the job application.

The current situation is that there is plenty of evidence that there is widespread discrimination on age when it comes to recruitment.

This chapter focuses on the recruiting and selection of older workers. The topics covered are:

1.   Background and current situation

2.   The business case

3.   Age-neutral recruitment

4.   Job descriptions, person specifications and application forms

5.   Advertising

6.   Interviews.

1. BACKGROUND AND CURRENT SITUATION

People aged over 50 have a real difficulty finding a new job, and many finally abandon the search. Government statistics highlight that the older the person the longer they are likely to remain unemployed. Six out of 10 people under the age of 50 who have been made redundant get back into work within a year. Only one out of 10 over the age of 50 find work within a year. Nine out of 10 people over the age of 50 who started job hunting after redundancy gave up after 12 months because of the response they experienced.

750 000 people over the age of 50 would like to be working if they thought there was a relevant opportunity to do so. Many who do return to work after redundancy or for other reasons face a substantial pay reduction compared to their previous job. This wage penalty has increased steadily over the last 20 years with 26 per cent of people over the age of 45 taking a pay reduction, compared to 12 per cent in 1980. These statistics reflect the prejudice shown towards older workers.

Nine out of ten older people believe that employers discriminate on grounds of age (NOP research – Code on Age Diversity). This statement is upheld by the fact that 55 per cent of managers say they use age as a criterion for recruitment (Chartered Management Institute Survey). The availability of training also decreases with age: there is a 50 per cent reduction in training levels for the over-50s compared with the 35–50 year olds (New Policy Institute).

A survey of 2072 adults (aged 15 and over) found that ageism is the most common form of workplace discrimination. Twenty-two per cent of people have experienced workplace discrimination and of these, 38 per cent said it was because of their age. Thirty-eight per cent of those said it happened during recruitment, 25 per cent during promotion processes and 25 per cent during selection (MORI Social Research Institute, December 2002).

In a survey of over 1000 people the Chartered Institute of Personnel and Development found that: one in eight workers had been discouraged from applying from jobs on the grounds of age; one in four thinks that employers are not interested in employing people over the age of 40 (CIPD, *Age Discrimination at Work*, January 2001).

This is a typical case study:

> A 66-year-old factory worker had to lie about his age when he applied for his present job. He had sent in numerous applications and although he felt he had the qualifications, was turned down. Eighteen months into his current post he was overheard saying that he was about to celebrate his 63rd birthday party that weekend. His boss, who was walking past, called him over and said, 'That is not the age you put down on your application form; why did you do this?' Jim asked him, 'Would I be standing here now if I had told you I was over 60?' His boss replied, 'No'.

The result of this is that highly skilled people end up working in less challenging areas, taking part-time work, or working in the voluntary sector. Others choose to set up their own businesses or consultancies. Either way, organizations could be losing out on real talent, knowledge and wisdom.

'It is time to recognize that 60-somethings are "not in their dotage" and still capable of doing high-powered jobs', warned Alan Johnson, former Work and Pensions Secretary. He has called for a culture change to stamp out ageism at work saying, 'When you get to 65 people are remarkably youthful and energetic and have got lots of ideas. The view that people are only fit to do a few simple clerical jobs when they reach 65 is wrong.'

The concept of age in the UK is not shared throughout the rest of the world. In the US it is common for lawyers and other professionals to continue to work well into their late 60s and early 70s. American legal companies in the UK benefit from partners in their 50s leaving or retiring from UK companies and coming to them at what they consider to be at the 'peak' of their career, bringing with them clients, wisdom, knowledge and experience.

This is not just happening in the law. The UK loses many of its outstanding academics to American universities. Professor Harry Koto, a Nobel-Prize-winning chemist was forced to retire from his post at Sussex University when he reached 65. He has moved to the US where there is no mandatory age of retirement and Florida has acquired a 'prize asset' (*The Times*, October 2004).

There are numerous examples of older people who, in spite of having taken further qualifications, are turned down from posts as unsuitable or incompetent before they have reached the short-listing. Some report taking five to ten years off their age and editing their CVs in order to feel confident in applying for jobs.

In recent years, however, some organizations, such as major supermarkets and retail stores, have developed policies to encourage the older worker to apply for work. Those organizations that have done this have reported real business benefits, particularly in customer satisfaction.

Companies in the financial services sector have also reported that customers value the help of an older person when it comes to financial advice. The Nationwide Building Society raised its retirement age to 75 as many customers said they preferred to discuss their finances with someone of the same age and someone who had had some financial experience.

It is estimated that the relatively low level of employment amongst older workers costs the economy between £19–31 billion a year, mostly in lost output but also because of reduced taxes and increased welfare payments (National Audit Office).

The Government is increasing employment opportunities and has set up the New Deal 50 Plus, a scheme that was set up specifically for older workers. They have helped more than 120 000 people into work. They are also increasing employment opportunities in other ways such as working with employers to raise awareness of an age-diverse workforce and helping older people manage interviews by improving their self-confidence and presentation. As reported by a recruitment agency working specifically with older people, one of the difficulties is that many older workers, having been employed for 20–30 years in one organization, have little experience of how to approach both filling in a CV and attending an interview. A particular problem that has been highlighted is that many organizations are recruiting new staff through on-line processes and many older people do not feel confident of their technical abilities. Equally a gruelling three-day interview in an assessment centre can be extremely daunting and not necessarily bring out the best in a person.

A number of our clients have said that they would rather apply for a lower level position than put themselves through some of today's employment procedures. This is not because they feel less able but because they have not been taught how to do those particular tests. One of our coaching clients equated it to taking the 11+.

When I was at school I was fortunate enough to go to a school that taught us how to pass the exam, my next door neighbour didn't and failed, although he was always brighter than me. It took him until he was 30 to realize that he could do it. He went back to college and now has a Ph.D. I thought we had got beyond all this. Unless something changes so much talent will be lost.

2. THE BUSINESS CASE

The business case for recruiting older workers is a powerful one. As has been discussed in Chapter 3 Demographic Changes, the demography of the workforce is changing and we are moving into uncharted territory, while a smaller older population of skilled workers increasingly come at a premium. Companies that put their heads in the sand and refuse to recognize this threat will put their future growth and profitability at risk, whilst missing out on the benefits of greater age diversity. Employment decisions based on age neither make good business sense nor will they be legal.

The business benefits of a mixed-age workforce are now widely recognized. There is clear evidence that both staff turnover and absenteeism are reduced and that motivation and commitment are improved in organizations employing people of all ages. By expanding the age group you employ, you will be recruiting from a bigger pool and therefore will automatically broaden your resource of talent, skills, experience and knowledge.

It isn't only the workforce that is changing but also the customer base. By changing your workforce to match that of the general population you will match the profile of your customers. According to Malcolm Wicks, former minister for pensions, businesses of all sizes are reaping the benefits. 'There are proven advantages to having a workforce of older, as well as younger, people,' he says. 'Among them are better productivity, reduced absenteeism, a wider customer base, and a broader range of skills and experience, raised morale and loyalty among staff, improved staff retention and reduced recruitment costs.'

Rachel's Organic Dairy based in Aberystwyth, Wales, is one of the many companies that agrees that recruiting older workers makes excellent business sense. HR manager Phil Evans explains:

We currently have 104 employees ranging from 17 to 63, with an average age of 38 – up ten years since 1998. There have been three main benefits of this. First, it has assisted us in reinforcing our company values, which include respect for individuals', and customers', sovereignty. Second, it has helped in lowering employee turnover rates, and third, it has allowed teams to develop mature and responsible attitudes (Diversity at Work 2005).

Evaluations of older workers show that a high proportion are flexible in accepting change in occupation and earnings and are often more flexible about the times they work. Many are able to work part time and have a better attendance record than the younger worker. They are also less likely to take time off for family, responsibilities, childbirth or caring for elderly parents, in spite of the latter being an issue for many (*Maturity Works*).

A recent UK report by the independent Institute for Employment Studies states that:

Quite aside from their experience, older workers are more committed and reliable, have better customer-facing skills, understand business better, and take less short-term sickness absence. Moreover, with few younger workers to pick from in the future, organizations are going to have to become better employers of these older workers, more able to attract them for their benefits, and accommodate them for their needs (The Fifties Revival, J. Kodz, B. Kersley, P. Bates. IES Report 359, 1999).

Dianah Worman, CIPD diversity adviser, says:

Age discrimination is costly to business, given that older workers achieve the same levels of performance as younger workers. In fact the business case for employing older workers seems more compelling as they are more likely to stay in their jobs for longer. The cost of replacing staff is more than £3500 on average.

The Institute warns employers that they need to start changing their ways: 'immediate knee-jerk damage-limitation responses – will be too late and may leave companies exposed to legal risks', it states in its document: *The Challenge of the Age.*

3. AGE-NEUTRAL RECRUITMENT

The term 'older worker' is generally used for people over 50. As discussed earlier this group finds it hard to get work because age discrimination is most common during recruitment and selection.

In order to have an age-neutral recruitment process you will need to review your current practices and take action in the following areas:

1. Job specification and selection criteria

2. Context: considerations for flexible working

3. Age considerations

4. Salaries and benefits

5. Sourcing the right people

6. Age-neutral application forms

7. Advertising

8. Short-listing using competencies as the criteria

9. Interviews and managing stereotypes

10. Selection.

You will need to review your current practices, policies and documents to ensure equal opportunity for all age groups. As we saw in Chapter 5 Changing Attitudes and Stereotypes, stereotypical thinking and discrimination is embedded in our culture. Unwittingly there may be negative messages given in your recruitment materials. Advertisements, for example, are one of the main barriers to older people during the recruitment process.

Exercise 9.1

Exercise 9.1 offers you an opportunity to take a look at the materials you use and to see if they are age neutral. This would be a good exercise to do with all HR personnel. We all perceive language differently so a number of views will widen the knowledge base.

4. JOB DESCRIPTIONS, PERSON SPECIFICATIONS AND APPLICATION FORMS

Job descriptions should already be age-neutral documents outlining the responsibilities, duties, activities and accountabilities associated with a particular role. This is unlikely to need to be changed in the light of the legislation though you might revisit your job descriptions to ensure that the language is not discriminatory in any way.

One of the dilemmas that you will be facing you as a result of the new legislation is how to gather information about people's suitability for a job. In the past you have been able to request a chronologically arranged CV with details of a person's skills and experience over time. You will no longer be able to do this.

In the person specification you will now need to specify the competencies you require for a role without seeking information with regard to length of service. HR and line managers will need to work closely together to identify relevant requirements.

We would suggest that you divide the person specification into two sections: one part to focus on competencies, the other to focus on personal information.

In order to produce the competencies specification you will need to identify the precise skills, knowledge and behaviour that an individual would need in order to undertake the specific role that is vacant. This enables you to match abilities with job functions. Within this section you will need to identify and describe the relevant knowledge and experiences a person will require to carry out the role effectively.

For example, if you have a vacancy in your organization for a conference organizer. Both of the competencies you might require would include: planning, communicating and co-ordinating others internally and externally, sourcing providers, managing risk, overseeing contracts and insurance, promotion and advertising.

A person of any age who had developed these skills inside or outside the workplace and was able to demonstrate these would be eligible to apply.

It is advisable to consider the individual's personal qualities and also the activities they have undertaken that would be relevant to the effective performance of the role. When it comes to the application form there should be space for this information. For example, detailing the requirement for a GCSE excludes older workers who may have had a CSE or O level in that subject but not GCSE. Any competency criteria must be essential to the job and inclusion of any unnecessary competencies can go against the principles of equal opportunity. In this way you might inadvertently discriminate against the older worker.

Age-neutral application forms

If you are to ensure that the recruitment process is truly age-neutral you need to produce an age-neutral application form so that those who are recruiting the candidate do not know their age or chronological career history. The line manager or decision-maker would therefore only see the part of a person's application form that is relevant to the role, that is, the part that asks for competencies. They will make their decisions based solely on this. In some positions it may be deemed necessary for the selectors to know the employment history. This will be acceptable if there is a geniune reason why it is needed.

It will still be necessary for organizations to record an individual's relevant personal details. For example, date of birth will be needed for pension and insurance reasons. HR will need to file the personal information separately and securely, as this should be kept confidential and not be common knowledge. We suggest that this is done on a separate application form and is not used in the selection procedure. Remember to only ask for information that is relevant to the post. Our recommendations for an age-neutral application form would therefore be that it was divided into two sections:

Part one (confidential document)

- Personal details, name, address
- Education and qualifications, including grades achieved
- Employment history giving details of all previous posts, including part-time and unpaid work. Current or most recent employer comes first
- Memberships of professional bodies or associations
- Courses or activities undertaken, both technical, professional and personal
- References.

Part 2 (open to selectors)

- Skills and competencies
- Knowledge
- Behaviour
- Supporting statement which can include personal qualities, hobbies, interests and ambitions
- Employment history without dates or chronology.

If your organization uses on-line applications these will also need to be updated. If computer literacy is not an essential skill for the post advertised you should consider making these application forms available in hard copy.

The HR department would need to use their discretion regarding what they share with the manager so as not to trigger prejudice or stereotypical thinking. The EFA have produced a draft application form (see useful organizations at the end of the book).

5. ADVERTISING

Advertisements are often the first point of contact a future employee has with your organization. The language you use is critical and will convey your company's attitude towards age. The perceptions made by the reader can discourage suitable individuals from even making the initial contact with your company. This will reduce the labour pool, creating missed recruitment opportunities for your business. In the first successful age discrimination case in Europe, in Eire in 2002, Ryanair was fined £8000 under the Southern Irish 1998 Employment Equality Act for using the term 'young and dynamic professional' in a recruitment advertisement.

Exercise 9.2

Exercise 9.2 offers you an opportunity to look at the words used and the underlying message portrayed. For example the word 'dynamic' is considered by many to be associated with youth but there are plenty of dynamic people in their fifties, for example, Bob Geldof who organized LIVE 8 in July 2005 and changed people's awareness of world poverty.

Placing your advertisement is equally important. You need to review the advertising media and location regularly to ensure that you are reaching a wide range of potential applicants. If you only advertise on the Internet or in magazines for the older person such as Saga you will be reducing the pool of talent available to you. A number of companies report that a usually forgotten but highly effective and inexpensive way to advertise is using the local resources such as the local paper or putting flyers through people's doors. Use positive representative pictures and language to ensure you appeal to the widest audience. B&Q and Asda have both succeeded in attracting and employing mature employees by changing their advertising strategies. More than 16 per cent of Asda's workforce is over 50, and more than 1000 employees are over the age of 65.

Exercise 9.3 is useful for managers who are responsible for writing for their department's job advertisements.

✎ Exercise 9.3

6. INTERVIEWS

Every part of the recruitment process will need to be reviewed and this includes your current interview practices. Managers and those who carry out your interview process will need training in age awareness.

One way to reduce ageism is to ensure that your interview panel is of mixed age to reflect the workforce you plan to employ. All those attending will need to be aware of the new regulations and although we are focusing on the older worker these regulations will, of course, affect people of all ages.

To avoid ageism at the initial recruitment stage, D & G, a call centre, introduced telephone interviews. The benefits of these interviews are two-fold; telephone interviews reduce any possible bias on age, and, as all their work is telephone-based, this interview can test the individual's telephone skills. This has increased the percentage of older workers that are invited to the second stage of the process.

Line managers' attitudes are particularly important, especially if the HR function is decentralized and individual managers have more responsibility for recruitment. Age can be used subconsciously as a quick method to assess a person. As we have seen in Chapter 5 Changing Attitudes and Stereotypes, stereotypical assumptions impact decision making. Managers may also be reluctant to recruit subordinate staff who are older than themselves, as discussed in Chapter 6 People Management (section 1 on Transactional Analysis).

Those responsible for interviewing will also need to be sensitive to age-related issues. These include the fact that large numbers of older workers do not have university qualifications because it was not the norm at the time. This is particularly true for women. It is equally less likely that they will have a masters qualification because very few people outside academia used to participate in these courses, whereas it is now a reasonably common practice for younger people.

Nonetheless, this doesn't mean that this group have not acquired skills and strengths. Many of them will have achieved high status, vast experience and been highly successful individuals. Therefore it is important to be open to judging them on different criteria that are equally valid and useful.

The environment you create for an interview and the type of questions you ask need to be carefully considered in order to gauge a person's capabilities accurately. Questions will need to be broad so as to be relevant to all age groups.

Exercise 9.4

With equal opportunity interviews it is essential that the questions offer an opportunity for all candidates to show their expertise whatever their background and education. Exercise 9.4 helps practise formulating age-neutral questions.

Exercise 9.5

The approach to the interview also needs to be age-neutral. Many of us find that although we know the theory, in practice we revert to stereotypical behavioural patterns that are indirectly discriminatory. The role plays in Exercise 9.5 give you an opportunity to explore this.

SUMMARY

This chapter has shown you how important it is to be aware of what is often indirect discrimination when recruiting staff. Many older workers feel anxious and demotivated when they see advertisements that exclude them purely on age. Most people feel disappointed and rejected when they are not successful following a job application. The individual then often justifies why this has happened. They may assume that it is discriminatory and start a legal proceeding against the company. Interviewers often have no intention of suggesting anything of a discriminatory nature but if they are not vigilant about the language they use they can do so indirectly.

These two factors together can cause explosive situations that are detrimental to organizations. Increasingly, as with other areas of discrimination, people will with justification be highly sensitive about this topic. When the new legislation is passed, litigation is likely unless you are really scrupulous when managing this emotive area of recruitment and selection.

Six tips

1. **Take some time to explore your recruitment material and ensure that any words that could be seen as age discriminatory are removed.**

2. **Place recruitment advertisements more widely than before. Consider where you might attract a broader age group of candidates.**

3. **Understand how it feels to be a very young or very old candidate.**

4. **Train those who may have to undertake interviews in age-neutral practices.**

5. **Identify a mixed-age interview panel.**

6. **Use competencies rather than experience as criteria for selection.**

AGE-AWARENESS EXERCISE

Carry out a word search exercise in your current recruitment and selection materials in order to analyse age discrimination in the language of policies, forms and advertisements. Notice words such as:

Age

Date of birth

Age-bands

Mature

Experienced

Years in a job

Aged between …

Young

Salary relevant to age and experience

Must have GCSE [a recent qualification]

Dynamic

Lively

 Exercise 9.2

AGE-NEUTRAL LANGUAGE

Brainstorm all the adjectival words you currently use in your job advertisements, for example:

Dynamic, bright, young mature or even graduate, etc.

How many of them are age-related or could be perceived to be so?

Produce a list of alternative words that attract the right candidate without being age discriminatory.

JOB ADVERTISEMENT

This exercise follows on from Exercise 9.2. This is ideally done with a group of 8–10. Divide the group into two.

Ask each group to write an advertisement for the following two posts.

Group 1
Imagine that you have job vacancies for:

(a)   A junior administrative clerk
(b)   A senior management post

Group 2
Imagine that you have job vacancies for:

(b)   A post room worker
(c)   A senior technical/ professional adviser

(You can chose whatever posts you think would be relevant to your organization.)

When they have written their advertisements ask them to swap these with the other group. Ask each group to look at the advert to check it is age-neutral and appealing. It can also be useful to talk to employees of different ages about the content of your job advertisements and find out what would attract or appeal to them.

JOB ADVERTISEMENT

Group 1
Imagine that you have job vacancies for:

(a)   A junior administrative clerk

(b)   A senior management post

Group 2
Imagine that you have job vacancies for:

(a)   A post room worker

(b)   A senior technical/professional adviser

Write an advertisement below that is age-neutral.

Note: words that may be seen as age discriminatory are as follows:

lively	ambitious
bright	funky
fit	graduate
mature	dependable
responsible	reliable
experienced	dynamic

```
ADVERT




```

INTERVIEW QUESTIONS

This is an exercise you can do with your interviewers to help them to prepare age-neutral questions.

Which of the following questions would you be able to use in an age-neutral interview?

1. What have you been doing since you left school?
2. What contribution could you make to this organization?
3. How would you undertake x task?
4. What GCSEs did you get?
5. How do you feel about having a boss that is younger than you?
6. Do you fit in with different age groups?
7. Where did you go on your gap year?
8. Which university did you go to?
9. How did you manage living on your own when you were at university?
10. We use a lot of technology around here, will you find that difficult?
11. We don't have a lift; can you manage three flights of stairs?
12. How do you feel about training?
13. We are looking for someone with experience; do you feel you have sufficient?
14. Don't you think you are over-qualified for this job and might get bored?
15. Do you have a current pension scheme?

(Questions 1, 4, 5, 6, 7, 8, 9, 10, 11, 13 and 14 are not age-neutral.)

It is always advisable to have a list of suitable questions available for the interviewer and ensure that they feel confident and capable of running an effective age-neutral interview.

Useful questions could include the following:

1. What skills would you bring to this role?
2. What motivates you at work?
3. What do you value in teamwork?
4. What is your preferred way of working?
5. Tell me about an occasion when you made a mistake and how you responded and rectified it?
6. What are your views on in-house training?
7. What contribution can you make to this organization?

INTERVIEW ROLE PLAYS

These exercises can be done with just two people or done in a larger group. In our experience it is often useful to have six to eight participants so a number of different perspectives can be gathered. When using these role plays it is important to:

a. get into role;
b. once finished, help people to de-role by moving out of the role;
c. have a discussion, as yourselves, about the effects of playing that particular role.

It is often very helpful to play a part that is not like you, so make sure that you try being the very young worker, the medium-aged worker and the older worker so that you are able to empathize with each.

Role Play 1
28-year-old young woman or man interviewing a 57-year-old opposite gender worker for a junior post in their department.

Role Play 2
Senior manager interviewing someone of a similar age for a junior post.

Role Play 3
Older manager interviewing a new university graduate (try this with somebody who is 22 as the graduate, and try this with someone who is 48).

Role Play 4
An older senior manager who has been in post many years interviewing a young person who has applied for the post of Head of the Department.

INTERVIEW ROLE PLAYS

Debrief

How did it feel to be the older person?

How did it feel to be the younger person?

What specific questions or words made you feel valued or devalued?

Were there particular age-discriminatory words or attitudes or behaviours used?

Have a discussion with the group about selection. Based on everything that has been said before, it is important that at the last moment you do not allow your stereotypical views, or those of your colleagues, to colour your decision making.

Ask yourself the question, particularly when you are faced with two different candidates of different ages: 'Would we be taking x if x and y were the same age?' If the answer is no, you need to go back to the drawing board.

181

CHAPTER 10

Performance Management

The appraisal season is just about to start. The HR department, initiated by Sally, has produced a new form that they want to pilot. They think this will help them to meet the requirements of the new Age Discrimination Regulations. The new system is competency based.

Maria is sitting at her desk with her appraisal form in front of her. She is trying to fill it in and has got as far as the personal development plan. She is stuck as to what to say. She would like to go on day-release training at college which lasts a year and would enable her to apply for other jobs within XYZ. However, she is convinced that her boss won't let her go as she is in her mid-50s. Although she plans these appraisal sessions, as soon as she gets into the room she loses confidence and forgets what to say.

Further down the corridor Simon is filling in his form. He knows he will be into an argument with his boss. He is going to sit it out until he retires. He is fed up with having to do personal development plans; he considers he has developed enough and he doesn't see why he should do any more at his time of life.

Bill, his manager, has just completed his appraisal training. He knows that he is in for a difficult time with Simon. He is wondering how he is going to use the new competency framework. Simon's work has to improve and Bill knows he has to think laterally if he is going to succeed.

Heidi is also planning her session with her direct report, Maria. In her opinion Maria tends to blow hot or cold, either wanting to do training that is not appropriate for her job, or not wanting to do anything to develop herself. Heidi thinks that she and Maria just don't seem to see things from the same perspective. Maria seems at times to willfully misunderstand. She seems content to stay where she is and have an easy life. Heidi knows that at times she finds it hard to understand people who don't want a challenge. She thrives on new and difficult tasks. She sits back and thinks for a moment about her appraisal three years ago; she had asked for some more responsibility and she had been given an acting head of department role which has changed her career.

Possible outcomes

All four people come away from the session dissatisfied; Simon and Maria feel that whatever they do nothing has or will change. Bill feels stuck and wonders if he is going to have to go down the disciplinary route – a costly and unpleasant activity. Heidi is saddened that Maria is not realizing her potential.

Appraisals or performance development reviews have been part of most organization's procedures for a number of years. In this section we will refer to them as performance appraisal reviews. They offer an opportunity for both an individual and their manager to look at the work the individual has undertaken over the last six months or year and create a development plan.

The specific purposes of the process are:

1. The performance appraisal review: this provides all staff with a framework within which they can review their performance (knowledge, behaviour and skills) and gain recognition for their contribution and achievements.

2. Objective setting: this ensures that all staff know the importance of their role and how their work and objectives fit with the aims and objectives of the organization.

3. Personal development plan: this offers a place:

   (a) for staff to discuss their development and training needs and to ensure that their training and development supports them to undertake their job effectively.

   (b) to give staff feedback and help them identify their short- and long-term career direction and goals.

This chapter focuses on how you can use the performance appraisal review and the personal development plan to enhance an older workers' skills and motivation and bring genuine rewards to the business.

The topics covered are:

1. The performance appraisal review
2. The business case
3. Overcoming blocks
4. Managing the performance appraisal review meeting
5. Empowering the older worker
6. Setting goals and objectives.

1   THE PERFORMANCE APPRAISAL REVIEW

We have explored in previous chapters why businesses will increasingly need to employ, manage and retain older workers. This is essential if they are going to successfully manage the demographic shifts and act within the law. In order to maintain a relationship with your older workers you will have to focus on training, career planning and performance appraisal. This chapter will explore performance appraisal and touch on training and career planning. These topics will be discussed in more depth in Chapters 11 and 12.

Research undertaken by The Institute of Employment Studies reports that there are numerous myths about workers of different ages. These include views that older workers have lower career aspirations and expectations; that they are more resistant to change; they are less able to cope with change; more difficult to train and less able to learn new skills, particularly new technology (Itzin and Philipson, 1994; Whithnall et al, 2004.)

It has been shown that attributes and competencies are not tied to age. However the evidence in the literature suggests that at present many older workers face a set of beliefs and assumptions held by their managers that limit their access to training.

In research undertaken by Meadows (2003) she concluded that there is no discernable deterioration in performance in the majority of different types of work, at least up until the age of 70. Critically, she found that the factor that impacted on level of performance was training – precisely what older workers are likely to be excluded from.

> *Only where older workers do not receive the same level of training as younger workers doing the same work, does their performance show differences. Older workers who receive job-related training reach the same skill standards as younger workers.*

The performance appraisal review is the place where career aspiration and training and development needs are identified. In the light of the Age Discrimination Regulations performance appraisal reviews need to be high on all managers' agendas if they are to facilitate effective performance management for all age groups.

Appraisal forms, like application forms discussed in Chapter 9 Recruiting and Selecting Older Workers, need to be age-neutral. It may be necessary for you to review your appraisal forms and procedures to ensure that they are age-inclusive. Useful exercises to help you to undertake this are Exercises 9.1 and 9.2. The form needs to use competency-based measures both to evaluate a member of staff's work and to ensure that appropriate training is offered to them. You will need to develop a competency-based system which focuses on the skills required to undertake a particular job.

Many of our older clients have commented how anxious they feel at their appraisals. It takes them back to school and memories of being called into the headmaster's office. They feel ill equipped and at a disadvantage. Many young people arrive at the workplace totally familiar with the system, as they have been brought up on records of achievement at school, which involve them discussing their development with their teachers.

The advantages of a competency-based system is that by focusing on the role and not the individual, it enables organizations to base promotion on measurable performance indicators rather than age, and base any redundancies on objective criteria, not on age or length of service. Furthermore you need to ensure that terms such as 'energetic', 'dynamic' and 'lively' do not appear in a section of personal attributes needed for a particular position as they may be indirectly discriminatory. Managers may well believe that these are not attributes found in the over 50s and therefore assume the individual has not met these criteria. It is important that your system does not feed into these beliefs and leave the older worker feeling inadequate. You will need to help your managers to challenge his or her own assumptions.

Many assumptions are made about older workers, their productivity and ability to learn. Their levels of performance need to be monitored just as closely as those of any staff. A number of our clients have said that their managers have lost interest in them and are waiting for them to leave. This makes them feel devalued and does not inspire them to work hard. From October 2006 treating older workers less favourably against the law.

Some of the assumptions we have heard younger managers make about their older colleagues are 'they can't learn new skills especially if they are technological,' 'there is no point setting them challenging targets during a performance appraisal review, they don't need to be developed because they are going nowhere – just waiting for retirement'.

The performance appraisal review process plays a crucial role in an individual's development and training plans. Their personal development plan is created during the appraisal review meeting. This plan details the individual's agreed way forward. The procedure needs to offer all staff an opportunity to fully participate in the process. In devising a system it is important you are aware of the issues facing the older worker (See Chapter 4 Understanding Your Older Workforce). The more preparation both parties undertake, the more effective the meeting is likely to be.

The following procedure, which allows the reviewee to fully prepare, is one we would recommend.

- The reviewer should set up a meeting with the reviewee at a mutually convenient time and give the reviewee a pre-appraisal form to complete.

- Both the individual and the manager need to assess before the meeting whether the individual has the necessary skills to perform this role, where there are difficulties, and what needs to be introduced, both to help them with their role and to develop their career.

- The reviewee and the reviewer should use the forms to trigger their thinking and subsequent discussion.

- During the meeting the personal development review (PDR) form is filled in and signed by both people and both are given a copy. This ensures that the system is totally transparent.

- The discussion documents can now be discarded (or kept by the individual who wrote them).

- The staff member, together with the reviewer should set SMART objectives for the coming year. See later in this chapter: Setting goals and objectives.

- Both of them must sign the objective sheet and they both keep a copy of this.

- The personal development plan is filled in during the last part of the meeting. This outlines both the training needs and career aspirations of the individual.

- The reviewee and reviewer keep a copy and a copy should be sent to the HR/ training department.

2. THE BUSINESS CASE

Many companies have had a covert policy of 'retiring' their older worker whom they thought was underperforming and many older workers have assumed this was 'the easy way out' and have put little effort into their development. Both are going to have to change if organizations are going to maintain their competitive edge and efficient services. The NHS is at present undergoing major changes in both its recruitment and retention policies to ensure it can maintain its present level of service.

Two very common questions asked when managers are considering the effects of the changes in the law are, 'How can I manage the exit of our older workers who are underperforming when they would have previously been retired?' and 'How can we make the most of the older workers' expertise without blocking potential career progression for junior staff?' The answer is through good performance management.

By basing performance management and development decisions on the grounds of ability and not age, employers will benefit in the following ways:

- They will create a more efficient workforce, which is necessary to overcome global skills shortages.

- They will develop valuable experience use existing talents and skills to the full and this in turn will improve stability, loyalty, motivation and productivity to maintain a 'corporate memory'.

- They will also benefit from improved staff development through the effective use of all employees in the training process.

It appears that the rate of absence increases significantly in both men and women in the four years prior to their retirement ages – 60 for women and 65 for men. On reaching retirement age those workers who choose to continue to work have much lower absence rates – around 2.5 per cent lower. This may mean that those who stay on are self-selecting and motivated and those waiting for retirement experience more illness. This may be due to stress leading up to retirement, possibly caused by a fear of leaving, or boredom with the task in hand. (Tim Barmby, Marco Ecolani and John Treble in *Sickness and Absence in the UK 1984–2002*, September 2003.)

Good performance management results in an engaged and motivated workforce who stay in post. It therefore reduces unnecessary business costs by minimizing recruitment expenses (search costs, and other costs associated with filling vacancies) and avoids the effects of inefficient recruitment decisions and inexperienced new employees. This will also reduce turnover and absenteeism (both proven benefits of employing an age-diverse workforce). It will also reduce early retirement costs and cut the expenses associated with legislative non-compliance, once legislation is introduced. All these measures will improve your corporate image and reputation.

3. OVERCOMING BLOCKS

It is essential that the performance development review be used to improve the working life of the individuals, their teams/departments and to enhance the business. As you can see from our scenario, our friends at XYZ Plc need to use the opportunity that presents itself in the form of the review to improve their working lives. The next section will look at ways to do this.

Maria raises a very common block for employees; that of losing confidence and therefore not expressing her true worth. An individual such as Maria needs to look at what stops her asking for what she wants. If she is able to increase her confidence and feel more able to express her views she has 100 per cent more opportunity to achieve her goals and that will bring with it benefits to the department and the organization.

For an appraisal to be totally effective the individual needs to know what they want, be objective and honest about their strengths and weaknesses and to approach the meeting in their adult ego state. The manager needs to feel secure in themselves and to be able to listen from their adult perspective. (See Chapter 6 People Management.) The manager needs to have a positive intention to support the individual and to keep their development the priority. The meeting is for the reviewee and only indirectly for the manager. The manager will have their turn in their own appraisal.

In order to do this the manager needs to rethink the approach. Career progression is not just promotion. Many of your older workers will have progressed to where they feel comfortable. This does not mean they want to feel bored. You need to consider some of the other options such as a mentoring role where they help develop and coach more junior staff or they move sideways into a different department or manage special projects. All of these ideas need to be considered by the manager prior to the review session. We have found in our work that both the reviewee and the reviewer can be anxious about the process. This is often expressed by managers who are younger than their direct reports, and also by managers for whom people issues don't come easily.

The confidence building exercise (Exercise 10.1) is useful for anyone who needs to work on this issue. The exercise can be done either as a coaching

Exercise 10.1

PERFORMANCE MANAGEMENT

session or with a group. Most organizations have appraiser training for their managers and some of the organizations we work with also offer preappraisal training courses for the reviewee. These courses enable the individual to learn the skills needed to use their review fully. These companies report that staff now look forward to these sessions and the business is benefiting from more motivated staff.

4. MANAGING THE PERFORMANCE APPRAISAL REVIEW MEETING

We each perceive the world from our own viewpoint. As we discussed in Chapter 6 Changing Attitudes and Stereotypes, these viewpoints are built on our beliefs, which develop through our interpretation of our experiences. We establish a unique set of filters based on these. We each interpret the world through a series of filters.

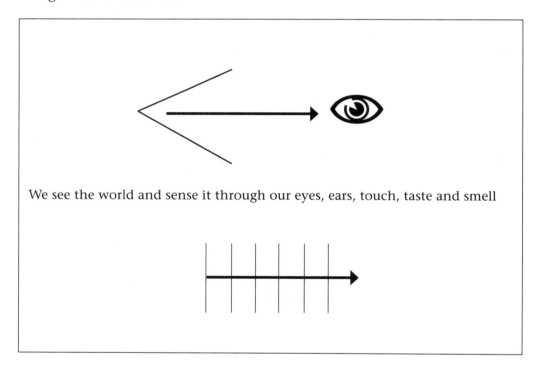

We see the world and sense it through our eyes, ears, touch, taste and smell

Figure 10.1   Filters

Our experiences effect how we see/feel the world. For example a male will see the world through the eyes of a man and a female will see the world through the eyes of a woman. They have no alternative. This will affect how they interpret situations. We all see the world differently and from our own unique perspective. As there are more than six billion of us in the world there are a lot of unique filters – no wonder it can sometimes be hard to communicate!

If we are to improve our communication it is essential to open ourselves to other possibilities. We need to listen and empathize with the other person and 'get into their shoes', that is, understand what it feels like for them and how they may see the world. This is discussed in detail in Chapter 6 People Management.

The more someone understands your perceptual filter the more they will understand why you are responding the way you do. The more you understand theirs the more easily you will communicate. One of the easiest ways to find out about another person is to ask them open questions (why, what, where, who, when, which and how). The more positive our attitude is when interpreting another's behaviour the more likely we will be in achieving a positive outcome.

Let's revisit our scenario. Heidi is aware that she and Maria have different perspectives. She knows that it would be helpful to understand Maria's point of view. At the moment she is speculating about Maria's motivation and making a lot of assumptions based on her own filters. This will colour her behaviour when she meets Maria at her review.

The type of interpretations Heidi might make about Maria are:

1. She is not interested in learning.

2. She has not really understood how her personal objectives fit in with the organizational objectives.

3. She is bored in her job and doesn't want to improve.

4. She wants to develop just to leave the organization.

5. She doesn't know how to ask for what she wants.

The list is endless.

Exercise 10.2 explores how our filters colour our perception of different situations.

Exercise 10.2

5. EMPOWERING THE OLDER WORKER

The purpose of a performance appraisal review, as we have discussed, is two-fold. One is to help the individual to assess their success so far and to understand where they might need to improve in order to achieve their goals. The other is for them to align their goals with the organization's goals and develop the necessary skills to achieve these. It should be a win–win situation where both the individual and the manager/organization benefit. It is not a competition. Many older workers may have been brought up in a period where it was common to engage in a win–lose style of debating/arguing. They may need help to develop consensual adult-to-adult communication.

PERFORMANCE
MANAGEMENT

WIN–WIN Communication

Respecting yourself

Giving respect to others

Expressing needs

Allowing others to express needs

Being able to say 'No'

Being able to say 'I don't understand'

Seeking a win–win solution

Figure 10.2   Win–win communication

If a manager is going to achieve win–win communication and help an individual to hear which things need improving they are going to have to be very skilled in giving feedback. Both Heidi and Bill will need to give Maria and Simon feedback on their work and listen openly to any feedback given to them.

We learn about ourselves and how others view us from the feedback we are given. Without this we would only see the world in one way and we would be very blinkered. The feedback anyone gives is coloured by their own experiences and perception. Giving positive and constructive feedback is a difficult and important communication skill.

Exercise 10.3

Exercise 10.4

6. SETTING GOALS AND OBJECTIVES

Bill is faced with a difficult task: he is hoping to motivate Simon and set with him some clear objectives to ensure they have an agreed way forward. Bill needs to find out from Simon what motivates him (see Chapter 6 People Management). He knows that if things are going to change Simon will have to develop new ways of working. He also needs to understand what makes Simon resistant to change. It may be useful for Simon and Bill to do the change questionnaire together. (See Chapter 7 Managing Change.) This will help them both to understand each other. It will also send a message to Simon that this is not just down to him. Knowing that the other person is equally involved and shares the responsibility can take a lot of the heat out of a situation.

Once Bill and Simon have discussed Simon's aspirations and agreed what areas Simon is going to work on they need to set objectives. The objectives must belong to the reviewee. If they are the manager's for the reviewee, the individual will feel they have been told what to do and may well ignore it. The most effective way to help an individual create their objectives is to ask the person what it is they want to do, or think they need to do, to improve the situation. Once they have told you and agreed you will have their total buy in and will achieve a win–win situation.

Exercise 10.5 on objective setting will help you to learn how to do this.

✏ Exercise 10.5

SUMMARY AND TIPS

This chapter has looked at an extremely important part of people management. The personal appraisal review is an essential tool for staff development, training and career progression. It is essential that all staff whatever their age feel valued and have an equal opportunity to learn new skills. It is important to help all your staff to develop their career and tackle new challenges, this is equally important for the older worker.

The importance of a performance appraisal review is not always understood by task focused managers who don't understand and don't value the time spent on people focused activities. It is essential that they are helped to see that without an effective motivated staff team they will not meet their targets.

This process is particularly important when you have either disaffected staff or staff who are not meeting their targets. For all the reasons discussed in earlier chapters there will most likely be an increase in staff who had hoped to retire and for many reasons can't. The one-to-one review interview offers the perfect place to re-engage and motivate the person to contribute.

Six tips

1. **Look at your appraisal system and paperwork, and check it for age-discriminatory words.**

2. **Look at changing your system to a competency-based system.**

3. **Give everyone an equal opportunity to learn whatever their age.**

4. **Make sure you understand what motivates the individual and find ways to enable them to achieve their goals.**

5. **Don't let stereotypical views about the older/younger worker affect the process or outcomes of the session.**

6. **See appraisal review sessions as the ideal way to set objectives that meet both the organization's and the individual's goals, and achieve win–win results.**

PERFORMANCE MANAGEMENT

CONFIDENCE BUILDING

This exercise is organized in two parts: the first to be done on your own and the second to be talked through with another.

CONFIDENCE BUILDING

STAGE ONE

Instructions for participants:

A. Think of a situation in which you feel totally self-confident and have a feeling of self-worth and answer the following questions:

a. What is the situation?
b. What do you say to yourself? (inner self-talk).
c. How do you feel? (feelings and sensations in the body).
d. What do you do? (as a consequence).

B. Think of a current situation in which you experience a lack of self confidence and self worth that you would like to and could change, and answer the following questions (it is helpful to think of the appraisal session here):

a. What is the situation?
b. What do you say to yourself? (inner self-talk)
c. How do you feel? (feelings and sensations in the body).
d. What do you do? (as a consequence).

C. Go back to the situation in Part B and using the information that you have about yourself from the situation in Part A ask yourself the following questions:

a. What could I say to myself? (a positive statement about self).
b. How could I feel differently? (for example, if you want to feel more relaxed you could breathe more deeply).
c. What could I and will I do differently? (what direct action could I take and will take).

STAGE TWO

If this exercise is happening in a coaching session, the facilitator takes the place of the partner. If you are working with a group ask them to choose someone to work with and to take 10 minutes each to share with their partner Part C of the exercise. The person who is listening can help the person clarify and specify exactly what they are going to do by asking OPEN QUESTIONS. (See Chapter 6 People Management.)

For example:

'What will you say to yourself?'

'How will you feel differently?'

'What will you do to feel differently?'

'What exactly will you do in the situation?'

INTERPRETATION OF SITUATIONS

This group exercise helps to increase awareness of our filters.

- Ask the group to divide into groups of four or five.

- Give them a number of situations and ask them to interpret them in as many ways as possible.

You can make this a competition by timing them for three minutes per scenario and seeing which group gets the most. Some groups enjoy this.

- After you have completed the scenarios let everyone look at the sheets of paper and have a plenary discussion on filters.

The learning point in this exercise is that unless you ask somone what they think, you will never know, as we all interpret people and situations differently.

Possible situations:

1. A person is regularly late to meetings

2. A person doesn't call you back when they said they would

3. An older person who is always quiet at meetings

4. An older person who always blows their own trumpet

5. A person who is unexpectedly offhand

6. An older person who is irritable

7. A person who never shares their ideas with the team

The reviewer needs to set the scene by creating a comfortable neutral environment, to be warm and open and put the individual at their ease.

Once they have brainstormed their initial thoughts, ask them to go back to the examples and answer the following questions. Once completed, discuss the experience in a plenary session.

✎ Exercise 10.2 | *continued*

During the session the manager needs to help the individual to consider:

1. What are their concerns?

2. What other pressures do they have on their time?

3. What might motivate them?

4. What are their drivers?

5. Are their priorities aligned to that of the business?

PERFORMANCE
MANAGEMENT

GIVING AND RECEIVING FEEDBACK

This exercise is ideally done in groups of 6–8 people. If you are working with a larger group divide the group into two:

Name	Car	Food	Musical Instrument	Animal

1. Draw a grid like the one above on the flip chart and ask the participants to write down the name of everyone in the group.

2. Ask them to write down for each individual what they would consider them to be if they were, for example, a food.

3. Once they have written it down, each person is given feedback from the other group members with an explanation why they have chosen that animal, food etc .

For example

I see you as an ant as you carry the world/team on your shoulders!

I see you as a cart horse as I know you would pull me out of any situation!

I see you as a delicious salad with an unexpected spicy sauce because most of the time you are lovely but every so often there is a snappy response!

I see you as a bowl of soup as you are very good at starting things but not so good at finishing them!

In the plenary session discuss what they have discovered about themselves and giving and receiving feedback. Many of your managers will think that giving feedback is much easier when the individual is younger than them. They often find it more difficult if they are the same age or older.

FEEDBACK ROLE PLAYS

These exercises can be done with just two people or done in a larger group. In our experience it is often useful to have six to eight participants so a number of different perspectives can be gathered.

When using these role plays it is important to:

1. Get into role.

2. Once finished, to de-role.

3. Have a discussion, as yourselves, about the effects of playing that particular role.

It is often very helpful to play a part that is not like you, so make sure that you try being the very young worker, the medium-aged worker and the older worker so that you are able to empathize with each.

Role Play 1
A 47-year-old woman or man reviewing a similarly aged, opposite gender worker who has been in the company as long as they have and hasn't reached the same seniority.

Role Play 2
A 29-year-old new manager reviewing a 50-year-old team member.

Role Play 3
An ambitious 35-year-old manager reviewing an older worker who doesn't want promotion.

Role Play 4
A manager reviewing an older worker who has made it clear they are counting the days until they retire. (Try this with it being six months and six years away).

Role Play 5
A 52-year-old worker telling their younger manager that they think they are not being offered the same opportunities as others in the team.

Role Play 6
An older worker telling their 'workaholic' manager that they want to work part time and to take on a mentoring role.

Have a discussion after the role plays to explore what they find difficult when giving feedback to an older worker, and develop some strategies to help them. It may be useful on any of your appraisal trainings to give the participants a handout on feedback.

GUIDELINES FOR GIVING AND RECEIVING FEEDBACK

1. Make sure the feedback is specific and clear, for example, 'yesterday when you were giving a presentation, during the introduction you appeared to be reading the notes and not looking at the group.'

2. Feedback is only relevant in the context of what an individual is trying to achieve. Make sure you know what the person's goals are.

3. Feedback needs to be non-evaluative and non-judgemental, for example, 'The dress you wore yesterday to go to the client meeting was not suitable because the skirt was too short', not 'I don't like the dress you wore.'

4. Feedback is only useful if it is given about something that can be changed. There is no point telling someone that his or her feet are too big!

5. Feedback must focus on an action or behaviour not on the whole person as though they are the action, for example, not 'You are stupid' but 'In X situation it would have been more appropriate if you had done Y.'

6. Make 'I' statements. It is important not to give second-hand feedback, for example, 'When X happened I felt Y.' Not – 'Mary said, "When you did X she felt Y".'

7. Feedback must be constructive. Nobody makes mistakes because they want to; it is usually because they don't have as yet the skills needed to do something differently. It is most helpful when it is linked to a possible solution.

8. Feedback will be listened to and acknowledged if it is given with a positive intention.

9. The feedback you give says as much about the giver as the receiver.

When receiving feedback:

1. Accept positively – that is, listen and don't negate it especially when it is positive.

2. Check that what you have heard has been said, for example, ask questions, paraphrase, repeat and check understanding.

3. Evaluate it, that is, check it out with others. Just because X says you are stupid doesn't mean they are right!

4. Choose if you want to do anything with the feedback, in which case set yourself a personal goal to achieve change.

OBJECTIVE SETTING

This exercise can be done on both appraisee and appraiser training. Objective setting is a skill that is needed by all. Managers must master this so they can help their staff to change their desires into objectives.

Objectives follow a formula, they must be:

S	Specific
M	Measurable
A	Appropriate
R	Realistic
T	Time related

An example would be: I want to run a five-mile charity fun run next April.

- Specific = five-mile charity run.

- Measurable = I will have run or I won't!

- Appropriate= five miles is in my physical capabilities.

- Realistic= with six months' training I will be able to achieve this.

- Time related = next April.

Take the following comments and apply the 'SMART' criteria to the statement below.

- X should work to improve his relationship with younger staff.

- We agreed that X would work to improve his technology skills.

- X will work on her use of the computer in the next six months.

- X should try to make a better presentation of himself.

- X will undertake more selling work in the next six months to increase the age range of her clients.

- X will try to pay more attention to the coaching and development of older staff.

- I have explained to X the need to show more interest in the older members of the team.

Lifelong Learning

'Oh dear, my boss has allocated me to go on a training course to learn about Excel spreadsheets. I know there will be all those young kids from Tech Support there and I shall just feel stupid,' Maria says to Raj.

He laughs, 'There's plenty you know that they don't!'

'Well, I suppose so but the trouble is my memory is really going now I'm older and I'll never remember what I learnt.'

'Yes, I know what you mean – I can never remember everyone's names and faces these days. But don't worry it's even a problem for the Chief Exec.: he couldn't remember my name the other day and I've been here for 25 years!' Raj commented.

'Well.' Maria says, 'I heard the Chief Exec. had private management training and asked the trainer to go in the back door so that no one would realize that he didn't already know it all!'

'Actually that is rather a relief,' Raj grins, 'At least we are not alone in not feeling confident about our skills.'

'No but us oldies hardly ever get the opportunity to go on training courses because they think we are past it anyway,' Maria grumbles.

'And when we do,' Raj laughs, 'we complain!'

Possible outcome

Maria goes to the training course lacking in self-confidence and stressed so is unlikely to learn well. The organization suffers from older people not keeping up to date and taking longer to fulfil their targets.

Many older workers have been neglected when it comes to training. Under the new legislation organizations must offer training to all age groups and not discriminate on the grounds of age. HR and line management will therefore need to review current policies and procedures to ensure that all age groups are treated equally with regard to training and development. The Regulations will have a specific impact on organizations providing vocational education and training to the wider community.

This chapter will focus on the measures you can take to ensure that your training practices are age-inclusive, and also to enable your older workers to feel confident of their ability to enjoy lifelong learning.

The topics covered in this chapter are:

1. Discriminatory practices

2. Return on training investment

3. Confidence in learning skills

4. Strategies to maintain lifelong learning for older workers

5. Applying individual intelligences to successful learning

6. Use it or lose it.

1. DISCRIMINATORY PRACTICES

It is interesting and disillusioning that despite much lip service to 'lifelong learning' many employees over 50 are not gaining access to training. In our own experience as trainers and coaches the overwhelming majority of people attending training courses are in their 30s.

The Bureau of Labor Statistics in the US calculated that older workers (aged 55+) receive on average less than half the amount of training than younger staff – even if one includes those in the age group of 45–54. Part of this problem can be attributed to the attitude of the organization, which may be covertly discriminatory about upskilling older workers.

Lack of training leaves older workers at a disadvantage not only in their own job but also within the job market as a whole. Organizations in many sectors need staff but older people can be excluded because they do not have the right qualifications. For example, this problem was highlighted recently in the teaching profession where those who may have been senior teachers or even heads were unable to find a new teaching post because they did not have a GCSE or A level qualification in the relevant subject. The criteria for these posts have changed: O levels have been replaced with GCSEs, and therefore extremely experienced teachers are being excluded from applying to posts for which they could well be suited.

Within the National Health Service it has been demonstrated that when older people leave their jobs and try to find new positions they can discover that their skills and experience are not relevant to the jobs now available in the labour market, 76 per cent of which are now in the service sector (Cabinet Office, 2000).

2. RETURN ON TRAINING INVESTMENT

Exercise 11.1

There has been a perception that training or upskilling older employees is a wasted investment. As one employer commented, 'It costs us a lot to train our staff. We can't afford to train people and see them retire within a few months.' A colleague replied, 'Well how many of those 28 year olds will still be with us in five years' time do you think?' This is certainly a debatable point.

Under the new legislation an organization will only be able to exclude an older worker from training if the training programme takes longer than the period of time a member of staff has until agreed retirement age, or if they can prove that there will not be any return on investment.

A report by David Simmons and Peter Urwin from the University of Westminster suggested that the practice of excluding older workers from training could be explained by human capital theory. This measures the impact of training in terms of the ability of the organization to reap the rewards of any enhanced productivity. If this cannot be proven through measurement then it is possible that the organization would decide that the associated costs of training may not be justifiable. With changes in the retirement age calculations will inevitably alter. Organizations will now have to prove that existing investment in training younger staff is being rewarded by increased retention. If not, to exclude an older worker from training could be regarded as discrimination. In fact, older workers tend on average to have spent 12.8 years in their current employment, which is longer than the average for younger age groups.

Continuous professional development

Many professional bodies now require their members to undertake a number of hours' training per annum in order to upgrade their knowledge and skills. This continuous professional development is a prerequisite for their membership to that professional body.

However, for many general management roles these rules do not apply and older managers can be left behind with regard to knowledge of up-to-date management and leadership practices. This undermines their confidence and their ability to manage well. Opening up training and development to all age groups will, therefore, enable staff to perform at their peak, continue to learn new skills and contribute more to their organizations.

Vocational education and training

All forms of vocational training including further, higher and other educational institutions, vocational guidance, practical work experience and all types of training which would help fit a person for employment will be covered by the Regulations. The Regulations apply to providers across the statutory, private and voluntary sectors. They also relate to bodies that accredit courses that result from vocational training. Vocational training providers will not be able to set age limits or age-related criteria for entry to training nor for the benefits offered to those they provide training to, for example offering help with costs to encourage participation among under-represented groups. The Directive allows for the setting of requirements in respect of age in certain circumstances, particularly access to vocational training for young people, older workers and persons with caring responsibilities. The Regulations also allows positive action to be taken towards access for vocational training if it prevents or compensates for disadvantages linked to age.

Vocational training providers will need to consider whether: there is a minimum or maximum age for entry generally or for access to specific courses; whether age is a consideration for applications for admission or access, and whether any fee discount arrangements are age-based. If that is the case then this will require justification. You will need to review whether you provide residential accommodation to students of all ages.

3. CONFIDENCE IN LEARNING SKILLS

Another reason for older people not attending training can also be the fact that many older workers feel less confident about attending training, fearing loss of face if they are shown not to know as much as their juniors might have expected of them. This can result in older workers avoiding going on courses or using imminent retirement as an excuse not to need training. Many, especially those who left school without any formal education, assume adult learning will be like school. They may benefit from individual coaching to enable them to join a course.

✏ Exercise 11.2

This is all the more reason to provide older workers with the confidence to attend courses so that they can gain the knowledge, skills and concepts about business skills and also management practices so as to help them raise the bar and continue to develop and grow. Learning new skills and information sparks new brain activity and neural pathways and it can be rejuvenating. Combined with their experience and the wisdom they gain over a lifetime of work these people can become, in one employer's terms 'the jewel in the crown'. He went on to say that the staff he had employed over the age of 55 brought perspective to situations and that training courses could provide a helpful opportunity for knowledge sharing.

A government report showed that the over-50s often arrived on training schemes with a lower level of prior formal qualifications but that they do as well as anyone else on the course. (*Training Older Workers*, Quality, Prevalence and Indicator Database (QPID), DfEE, 2000) However, lack of confidence in the ability to learn new skills can be a very real barrier to self-selection and can result also in an older participant on a training programme holding back.

Inevitably lack of knowledge and skills can have a negative impact on performance and it is therefore in everyone's benefit to ensure that all staff are equipped with the necessary training. This is not a 'soft' option and with the introduction of the Age Discrimination Regulations it will be essential for organizations to ensure that their older workers are included in these development programmes.

4. STRATEGIES TO MAINTAIN LIFELONG LEARNING FOR OLDER WORKERS

The next section will provide some specific actions and skills that you can offer your older workers in order to help them to feel confident in their ability to continue to participate in lifelong learning.

When the exercise has been fully analysed it should be possible for you to give an opinion as to whether older workers:

(a)   are less productive than their younger counterparts post-training

or

(b)   stay in the company for a shorter time post-training than their younger counterparts, thereby indicating reduced return on invest-ment.

If it is shown that return on investment is reduced then you may have reason to exclude older workers from training programmes. However, you will have to weigh this information against the fact that training and upskilling can enable a person to work faster and more effectively, to feel more confident about themselves and to experience increased motivation and morale.

Some companies experiencing these problems have negotiated deals with their older staff whereby if the company pays for training and the employee leaves earlier than the normal retirement age the individual may agree to repay the costs incurred by their employer. This will have to be changed to a period of, for example, five years.

The likely prospect that many staff will continue working further into old age would certainly make individual investment in human capital more attractive as the period during which returns would be reaped would inevitably be extended.

5. APPLYING INDIVIDUAL INTELLIGENCES TO SUCCESSFUL LEARNING

Success breeds success. If older people are feeling less confident of their ability to learn this may adversely affect their success in doing so. It therefore helps them to learn to value the success they have already achieved, and identify where their current skills and strengths lie so that they can use these strengths as a springboard for personal learning and career development.

It is vital to help people to recognize that going on a training course is not a sign of weakness. Encourage older workers to enjoy their strengths and tackle new skills.

In order to help people to learn effectively it can be useful to help them to identify their own specific learning style and strengths. As many people still assume that intelligence relates either to mathematical intelligence or logical and linguistic intelligence we believe that the model of multiple intelligences originated by Howard Gardner works well to enable a person to identify their own unique approach and value their personal contribution to the workplace. Many subjects at school do not include the type of life skills – such as communication or creativity – that are useful in the workplace. Nor are many people taught the essential skill of understanding how to learn to learn.

6. USE IT OR LOSE IT

Many older people become worried about losing their memory and this inevitably detracts from confidence in their ability to continue to learn new skills. This exercise is designed to give them some information and techniques to ensure that they maintain a good memory.

Exercise 11.3

The brain is like any other part of our body: if we use a skill then it continues to function well; if we don't then our abilities decline. It is important to inform older people that recent research demonstrates that older people are perfectly capable of continuing to learn.

In studies it has been shown that although young people pick up some skills more quickly, older people can retain the perceptual understanding of the skill sufficiently to be able to revisit and re-access the skill at a later stage.

In fact the biggest problem of memory in old age is a set of limiting beliefs. Statements such as 'when I get older my memory will deteriorate'; 'brain cells die off as you get older' actually impair ability because they cause stress. Stress can negatively impact one's memory. (See Chapter 8 Health and Wellbeing.) Therefore if a person is loses self-confidence and is stressed, the brain can go into 'survival' mode so that thoughts and memories about non-survival items are less readily retrieved. A state of relaxed alertness has been shown to assist the natural methods of the brain to recall information.

Few people are given memory skills in school and this will be particularly true of the older age group as this concept has only been introduced into education recently. In order to support older workers to learn successfully it can help them to realize that memory works through a combination of sensory information, associations and imagination.

SUMMARY

This section has provided information and exercises to help you to understand the rationale behind training decisions in order that you can enable older workers to be included more frequently on training programmes. It has also given you some exercises to enable individuals to gain insight and confidence in their own specific type of intelligence and the way they learn. Finally we have demonstrated that the use of colour, imagery and stories can enhance the ability of an older person to retain their memory.

It benefits a business to have all employees feeling confident about their ability to learn and retain new skills and information. It has also been shown to enhance morale and motivation and keep older people more actively involved in the business.

Six tips

1. **Encourage your older workers to participate in training courses.**

2. **Ensure that all training is offered to all ages.**

3. **Give older people skills and information on memory retention.**

4. **Help older people to recognize that different people have different types of intelligence to contribute at work.**

5. **Make learning new skills a fun activity.**

6. **Ensure that older people do not see their participation in a training course as a sign of weakness.**

MEASURING RETURN ON TRAINING INVESTMENT

Although it can be difficult to gain an accurate measurement on your return on investment for training you should be able to undertake a survey on post-training retention rates. This should provide you with information as to whether it is accurate to say that older workers stay for a shorter period than their younger counterparts after training. The question is: is the person trained staying long enough after training for the organization to reap the reward on the investment?

The aim of this exercise is to help you have the evidence you may require to demonstrate the rationale behind how you spend your organization's training budget and on whom. This may be particularly relevant should any older worker feel that they are being unfairly excluded from training or skills development, or should senior managers query it.

Follow this procedure to gauge the return on investment:

1. Take the training records to which you have access and consider which training investments represent those from which you and your organization have the greatest expectations in terms of productivity or length of service after the course. For example, do you send your potential managers on an expensive management training programme in the expectation that your company will reap the rewards when they become senior managers? Or do you have some specific skill set training in the expectation that participants will be able to save time and increase productivity as a result?

2. Study carefully the goals and reasons for sending participants on these programmes.

3. Gather information on the age ranges of individuals attending training.

4. Analyse the evaluation forms post-training and also the appraisals of participants in the months or years after they undertook the development or skills programme.

5. Analyse whether there is any evidence that could demonstrate that specific cohorts of staff could be said to be more productive post-training than other age cohorts and, if that is the case, identify the reasons.

6. Identify whether any age cohorts of participants were shown to leave the organization earlier than other age cohorts.

7. Consider whether there are any other factors that you should take into account.

Plot these results by age so that you have information should any older worker consider themselves excluded on account of age. In the case of having to give evidence to any tribunal, you will need to prove your case that there is less return on investment (ROI) on training older people than there is younger people. It is useful to have that information on record.

BUILDING CONFIDENCE IN LEARNING TO LEARN

The aim of this exercise is to provide information and questions that help an individual to consider how they learn and function at their best in the learning arena, so as to give them greater confidence in their ability to continue to learn. This exercise can be done in an individual one-to-one session or within a group setting.

Explain that Professor Howard Gardner of Harvard University has developed a theory of multiple intelligences and shown that different people demonstrate different ways of being intelligent and capable, regardless of age.

Explain that the aim of the questionnaire is to help them identify their personal strengths within a variety of areas so that they can build on these strengths, and also identify areas they may wish to develop in the future. Depending on the group you are with, explain that purely academic or professional qualifications demonstrate a specific intelligence in certain areas but that there are many more ways in which a person can succeed in life and be 'intelligent'. The following list is not complete but is designed to help a person start to consider and value their personal strengths.

It is important, when completing this exercise, to take note of the following: there are many ways in which people can be intelligent, beyond those recognized in school. Value your strengths and realize that you have developed the ability to learn different subjects throughout your lifetime whether or not you have achieved traditional 'qualifications'. Build on these strengths to enjoy the ability to carry on learning for the rest of your life!

MULTIPLE INTELLIGENCES

Consider the description statements below to help you understand the type of intelligence you possess and your strengths and weaknesses. Place a tick or cross next to any statement that applies to you.

BODILY KINAESTHETIC INTELLIGENCE is the ability to engage competently in sports, dancing, body work and any area where physical mobility is necessary. Your physical stance is as important a part of the message that is sent to business associates and clients as your verbal communication. Your physical conduct within the workplace is an important part of your image. The way you walk into a room, or walk to the coffee machine says a great deal about you.

1. *I regularly practise a sport or physical activity.*
2. *I prefer to practise a new skill rather than sit and read about it.*
3. *I like working with my hands at concrete activities such as sewing, weaving, carving, carpentry or model building.*
4. *My best ideas often come to me when I'm out for a long walk or a jog, or when I'm engaged in some other kind of physical activity.*
5. *I would describe myself as well coordinated.*
6. *I like to keep physically active during the day.*

I have scored ...... /6 for kinaesthetic intelligence.

INTERPERSONAL INTELLIGENCE is the intelligence of communicating with others, enjoying the company of other people both at work and socially. This is a very crucial intelligence in today's world, especially where you are working with teams.

1. *I'm sociable and enjoy spending time with friends.*
2. *I like to work in teams to solve problems and challenges.*
3. *I enjoy teaching people and learn well when working with others.*
4. *My interpersonal skills help me to lead others.*
5. *I feel comfortable in the midst of a crowd.*
6. *I like to get involved in social activities at work and home.*

I have scored ...... /6 for interpersonal intelligence

MULTIPLE INTELLIGENCES

INTRAPERSONAL INTELLIGENCE is the ability to understand oneself. The ability to make decisions according to a good understanding of who you are and what is important to you

1. *I enjoy spending time alone thinking about what is important in my life.*
2. *I am clear about my personal values and make decisions based on these.*
3. *I have set personal goals.*
4. *I have taken time to consider my strengths and weaknesses.*
5. *I can manage difficult times with resilience.*
6. *I enjoy activities I can do alone.*

I have scored ...... /6 for intrapersonal intelligence

LOGICAL-MATHEMATICAL INTELLIGENCE is the ability to understand and manipulate numbers as well as exhibiting competence in logical thought. This intelligence includes appreciating abstract relationships. In the workplace it can be demonstrated by your ability to approach tasks in a logical way, scrutinize reports and analyse budgets.

1. *I consider myself good at maths.*
2. *I enjoy structure and logic.*
3. *I find the rigour of scientific experiment interesting.*
4. *I notice logical flaws in the ways others operate.*
5. *I like to achieve the right decision.*
6. *All things have a rational explanation.*

I have scored ...... /6 for logical-mathematical intelligence

MULTIPLE INTELLIGENCES

MUSICAL INTELLIGENCE relates to people who exhibit a good sense of rhythm. This intelligence can also include ability to listen carefully to the subtleties of the tone of voice. This can help you understand others through listening to the tone and pace of people's voices, developing the musical tonality of your own voice.

1. *I enjoy having music playing.*
2. *I sing in the shower.*
3. *I play a musical instrument.*
4. *Songs play an important part in helping me remember things.*
5. *I notice the tonality in other people's voices and can pick up their feelings from voice tone.*
6. *Once I hear a tune I can often sing it.*

I have scored ...... /6 for musical intelligence

LINGUISTIC INTELLIGENCE is ability with language, the ability to use words and communicate articulately through language and foreign languages.

1. *I enjoy reading.*
2. *I like doing crosswords and word games.*
3. *I can learn through listening to cassettes and language tapes.*
4. *I enjoyed history and English at school.*
5. *I enjoy listening to the radio.*
6. *I can remember information by using rhymes.*

I have scored ...... /6 for linguistic Intelligence

MULTIPLE INTELLIGENCES

VISUAL/SPATIAL INTELLIGENCE is the ability to perceive the world in three or more dimensions resulting in competence to work with inter-relationships of networks and systems. You use your spatial intelligence at work in the way you design and lay out your working environment.

1. *I am good at art and design.*
2. *I can picture how a building will look before it is completed.*
3. *I enjoy using a camera and video.*
4. *I can imagine things in three dimensions.*
5. *I prefer learning through pictures and designs than words.*
6. *I have a good sense of direction.*

I have scored ...... /6 for visual-spatial intelligence

INTUITIVE INTELLIGENCE is sensory knowledge which enables you to sense the unseen and the unspoken. It is helpful to be aware of unspoken messages at work.

1. *I can intuitively sense that a person's words do not tally with their body language.*
2. *I pick up internal messages about situations.*
3. *I come to decisions through gut instinct.*
4. *I know who is going to telephone me before the phone rings.*
5. *I get a feeling in my stomach when I don't trust someone.*
6. *I may not be able to explain logically how I come to a decision.*

I have scored ...... /6 for intuitive intelligence

MULTIPLE INTELLIGENCES

TECHNICAL INTELLIGENCE is the ability successfully to use technology, that is, computers, telecommunications, fax machines, videos, mobiles, DVDs and so on.

1.   *I can understand the logic of computers.*
2.   *I find it easy to programme the timer on a video/DVD.*
3.   *I can utilize fully several applications on my mobile phone.*
4.   *I feel confident of my ability to learn to manage new technology.*
5.   *I feel comfortable that I can correct problems if technology breaks down.*
6.   *I am fascinated by how technical things work.*

I have scored ...... /6 for technical intelligence

CREATIVE INTELLIGENCE is the ability to come up with new ideas, concepts and solutions. Creativity is not just for artists: it encompasses finding new ways to do things, developing new products or services.

1.   *I can think laterally around problems.*
2.   *I have many ideas in my head.*
3.   *I enjoy brainstorming solutions with colleagues.*
4.   *I can imagine the future.*
5.   *I like to take risks and try new things.*
6.   *I don't see the point of doing things the way they have always been done.*

I have scored ...... /6 for creative intelligence

MULTIPLE INTELLIGENCES

FINANCIAL INTELLIGENCE is the ability to know how to manage the flow of assets and to build and create wealth.

1.   *I am good with money.*
2.   *I understand how to build a business or service and make it successful.*
3.   *I have some entrepreneurial flair.*
4.   *I have a good business sense.*
5.   *I can understand management accounts.*
6.   *I make good investments of assets.*

I have scored ...... /6 for financial intelligence

PHILOSOPHICAL INTELLIGENCE is the ability to bring wisdom into the workplace and seek and find a sense of purpose in life.

1.   *I like to reflect on the major issues of life.*
2.   *I am able to learn from difficult situations.*
3.   *I can see the 'big picture' and not get bogged down in detail.*
4.   *I help others learn from mistakes and move forward.*
5.   *I gain consolation from reading the ideas of philosophers.*
6.   *I can see a sense of purpose in my life.*

I have scored ...... /6 for philosophical intelligence

Add up the number of ticks you have put beside each form of intelligence and write the number on the Mind Map overleaf so that you get an overview of your own personal ways of being intelligent. 6 is a high score, 0 a low score:

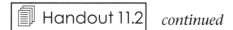
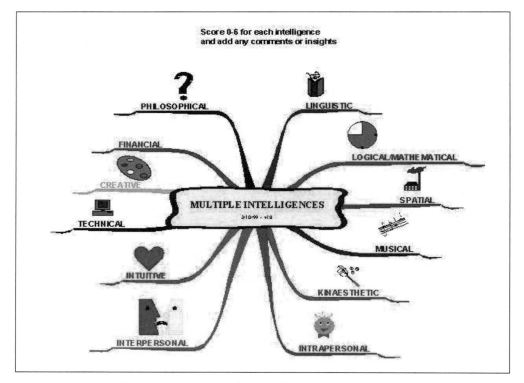

Figure 11.1   Multiple intelligences

(based on the concept of Multiple Intelligences developed by Professor Howard Gardner)

Once you have considered these statements, write down the numbers on the MindMap® above, and then write some comments and reflections below on your own personal and unique contribution to the workplace. The MindMap® was invented by Tony Buzan and is a visual method of recording facts, figures, ideas and information. A MindMap® enables a person to collect a large number of facts on one page which both aids recall and allows a person to get the overview of the key points of any situation.

Your intelligences influence your learning styles. In order to continue to develop your skills in lifelong learning it is likely that you will learn most effectively applying your strongest intelligences. For example, if you are kinaesthetically intelligent you will learn through doing new things physically; if you are linguistically intelligent you will learn best through reading. This will help you to choose training courses that meet your learning needs.

Write your comments and actions in the box below:

MEMORY EXERCISES

This exercise can be done in an individual coaching session or to a group training course.

Smiles Sharpen Memory is a mnemonic we have developed to illustrate the essential ingredients of effective recall.

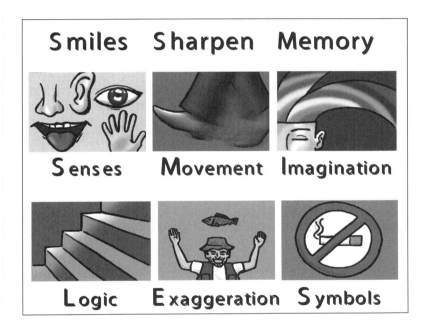

Figure 11.2   Smiles Sharpen Memory 1

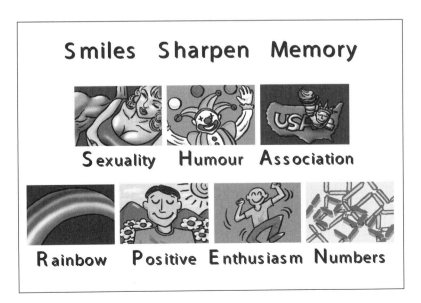

Figure 11.3   Smiles Sharpen Memory 2

Each of these 13 principles mirrors the way the memory naturally works – for example, take a moment to recall your early school days: What flashes into your mind? It is unlikely to be black and white words on an A4 page: it is much more likely to be pictures, sounds, movement, smells and emotions as this is how the majority of people's recall system works.

Once people have recalled their school days, have a discussion about what they discovered regarding how the memories came into their mind.

As a person thinks about a particular subject or piece of information they want to recall, it is necessary to turn the information into sensory, associative, colourful and logical information. If a topic is boring, our mind is less likely to recall it: we therefore have to find a way to make information interesting. These memory principles have been used – in one format or another – by many of the memory experts over generations. They can help people recall facts and figures, names and faces.

For example if you were needing to remember facts you would:

- imagine a colourful sensory picture of the information;

- make it humorous, possibly sexy and positive in order to make it more interesting;

- remember how many pieces of information there are to remember;

- feel enthusiastic about your ability to remember them.

It is important to use these principles with anything you are trying to remember. Creating a memorable story where you link and associate one piece of information with another can assist recall. For example below you will see a list of things you need to remember to pack for a business trip:

1. passport
2. pen
3. camera
4. shoes
5. briefcase
6. calculator
7. clothes
8. tickets
9. book
10. swimsuit.

Try this now by reading this short story:

Feeling <u>enthusiastic</u> about your ability to learn you start to imagine a large (exaggerated) red <u>passport</u> that you are holding in your left hand. In your right hand you hold a multi-coloured <u>pen.</u> Your <u>camera</u> is hung around your shoulder and you can feel the weight of it and you can feel the camera bump against your hip. Picture a pair of your <u>shoes</u> walking of their own accord into your <u>briefcase</u>. Your <u>calculator</u> is meantime singing a pop song that counts the number of <u>clothes</u> you want to take on the trip. Finally you picture yourself in a very sexy <u>swimsuit</u>, <u>tickets</u> tucked into the waistband, lying on a lovely warm beach reading a fascinating <u>book</u>.

Now read through the story quickly again using the memory principles; then close this book and write down the list of ten items on a piece of paper.

You can gradually apply this story technique to learning many items of information at one time (for example, 20–50 to begin with).

With technological advances people tend to use their memory less as mobile phones and computers recall information for you. Encourage people to keep practising by testing themselves and trying to remember new facts and figures, names and faces. Continuous practice will sharpen memory capability. Smiling will alleviate stress and make memory improvement more fun. Notice successes and build on them; the human brain can recall information perfectly if it is given the right tools to do so.

CHAPTER 12

Leadership, Promotion, Career Development and Succession Planning

Sally is sitting at her desk chatting with two of her HR colleagues. She has tried twice to recruit someone for a highly technical position and has failed to find anyone. She has also contacted a couple of her HR buddies from other companies who have said that there is a real shortage in that field. She says to Deepak,

'It makes me cross that we gave early retirement to George and Maurice. It cost us a fortune and now we need them.'

Deepak replies, 'I never thought there would be a day when you said we needed them. You and some of the others were so keen to retire them.'

'Yes, I remember,' says Sally, 'They were very skilled but we needed to cut costs and they were the obvious people to go.'

Deepak says, 'Yesterday I had Mary and Heidi in here complaining that they will never get to the top in this company because the next two managers up from them are both mid-50s and will be here for the next 10 years. They like it here but think they have to consider moving to a competitor – they are both very ambitious women.'

Sally responds, 'It is a real dilemma, isn't it? The law says we can't retire people early so we won't be able to use that solution any more but we are going to have to find some way to keep our highly competent skilled staff. Unless we tackle this and put in proper succession planning we are going to forever find ourselves in difficulty. Deepak, do you think I should phone George and Maurice and ask if they want to come back?'

Possible outcomes

Mary and Heidi could leave for a competitor company, taking their skills and knowledge with them; their managers remain, who may not be as skilled as them, and block promotion; departments have to manage without the necessary skills and the company pays expensive fees to recruitment agencies. George and Maurice return and the company pays both pension and salary.

As the baby boomers chronologically head for retirement over the next ten years organizations risk a mass loss of skills and professional experience. Many areas of the UK – such as Scotland and the South East of England – are already experiencing skills shortages. There will be those employees who want to remain at work for financial or social reasons but are no longer challenged or motivated sufficiently to contribute as fully as they did previously. If allowed to stay in post, these people could block the progress of younger staff wanting to step into their shoes.

HR and line managers are therefore going to need to focus their attention on three things that require strategic and long-term planning:

1. Retaining the skills and knowledge required to ensure continued success within their sector.

2. Helping the business and individuals within it to create long-term succession plans.

3. Supporting individuals to create a career–life plan that aligns with their values and aspirations so that they continue to contribute fully while in the workplace but equally do not hold on unnecessarily long in post, jeopardizing the promotion of others.

This section covers the following topics:

1. Resourcing skills and knowledge
2. Long-term succession planning
3. Promotion and career–life planning
4. Promotion and role change
5. Mentoring: retaining and sharing knowledge
6. Changing direction
7. Managing promotion issues
8. Strategies to manage leadership and career planning.

1. RESOURCING SKILLS AND KNOWLEDGE

The trend for giving older workers early retirement that took place in the 80s and 90s has resulted in a loss of skills and knowledge in certain business areas. Similarly older workers were frequently targeted for redundancy when cutbacks were required, with a similar result. Many organizations – particularly in the technology and financial sectors – have come to regret that they had encouraged their older workers to exit young.

Inevitably there is some correlation between length of working years and professional knowledge and understanding. This does not mean that younger people do not have an input but it does mean that older staff have experienced the whole business cycle and are able to put current trends and events within an economic perspective. Whilst this is not infallible it is nonetheless a valid perspective. When this information walks out the door it can take years to rebuild.

Recruiting senior level people of any age bracket is extremely expensive and it is therefore wise for organizations to identify what knowledge, skills and expertise their business is likely to require over the next five to ten years and ensure that they have an adequate pool of talent to meet these needs.

Many businesses take knee-jerk reactions when there is an economic downturn. The 90-day accounting system focuses management minds on the immediate figures and does not encourage them to look at the 'hidden' costs involved in redundancy and early retirement schemes.

HR will need to persuade their organization to do a skills and knowledge audit, analysing what exists within the business currently, and introducing scenario planning for the future and the possible needs of the business in five to ten years' time. From this data they will be able to consider whether there are certain people whom they need to motivate and retain; others who could share their knowledge and experience with colleagues; others who need help in creating their life–career plan; and possibly others who may benefit from a phased retirement plan.

Resourcing an organization is like a jigsaw puzzle. The picture on the box today may have changed beyond recognition in five to ten years' time. As one piece moves out there needs to be another to take its place in order to build that new picture and ensure a company's long-term and continued success. Considering how best to utilize the older workers and at the same time plan that there are no gaps of expertise is a detailed and thought-intensive process. It should not be left until the moment there is an economic downturn or someone decides to leave.

2. LONG-TERM SUCCESSION PLANNING

Long-term leadership and succession planning is surprisingly rare in organizations. In today's world it is, however, absolutely crucial as numerically there will be fewer younger people to step into the footsteps of those who move on. Equally management need to recognize that the younger generations are motivated by different factors to their predecessors: we find that younger men and women alike are looking at the current leadership practices at the top and saying they do not want to work extended working days out of habit rather than necessity. This is extremely dangerous for the continued success of an organization which inevitably survives through the energy and dedication of those who have a drive to get to the top.

There are now countless examples of younger people opting out of business to travel or to take a learning sabbatical. Equally as family life has shifted, fathers as well as mothers are wishing to spend more time with their children and view life at the top of organizations as over-demanding and unattractive. They do not have the overriding need for security that many of their parents brought up in the 50s did.

Women are still not reaching leadership roles as easily as they might like. Balancing family and work is demanding and many take time out to have their children, which hinders their ability to get to the top through the normal routes. Equally when they have had their children they may opt for work that does not involve travel and this may in some businesses relegate them to the 'back office' where a leadership role is less likely. Losing women after childbirth is expensive and dangerous as these same women frequently set up their own consultancies – which gives them more autonomy – and can become a direct competitor. Offering flexible and new ways of working can therefore help you retain skilled women in your organization.

Values have shifted and people are time-hungry and seeking purpose. They seek fulfilment and self-actualization. This is leading people in their 50s to leave professions and undertake a year of Voluntary Service Overseas (VSO); people of all ages are opting out of the large organizations and setting up small businesses or consultancies leaving highly paid jobs for work that gives them autonomy and flexibility. Organizations are going to need to consider this situation seriously and consider how they can ensure that they retain their top talent and maintain leadership capability in strategic posts.

3. PROMOTION AND CAREER–LIFE PLANNING

Older workers frequently report that unless they have got into senior management positions by their early forties it is unlikely that they will be promoted or developed after that time. For some this means having to face up to disappointment in the knowledge that their opportunities for promotion are now severely curtailed. For others this can mean that they give up trying to work hard and just 'hold on' to their current post, doing the basics and no more in order to wait for retirement and their pension.

As it is important for the organization to identify what skills and competencies will be required to meet business needs in the future, so also it is important that individuals are encouraged to consider their career–life plan. Very few people do this beyond their personal development plan, which is very work focused and does not necessarily take into account an individual's personal situation, financial status, values and aspirations. When a person is supported through a process of evaluation about themselves and their lives they can make more informed decisions regarding their future within an organization.

Not only is it factually an issue it is also an issue attitudinally (See Chapter 3 Demographic Changes). Nine out of ten older people believe that employers discriminate on grounds of age; 750 000 people over the age of 50 would like to be working if they thought there was a relevant opportunity to do so. This is a terrible waste of talent that could be supporting your organization. These people will be essential in businesses in the light of the demographics. (See Chapter 3.)

Three quarters of UK firms have no workers over the age of 60 (Norwich Union research) and the average age of retirement in many firms is 50–52. In the context of greater health and longevity these figures demonstrate that organizations are offering retirement packages at a very young age, thereby losing knowledge, skills and 'corporate memory'.

> *Although 25 per cent of those who were made redundant or given early retirement packages in their 50s wanted to work one year later 98 per cent of them had given up looking, due to the barriers they experienced* (Sheffield Hallam University).

Those returning to the labour market following redundancy or other gaps from work face a pay reduction compared to their previous job. This wage penalty has risen steadily over the last twenty years. In the case of under-50s the discount on the level of pay in a new job is 12 per cent compared to pay in the last job. For those over age 45 it is now 26 per cent, up from 12 per cent in 1980 and reflecting prejudices about older workers (*The Journal of The Centre for Economic Performance*, 2001; Campbell, London School of Economics (LSE), 1999).

Employers stand to gain significant benefits from ensuring they adopt non-ageist employment practices. This is especially so against a backdrop of skills shortages and the changing demographic position, with older workers forming a larger proportion of the workforce and customer base.

> *In almost all occupations workers over 50 are no less productive than people aged 25 to 49. The World Economic Forum Report addressing the older population issue in the UK argued that a third of a percentage point a year rise in 50-69 year olds in work would be enough to solve any economic problems in the future* (World Economic Forum Report, 20th January 2004).

Interestingly although it can often be assumed that an older member of staff no longer sees their work in terms of a 'career', this is not borne out by research which demonstrates that the over 50s frequently view their work in the context of a career timeline, as they always have. Younger people do not always plan a future 'career' but move as the opportunities present themselves.

4. PROMOTION AND ROLE CHANGE

To address talent retention and continuing promotion opportunities for the older worker the HR department will need to look at lateral uses for a person's skills and the potential that they still have to develop new and strong capabilities.

The 'old fogey' stereotype can be misleading as a recent survey showed that, while people imagine that young people are the most successful entrepreneurs, many businesses and consultancies that have been set up by those in the over-50s age group are, in fact, highly successful. Their experience within the workplace can have enabled them to learn good money management and take the practical and innovative steps required to make a new business work. (*Director* magazine, October 2004, beer mat entrepreneur.)

Similarly, contrary to stereotypical thinking about how an older person who has been in a particular line of business for many years will not be able to make the switch to a new area, there are again many examples of older people finding it revitalizing and rewarding to be given a new challenge later in life. In fact the feedback we have received from older people records strongly how they wish to be given new opportunities so that their present skills and experience are utilized and at the same time new areas of thinking and experience are opened up. A strong message was that they do not want to be treated 'as a number' or as a one-dimensional person. Just because they have spent 25 years in the audit department does not mean that they wouldn't want to be considered for a role in marketing applying transferable skills.

If this is the case then there is no reason why an older person should not be promoted to set up a new department, or drive a new project. In the light of the law everyone qualified must be considered for all positions. It is therefore important to base promotion on ability and performance of the individual and not make assumptions as to their competence based on age, as was discussed in Chapter 10 Performance Management.

5. MENTORING: RETAINING AND SHARING KNOWLEDGE

In our own surveys many of the older people were asked about giving advice to younger colleagues: 'People respect the fact that you've seen a lot of situations before and that you have experienced different business environments and cultures.'

Others responded that 'clients value advice and experience. It makes you feel good when you know you have helped someone whether inside or outside the organization.'

In managing older workers it will be important to understand these motivators and to generate a culture where people do feel they can ask for advice and receive it.

An excellent way to ease many of these problems is to introduce mentoring, where an older person can gain fulfilment from supporting the success of a younger colleague.

Mentoring systems are working well in many organizations. Mentoring is not the same as coaching. Coaching is a specific process, facilitated by a trained person, where the client is assisted in identifying and achieving their goals. Mentoring is a knowledge-sharing process. A more experienced member of staff will make themselves available for a meeting, or phone call, or email where they can give advice, or talk about their own experiences of a variety of situations that the younger person may be facing. The mentor's knowledge of the business and of the actions that have worked and not worked in the past can be extremely helpful to someone being challenged by a situation for the first time. A person will need some training to become a good mentor as occasionally people mistake this for simply 'telling' the younger person what to do rather than sharing their own experiences and then allowing the younger person to approach the situation in the way they choose.

Through mentoring, rather than lose senior people as they get older because they feel they have 'outstayed their welcome' or see retirement as an attractive option, you can retain their knowledge and skills at the same time as bringing new talent up through the ranks. The older person can spend a period of time mentoring and supporting the younger person's development. This sharing of skills and knowledge results in a smooth succession transition. This can be rewarding for all concerned.

6. CHANGING DIRECTION

Occasionally you will be faced with a member of staff who blocks progress and does not buy into either mentoring or moving sideways into another role. Where an individual holds on out of fear of change, antipathy towards retirement, or general comfort and complacency, it can cause a blockage for the promotion of others. These people can become saboteurs and prevent communication and knowledge flow due to their closed attitude.

In this case it may be advisable to introduce a coach to help the person face up to their fears, challenge their perspectives and enable them to make positive decisions about whether they want to stay at work or not. It is helpful to let them explore all the options. Many of the people we have worked with have taken steps sideways which have both given them a challenge and allowed younger people to move into more senior positions. This has been further dealt with in Chapter 10 on Performance Management.

7. MANAGING PROMOTION ISSUES

People grow up seeing older people as authority figures. Therefore when a younger person is promoted to a leadership role over and above someone who has been a long-standing member of staff and expected to get the role themselves, it can cause problems.

This is not an unusual situation these days and on the whole our research has shown that older people are perfectly happy to be managed by a younger person provided they respect their capabilities. Despite this there may well be a period of adjustment when those involved come to develop a working relationship that allows all parties to flourish.

Younger staff, for their part, have, however, reported that they can find it quite difficult to manage older people who may be the same age as their parent or even grandparent. In this instance they may need help to feel confident and secure of their skills and competencies and to put the concept of age aside. They will need to view their actions in the context of 'the role' and what the role demands, rather than viewing decisions and actions in a personal and subjective way such as 'I am younger than them and they have been doing this work for ages – how can I delegate in this situation?!'

We have dealt with these intergenerational situations in more depth in Chapter 13 on Intergenerational Working and Chapter 10 Performance Management.

Senior management 'clique'

The 'old boys' network' still exists to some extent. It may not go back to schooldays but there are certainly circumstances when only an 'inner circle' gets promoted. It has been shown that many boards and non-executive directors are made up of old friends. This is happening less frequently because of equal opportunity laws.

Often the people involved have not considered the situation objectively but have offered a post to a trusted acquaintance with whom they feel comfortable. It is important for the HR department to be aware of this tendency and help senior management to broaden their view regarding options, as it could prove to be discriminatory. It has also been demonstrated that where old colleagues or friends join a board they are not as challenging or objective as they may need to be. A real mix of ages and approaches on a board makes for far more innovative and creative performance at the top.

Shunted sideways

We have observed that an older person can get shunted sideways to keep them quiet as they undertake their last few years towards retirement. 'Let's put old Gerald into that little project we have going on. It should just about see him through to his retirement and won't put him under pressure.' Whilst this may be a relevant action for some people who have expressed a desire for an 'easy life' it will absolutely demotivate others who continue to want new challenges, and to feel their contribution is valued. It is always important to check out a person's motivations as otherwise you are unlikely for them to perform well. You could refer them to their career–life plan and help them to find a way to enjoy their days rather than plough through them resentfully. You might also give them the opportunity to take the initiative and in identifying improvements that could be taken within their role or department so as to involve them and accept their ideas.

8. STRATEGIES TO MANAGE LEADERSHIP AND CAREER PLANNING

The two exercises at the end of this chapter will start the process of promotion and succession planning within an age-neutral context.

Exercise 12.1

Exercise 12.2

SUMMARY AND TIPS

This chapter has explored the different ways that businesses will need to prepare and implement career and succession planning. It will be necessary for you to review your current promotion policy to ensure that it is age-neutral. If you have grading systems are they based on age or length of service or on specific capabilities and performance criteria? You will need to ensure that your policies are equal to all age groups. How do you currently make decisions about promotion and reward? You will no longer be able to do this on the basis of age so you will need to select fair criteria for promoting and incentivizing people in the future.

Six tips

1. **Know what skills, knowledge and competencies your organization will need in future to be successful.**

2. **Identify a pool of talent who can become your leaders of the future.**

3. **Help long-serving leaders and senior management to enjoy the process of 'letting go' and developing new talent.**

4. **Help everyone see how essential it is to the future success of the business not to lose the existing knowledge base through stereotypical practices such as early retirement or offering redundancy to older workers.**

5. **Ensure that your promotion and reward policy is age-neutral.**

6. **Help individuals realize that older workers still have unlimited potential so that they can continue to offer them challenges that motivate and excite them, hence reducing the likelihood of your losing their knowledge and skills.**

SCENARIO-PLANNING KNOWLEDGE AUDIT

Part one

In order to ensure that you are able to provide the organization with the right skills and knowledge base that will be required to maintain the company's success it is useful to brainstorm the likely scenario in which the organization will be operating in the next five to ten years.

Involve people from different departments in this brainstorming session and ensure that it is 'blue sky' rules in that there is no critical or analytical thinking until the creative flow has come to a natural end. Be innovative and as far-reaching as possible – outrageous or crazy ideas are good!

Ask questions like:

- What might the world be like (1) politically (2) socially (3) technically (4) economically (5) environmentally?

- What might your current customers need and want?

- How could you develop your products and services to meet this changed world and the needs to your future customers?

- What is the strategic intent of some of your competitors within this context?

- What is the ideal picture of your organization within this context?

- What skills, knowledge base, experience and talents might be required to ensure this success?

Part two

Now that you have identified the skills and knowledge base that you are likely to require for future success you will need to go back to your workforce profile and identify future talent that will be able to provide you with the required competency framework for leadership. In view of the Age Discrimination Regulations it is important that this is an age-neutral process.

When you have identified the potential talent bank for leadership and senior positions – who may be within the senior teams, or a high-potential young person, or, indeed, someone external to the organization – it is now up to you to develop and promote that talent to ensure that they are ready to enter the leadership position as and when it becomes vacant.

Within this process draw the current occupant or occupants into a developmental relationship with your potential talent bank. Jack

Welch, former Chief Executive of General Electric, has reportedly identified four potential heads to take over his role. As this relationship develops it is important to help the present incumbent 'let go' of control and of thinking that they know best how the department or company should be run. They can be helped to see that the new person (whatever their age) has a right to developing their own way of doing things. This has been shown to be particularly the case within family businesses where the older person tends to find it difficult to give way to a son or daughter waiting in the wings.

Encouraging the 'letting go' process is vital for a successful succession plan. This might include working from home for part of the time, or altering hours to become a part timer, or generally working in a more flexible way so as to allow the new person to find their feet and not develop too dependent a relationship.

The process we have described here can take as much as five to ten years of nurturing development. Transparency of intention can be important so that others can support you within this journey.

CAREER–LIFE PLANNING

This is a timeline exercise to help individuals consider their careers within the broader framework of their lives. This can either be done on an individual basis or in a small workshop setting. Make sure that the room in which you hold this session is large enough to allow a person to walk some 10–15 paces.

Introduce the concept of planning one's life and career.

- Put the group into threes and ask them to consider the benefits of planning a career within the context of personal values, life and family needs. Give them five to ten minutes.

- Flipchart their responses.

- Draw out in a discussion whether any of those in the group have already made a career–life plan. Discuss why some did and others didn't. Was this something that was suggested in the Careers Department of School or University? Were they ever given help in setting life and career goals previously?

- Discuss the benefits of goal-setting versus 'leaving it to chance' and discover how many people have followed a real career path or have actually responded to circumstances as they arose – for example, have people driven their career path or have they been pushed and pulled by others and events along the way?

- Explain that you are now going to do a 'timeline' exercise where you are going to ask them to walk along an imaginary timeline of their life and career, considering what they have experienced and achieved so far and what they might want to achieve in the future.

- Explain that this will be a visualization exercise where you will be taking them back through their lives, starting at their schooldays and walking them through the major events and roles they have experienced up until today.

- To help them understand visualization ask them, as a group before they begin, to think of their first schooldays. Ask them what happened in their mind and get them to share this as a group. You are likely to find that the majority of people (usually 90 per cent) get pictures of some aspect of their school. Others will say that they also experience emotions; others sounds of the playground; others the smell of antiseptic or cabbage! All this helps them to understand that the brain naturally recalls and imagines information in a sensory format and not in words. The mind will immediately build memory pictures or, if asked, imagined pictures. Explain to them that the brain is doing this every time they go on a new journey – it is imagining where to go and what it might look like. The timeline exercise will be using the power of the mind to build these sensory pictures which will include memories of the past and imagined scenes in the future.

- Explain that this is an exercise where they are not required to talk, as you will be leading them through the process and they will need to take the focus of their attention internally to notice and observe their own emotional and thinking processes as they walk along the line.

- Ask them to stand up and imagine a path that represents their life. Ask them to stand in a position that they feel represents a time when they were seven years old.

- Explain that it can help to close their eyes so that they can pay full attention to their inner world of thought, memory and emotion as they undertake this exercise.

Now lead them through the process. You can read the following to an individual or group and/or adapt it to a specific situation.

Remember yourself as a 7-year-old child. Think about your life and what your dreams and goals were at that time. What did you really enjoy doing? Notice what is coming into your mind.

Take a step forward and as you do so think about how life changed between the ages of 7 and 14 and become the 14-year-old you.

Stand in this position for a moment or two and consider what changes have happened to you – do you have the same dreams at this age as you did when you were 7? Have you achieved some things of which you are proud? What skills did you have at that stage of your life? Have you been thinking about what career you might undertake?

Now take a step forward again and imagine yourself as a 21 year old. What has changed this time? What have you now achieved? What do you now enjoy doing or thinking about? Have you firmed up your ideas about work and the type of role you would like to have? Perhaps you have already started work.

Now take a step forward again and step into your life today. Look back over the preceding years and consider what your achievements have been; what has made you happy; what has made you unhappy; what disappointments you may have experienced; what your dreams are today. Get a holistic view of your life including personal life within the context of your work life. Have you had a career plan that has brought you to this place? Have events just presented themselves and you have taken advantage of them? Were there some opportunities that you regret that you did not take? What stopped you? What resource would have helped you? Stand in this position for several moments and notice what comes into your mind.

Now start to think about your future. What are your dreams for your future? What values would you like to live by? What would you like more of in your life? How can you happily combine your working life with the life you want to lead outside work? What emotional state will help you create this life? What other resources or help might you need?

| ✎ Exercise 12.2 | *continued* |

Now step forward into the future imagining you have that emotional state and those resources and see how that feels and what comes into your mind. Can you plan your career in a way that enables you to lead the life you want to lead?

As you take a further step forward into the future, see what else might be happening around you? Who else do you need to take into account? Is there a partner, children, parents? Consider what might influence your life. What talents do you think you might have that you have not yet developed? What would your dream be for your future career?

Go forward another step and make sure you are now five to ten years into the future. Now turn around and look back. What might have happened in this time? What emotional state will help you to create the life and work situation you want? What actions do you need to take? What support and help might you need? What resources? Stop and reflect on this for a moment.

Now walk slowly back towards the point that is 'today' and as you do so feel confident of your ability to create a good life and career path for yourself. Stop when you have reached today's position. When you are ready become aware of the room and then sit down.

- At the end of this timeline session ask the participants to share in pairs what their experiences were and how they might use the thoughts and images that came into their heads in order to help them move forward and create a career–life plan for their futures.

- When they have had five to ten minutes in pairs draw the group into a general discussion of experiences, findings and goals.

- At the end of the session give each person a piece of paper and give them ten minutes to write down their plans.

- Finish the session with each person sharing one aspect of their plan with the group.

Reproduced from *Age Matters* by Keren Smedley and Helen Whitten, Gower Publishing, 2006.

LEADERSHIP, PROMOTION, CAREER DEVELOPMENT AND SUCCESSION PLANNING

Intergenerational Working

The HR department in XYZ plc are having an Awayday. They are reviewing the work they have been doing over the last year and planning the work for the next 12 months. Sally starts the ball rolling saying, 'I seem to be spending a lot of time with my designated departments on dealing with complaints by managers about older members of staff.'

Richard continues, 'Me too, there seems to be a lot of prejudice around, this is going to have to be tackled before the Age Discrimination Act comes into force next October otherwise we'll be in trouble.'

Marlene joins in, 'One of the areas I am finding difficult to manage is the complaints from older workers that they are patronized by managers who are young enough to be their children.'

Sally agrees with this and adds, 'Well I often hear from younger members of staff that the older workers won't listen to any suggestions. Before they are halfway through an idea they are told it's been done before. Take my current problem with Simon and Bill, I can't say which of them is worse, it is certainly six of one and half a dozen of the other. I don't think either of them is being very nice to each other.'

Richard says, 'It is amazing to think that so many people now go to university compared to my day. I think that is part of the problem. The young come in with the qualifications, get senior jobs and think they know it all.'

Michael replies, 'And we think we're not prejudiced! Just listen to you Richard! Ageism is going to have to be our focus for the next year; we are going to be faced increasingly with older workers who stay longer at work and younger more educated staff overtaking them in the hierarchy and we need to find ways to enable them to work together.'

Possible outcomes

The staff of XYZ go on complaining and a disproportionate amount of time is spent by HR on dealing with these issues. Younger managers leave because they can't manage their older staff. Older staff put in complaints against younger staff. People work in an unpleasant environment, which can only reduce their productivity.

In many instances in our scenario examples throughout this book, the older worker has been the more 'junior' staff member. In reality in most organizations there is a mix of older and younger workers within both management and staff roles.

A number of the older workers we coach have expressed concern and disappointment that unless they are in senior management positions their experience is not taken into account when decisions are made. They are not suggesting that because they have been at work for a large number of years everything they say has to be taken on board. However, people do learn from experience. One of our clients reported that they hear themselves saying 'you can't do that, it doesn't work, we have done it before, and so on' just out of frustration at being 'invisible'. They know this will not enhance joint co-operative working but they get caught in the trap of complaining as they feel unheard.

This chapter focuses on how to work effectively in intergenerational teams. The topics covered are:

1. The historical perspective

2. The current trends

3. New models of working

4. The business case.

1. THE HISTORICAL PERSPECTIVE

If we take a moment to look at the situation historically, the expectation of most workers was that they came in at the bottom aged 16 plus, and worked themselves up through the company. Some would be promoted to a higher position than others but the likelihood was that when they reached 60 or 65 their boss was of a similar age. There were, of course, always people who started in a company at a different level because of higher education and those who were related to the boss! There was generally less development training offered in the workplace. For most it was sheer hard work and determination.

Most people's learning about relationships, communication and values takes place within the context of the family. In the late 1940s and 1950s when the baby boomers were born, people's roles and the way they were expected to behave were very clearly defined. There was a definite hierarchy between the generations. Certain behaviours were expected; for example, a younger person was expected to get up and give their seat to an older person if the bus or train was full. There was a very clear definition between children and young people and adults. A young person would never call their next door neighbour by their first name: it would always be 'Mr' or 'Mrs' or 'Miss' and the surname. Even in families aunts and uncles would never be called by their first names and close family friends were given honorary titles of aunt or uncle to show a special position. It was considered rude if these conventions were not kept.

Families were very hierarchical with grandparents at the head. Even within peer generations there was a hierarchy with older siblings often left to look after younger ones and therefore expecting similar respect. Just being a member of one of those groups gave you certain roles and expectations.

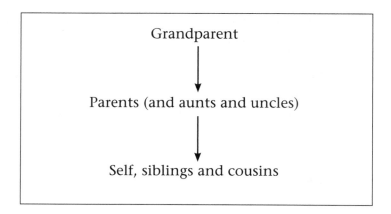

Figure 13.1   Hierarchic model

2. THE CURRENT TRENDS

Today's world is somewhat different. The youth culture has promoted an idea that younger people are better, more full of energy, more technological and more business minded. This has led to many being taken on or promoted when very young.

Organizations such as British Telecom (BT) and John Lewis have both recently reported taking on managers in their mid-twenties who have specific technical skills but little experience to manage teams. Some have to manage teams of more than 30 people who are aged between 30 and 55. This policy has of course some advantages but brings with it a number of issues.

The Employers Forum on Age has pointed out in a report based on research undertaken in 2004 that the over 55s will soon outnumber the 25–34 year olds. Therefore many will be faced with bosses who are both years younger than them and better educated. It is all very well joking about policemen getting younger every day, the test is how does this get managed in the workplace?

Alongside this scenario many organizations find that they lose highly motivated and talented 35–45 year olds who know that the only way to get to the top is to move into 'dead men's shoes'. With the welcome increase in longevity and the changes in retirement laws and pension practices this could for some be well past their preferred date for retirement and too late for their juniors to enjoy senior positions. Companies that continue to follow this practice will find themselves with a skills shortage of talented people when the older person finally retires. Both these scenarios need to be explored in organizations and clear succession practices introduced. (See Chapter 12 Leadership, Promotion, Career Development and Succession Planning.)

Customers' and clients' profiles are also changing as the population becomes older. Many organizations will be dealing with customers who are in different generations. This will affect both the ways the customer is communicated with and the products that the customer will want. This needs to be addressed if organizations are to maintain a competitive edge.

In a study undertaken by TNS, the market research company, it was reported that for many young people getting onto the career ladder is not a high priority. Only 16 per cent of those interviewed put career as a top priority; the large proportion saw work as important but not dominant. Socializing was high on the agenda. Many young people are rebelling against the work ethic of the Thatcher generation when the focus was on finance and economics. Today's young people are more concerned about personal development and work–life balance.

Another trend is that many young people do not settle down into long-term relationships or raise a family till later in life. So there are more years for a carefree social life. Figures from the Office for National Statistics show that on average women are not getting married until they are 29 as compared to 23 in the 1960s. There is also a similar increase in age for men. It is not that people do not take their careers seriously it is just that they may not start on the ladder till later.

It is not just the young who want to have a different pattern in their working lives; this is true of the baby boomer too. Many of this group are unprepared to fall into the stereotype of an older person and do not plan to retire in the conventional way. This will include finding ways to continue to work as well as having time to travel and pursue other interests. Many will have other external demands such as caring for elderly relatives that also have to be fitted into their life style. (This is discussed in Chapter 14 New Ways of Working.)

If older people are going to continue to work, in either a full- or part-time capacity, it is likely that they will have a younger boss at some stage and they need to find a new way to relate so that both can benefit from the relationship.

3. NEW MODELS OF WORKING

How does the older worker deal with issues of ego and an acceptance that someone younger than them has reached a higher position? How do young leaders make decisions with confidence without feeling too young and inexperienced? How do both these groups work together to accept their differences and embrace the respective knowledge that they both have? In Chapter 6 on People Management we explored the idea from Transactional Analysis. It is all too easy to fall into this trap of parent, adult and child in the workplace because a person looks like they would fall into the age group of your grandson or grandfather. It is important to consider how we can move away from this into an age-neutral model.

The model below looks at a different way of exploring one's position in the world. The relationships are based on the relative relationship to others, and have nothing to do with age.

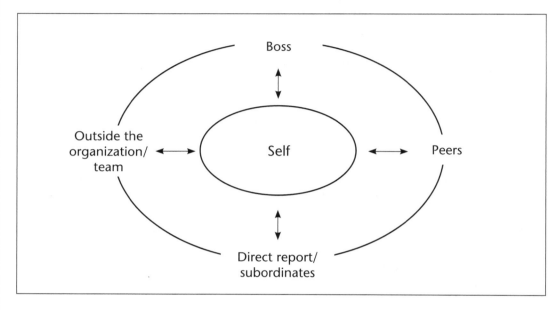

Figure 13.2   Relationship map (based on J. Mitchell's model)

We will all have had the experience of being in all four positions shown in the relationship map. For example, if you are a parent, you have above you your parents; to the right, your siblings and cousins; below, your children; and to the left, non-family members. You will have had the same experience at work. You have a peer group, the world outside, for example, the customers, a boss and, for many, direct reports. Our position in the map changes with our different relationships. Each position has a particular responsibility.

- The responsibility upwards is to make a full contribution.

- The responsibility downwards is to create an environment in which others can fulfil their potential.

- The responsibility to the right is to build an environment of trust and co-operation.

- The responsibility to the left is to enhance the reputation of the organization.

The model looks at responsibilities rather than age or expectations of age. If this idea is taken on board it offers a different way to explore the relationships which are not based on the natural order of things where only the older person could tell the younger person how to do things and that the younger person should only speak when spoken to!

This has already shifted within families and generations. For example, the parents of baby boomers generally assumed they 'knew best' whereas baby boomers tend to relate to their children in a more consensual way, accepting that the younger person has valid ideas.

In a number of our scenarios we have seen that none of our characters are meeting their responsibilities, as described in the relationship model above. Simon is quite clearly not contributing fully, as he could be working much harder and producing work of a higher quality. Bill is totally fed up with Simon and is not even attempting to create an atmosphere and environment where Simon can excel. The peer group spend a lot of time expressing how right they are as they are older and how unfair their deal is. They are unlikely to be working co-operatively with younger members of the team. They are, as we have seen, not promoting the company at all when they are meeting friends outside.

4. THE BUSINESS CASE

If an organization is going to recruit good staff it is important that the company has a good reputation in the market place. The individuals in the organization are ambassadors for their place of work. It is a well-known fact and a source of government and citizen concern that there is a shortage of trained nurses in the National Health Service. A specialist team working with a difficult health issue had had two vacancies in their department for a long period of time. The team members were all in their fifties and had worked together for a long time. They were delighted when two highly competent and able younger nurses applied for the jobs and were appointed. They brought with them new skills and a new ways of working that the team welcomed.

The team had already booked a team day with an outside facilitator before they were due to start and asked the new staff members to join them. The intention was for them to have time out of the office to get to know one another and be part of future planning – an honourable intention. The team however did not use the day in this way. They spent a lot of time focusing on the difficulties and how hard the job was. Whenever the new staff made an innovative suggestion they negated it by saying things such as 'you'll never be able to do that here', 'tried that, doesn't work', ' sounds like hard work – I am just waiting to retire'. The outcome was that the new staff members wrote that night saying that they had reconsidered and would no longer be taking up the positions. If a negative message is given about an organization it often brings a negative result. This is a very good example of intentions versus behaviours as discussed in Chapter 6 People Management.

All organizations have a customer base. They are sometimes not called this, for example patients in a GP practice or pupils in a school. In some environments such as a school the customer age group is fixed while in others such as the GP they see people of all ages nought to a hundred!

In most organizations there is a very mixed customer base. Supermarkets have customers that range from children to adults in their nineties. Each of these groups has different needs and this is reflected in the variety of products.

A number of large British retail outlets such as Asda, B&Q, Tesco and Sainsbury's have recently removed the retirement age for their staff. This has enabled them to employ a staff group that reflects the customer base. Many customers report preferring to ask someone of their own age group questions than someone they believe may not have the same understanding.

Sainsbury's are actively recruiting the over-50s. They believe that their development of a more mixed-age workforce has lead to:

- improved customer satisfaction by more accurately reflecting the profile of their customers;

- a more flexible workforce;

- a better motivated workforce which feels more valued and therefore more willing to contribute to business success;

- reduced business costs through increased productivity.

In Chapter 5 Changing Attitudes and Stereotypes we explored the ideas, beliefs and values that people held about the different age groups. The breaking down of these is essential if all groups are going to be able to work with one another. Many organizations employ a wide age range and are conscious that sometimes difficulties arise because of the lack of understanding between the generations. Many organizations may not as yet have looked at how this can be an asset. Also while many of us are carrying around old working patterns, values and attitudes in our heads we have not caught up with the societal changes that are already happening.

Much of the work that has been done on intergenerational working has been in the community in both educational and health projects. There is a range of diverse and innovative mentoring work being undertaken with older people. Lessons can be learnt from these projects and they can be modified to fit the organizational environment.

🖉 Exercise 13.1

🖉 Exercise 13.2

🖉 Exercise 13.3

🖉 Exercise 13.4

🖉 Exercise 13.5

🖉 Exercise 13.6

A mentor is defined as 'one who is experienced and seeks to develop the character and competence of a younger person; interaction occurs over an extended period of time.' (Neumann et al., 1997)

It has been seen that intergenerational activity helps to reduce the barriers that exist between older and younger generations. It can help to break down these misconceptions and stereotypes through the mentoring relationship.

The exercises in this chapter will look at ways to address intergenerational issues in the workplace.

SUMMARY AND TIPS

This chapter has focused on intergenerational working. This is increasingly going to be part of the work environment. It draws on a number of issues raised in other chapters such as stereotypes, demography and work–life balance.

If people of all ages are going to be able to work together and to benefit from the wealth of experience that each generation brings, they are going to have to put assumptions and beliefs aside and really get to know their fellow colleagues. Creativity and innovation will be greatly enhanced through the diverse experiences and perspectives existing within intergenerational teams.

Every generation is young during a particular era. Thoday's youth had very different experiences to those brought up in the post-War era. Lessons learnt over the years must be valued and understood and then modified to fit into today's environment.

Six tips

1. **Understand your workforce for who they are, not for their age.**

2. **Profile your organization to ensure your staff profile reflects your client group.**

3. **Set up groups where people can explore the ideas of intergenerational working and how they can use the different skills to enhance productivity.**

4. **Broadcast the benefits of a mixed-age workforce.**

5. **Organize some social activities that would appeal to all.**

6. **Help your older workers to sell their experience in a way that is positive and future thinking.**

AGE AUDIT

This exercise specifically useful to the HR department. It would be useful for one person to complete the research and then to discuss the strategy as a team.

The first step is to profile your organization (See Chapter 1).

Audit your workforce and the make-up of your teams.

How many managers are in their 50s, 40s, 30s and 20s?

Does the managerial group match that of the staff?

Does your managerial group match the customer base?

Does your staff group match your customer base?

Have you put in place any strategies to improve intergenerational working for example, mentoring?

Having done this it would be useful to look at whether your workforce profile is one that will optimize the organization's productivity. Come up with some action points to rectify this.

Action points

RELATIONSHIP MAP

This exercise can be done individually or in groups, at any level. It offers individuals an opportunity to explore where they are on the map and how that changes in different roles and to explore how they manage these relationships.

 Handout 13.2

RELATIONSHIP MAP

Below is a blank copy of the relationship map discussed in section 3.

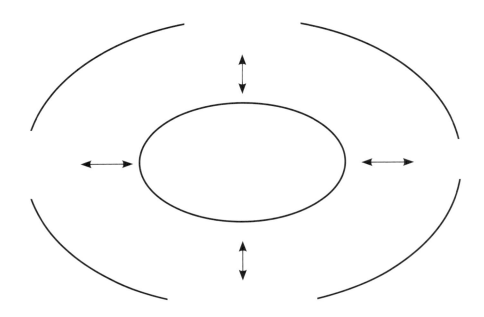

Steps

1. Put yourself in the centre of the circle. Put the names of your colleagues in the other positions.

2. Examine these to see if there is an age element.

3. Look at the relationships and identify the ones that are good and the ones that need improvement.

4. Examine what are the factors that make good/less good relationships and make a list of these.

5. Find someone to share the factors that make good and not so good relationships and explore ways these can be improved.

6. If there are difficulties in some of the relationships that are age-related, some of the other activities suggested both in this chapter and in others would be useful to look at.

If you are doing this exercise in a group follow the steps 1–4. Ask the participants to get into groups of three to discuss step 5. Come back to a plenary session to discuss and look at step 6.

CREATIVE INTERGENERATIONAL WORKING

This is a group exercise. It can be done with a group on a training course or with a team. It is an ideal exercise to use as an ice breaker.

Preparation

- Take five sheets of flip chart paper and write an age from the following list on the top of each sheet: 5, 20, 35, 50, 65, 80.

- Divide the group into six small groups and give them each a different colour pen and a piece of flip chart paper with one age on top.

- Tell them they will have three minutes to write down all the ways they think a person of that age would answer the following question below, however 'off the wall'.

Question:
What would help the generations work best together?

After three minutes you will swap the sheets and they will have a turn at a different age.

When the papers have been to each group put the papers in the middle of the room and have a discussion about what ideas would help your organization.

Exercise 13.4

INTERGENERATIONAL PROBLEM SOLVING

If there is to be an age-inclusive culture and one that uses the skills of all age groups and develops practices that meet all of the staff's needs, it is important to find out what staff think would make good intergenerational working.

One way to do this is to set up small intergenerational problem-solving groups to discuss these issues and to create some ideas for guidelines that can be issued to all to enhance working practices. The following guidelines will help you to run a successful problem-solving meeting.

The first step is the preparation:

- arrange a group of five to seven people;
- make sure they all know the purpose of the meeting and have had time to think about the issues;
- use a small room with a round table;
- have a co-ordinator who records ideas and maintains ground rules;
- choose a 'high energy' time.

Group session

This is divided into three stages:

The Generative stage

- pose the question – How can we create an effective intergenerational work environment?
- set a time limit;
- brainstorm and record all suggestions;
- quantity not quality;
- use ideas as triggers for others;
- freewheel;
- stop if ideas dry up.

The Practical stage:

- list positive and negative attributes for each suggestion;
- eliminate suggestions that have a predominance of negatives;
- repeat the process several times, gradually eliminating options;
- gain agreement for the solution.

Reproduced from *Age Matters* by Keren Smedley and Helen Whitten, Gower Publishing, 2006.

INTER-
GENERATIONAL
WORKING

✏ Exercise 13.4   *continued*

The Evaluation stage:

- collect all the data from the groups;
- have a meeting with HR and the senior management;
- create guidelines for new working practices.

INTERGENERATIONAL TEAM ACTIVITY – TEAM CONSTRUCTION GAME

Very often issues come to the attention of HR when things have gone wrong. It is important to have a discussion with the people involved to see if the situation can be rectified just between themselves. It is common to find that issues that affect one team member directly will affect others indirectly.

A useful and non-emotional way of looking at intergenerational issues in a team is to set up a group activity where you can observe the group and give feedback on the way the team works. Observe whether people's different approaches are because they think differently as explored in Hermann thinking styles, or whether it is to do with age. Ideally video the team whilst they are working, as they are then able to give one another feedback. The following exercise is a fun team activity, which will give you the opportunity to explore this.

Circulate Handout 13.5.

Show the group the video afterwards so they can focus on the way the team worked and how they used each other's strengths and agree ways to move the team forward.

TEAM CONSTRUCTION GAME

You have 30 minutes to construct a track made of straws. You may use any of the materials to construct a surface along which a table tennis ball can travel. The team with the most interesting track will be declared the winner.

Rules

1. You may only use the materials provided.

2. The bag containing the materials may not be used.

3. The ball must be in contact with the straws' surface during its run.

4. The ball should travel as far as possible horizontally and incline at least six inches vertically.

5. The ball must not touch or be touched by any other surface during its run.

6. At no time should the ball come closer than two inches to the base.

7. You cannot use any outside person to help, only the team members.

8. No one should take any safety risks during the activity.

Any group in breach of rules will be disqualified.

Materials provided
100 straws
1 table tennis ball
2 pencils
1 ruler
1 pair of scissors
1 rubber

Reproduced from *Age Matters* by Keren Smedley and Helen Whitten, Gower Publishing, 2006.

ASSUMPTIONS AND REALITY: AGE FEEDBACK EXERCISE

Very often the differences between us are in our assumptions about how others see us.

The following feedback exercise gives people the opportunity to really understand one another and how they are seen. This opens up the possibility to recognize one another's strengths and weaknesses, and a way to develop good working relationships.

This exercise must be done in a quiet space where the group has an opportunity to process the exercise so all comments are fully understood.

Each person is asked to fill in a a copy of the handout sheet for the other person in the room.

Ask them to partner with another person in the room and spend ten minutes telling one another how they see them, and then swap over.

Do this with the entire group.

Check that everyone is happy with what has been said.

In the plenary session, look at the assumptions made and how these affect your working practices.

Reproduced from *Age Matters* by Keren Smedley and Helen Whitten, Gower Publishing, 2006.

AGE FEEDBACK EXERCISE

1. a) Because I am older than you I see you as

b) Because I am younger than you I expect you see me as

Or

2. a) Because I am younger than you I see you as

b) Because I am older than you I expect you see me as

Or

3. a) Because I am approximately the same age as you I see you as

b) Because I am approximately the same age as you I expect you see me as

CHAPTER 14

New Ways of Working

Maria, Flora and Salma are meeting for their monthly get-together. Salma arrives late and stressed.

'Sorry I'm late. I have had to go round for the second time to the parents. Dad's not very well; Mum thinks that it is my role to support them all and she should not be expected to manage anything by herself. She is a perfectly able woman but becomes totally incapable in all of these situations.'

The competition now begins!

Maria says, 'I know you've got a problem with your parents but my Mum is on her own, diagnosed with Alzheimer's and there's no-one else to do anything. How on earth do I manage Mum, work and the children? I get no help from work at all and my manager's about 12 years old and doesn't understand the pressures I am under. How can she – what does she know about life?'

Flora says, 'Come on Maria, you are being totally unfair. We didn't understand the pressures of older people when we were in our mid-30s: how could we?'

Salma pipes up, 'We understood some of it because we all had children by then and we were already having to be responsible for another life. It meant we just couldn't stay late however urgent the project because the nurseries closed and we had to pick them up.'

'Yes but at least we had our kids when we were younger,' said Flora. 'My manager is expecting her first child and she is coming up to 42. She is exhausted and it must be harder for her. Just imagine how long she's going to have to work if she is going to get the children through education and have any money and free time left for herself.'

'What I worry about,' Maria sighs, 'is helping my children to pay their college fees without getting into debt; and at the same time trying to help Mum to pay for the kind of care that she needs, which costs a fortune.'

'I thought your Mum had a bit of money?' Salma asks.

'No,' Maria replies, 'the only thing she has is her home and I had always thought that would help towards my pension. The one thing Mum's always wanted was to leave her children some money. She worked very hard.'

'All I ever wanted was to get back to full-time work after the children went to school and to really fulfil my potential. But here we are all torn in numerous directions, feeling so exhausted that I'm beginning to wish I could give up but I can't afford to, and the way pensions are going I'll be working till I'm 95!'

Possible outcome

Salma becomes stressed and exhausted, taking extended sick/compassionate leave to help her elderly parents. Maria feels increasingly squeezed between the older and younger generation and her fears about the future of her job. A perfectionist, who has always produced high-quality work, Maria starts to make mistakes. Flora's manager takes extended maternity leave and Flora, who feels it is really important that women are allowed to do this, takes on her workload and becomes exhausted.

This section will explore how organizations can support their staff through life changes and difficult periods, by developing new ways of working so as to ensure a consistent high quality of work and productivity. Work–life balance is a key issue of today's world. Commitments outside work are a fact of life and people have little practical support to manage these home and life pressures. We all, at one stage or another, have some of these situations to manage: families to attend to; washing machines that break down; children or pets who become ill; elderly relatives who need to be taken to the hospital.

Inevitably this can impact on productivity at work. There is already a recognition that the organization, whilst not being directly responsible for an employee's private life, will nonetheless benefit from providing support to their staff at difficult times. (See Chapter 8 Health and Wellbeing.)

This chapter will explore some of the options available to organizations in order to help retain staff and maintain productivity by introducing alternative ways of working.

This chapter covers the following topics:

1. Evaluating the 9–5 culture

2. Work–life balance

3. Caring responsibilities

4. Flexible working

5. Training managers

6. Senior managers as role models

7. Adjusting rewards and benefits

8. Individual responsibility

9. Support systems and practices.

1. EVALUATING THE 9–5 CULTURE

The current patterns of working – which were developed centuries ago now – are seen by young people as outdated and impractical. They see people rise early, take a train for as much as four hours a day, sometimes with several changes, and spend eight or more hours at a computer that they could easily have accessed from home. Therefore it can be argued that people are putting themselves through unnecessary strain by the current working practices which restrict them to being present in an office for a specific amount of time each day. In reality people can now work from home, in cars, trains, planes and on the run.

As people get older they comment that one of the most tiring aspects of work is commuting; and that they would welcome either a shorter week or the ability to work from home from time to time. Unfortunately managers are often not trusting enough of their staff to allow this to happen, although the majority of people who work flexibly or from home generally take a responsible approach to work and increase productivity.

2. WORK–LIFE BALANCE

🖉 Exercise 14.1

🖉 Exercise 14.2

Work–life balance is relevant for all age groups. In the context of the older workforce if organizations are going to retain their older and valuable staff members and use available talent and personnel, new ways of working are a key solution. Flexible working – of which there are many options – and a culture where work–life balance is valued and can be seen as inherent in current practices – can support retention, motivation and performance within this older work group.

We have explored in Chapter 4, Understanding Your Older Workforce, some of the pressures that are likely to be affecting the 50+ worker's ability to perform at their peak. Not all of these will affect everyone and some, of course, will affect people in a much younger age group as well.

We have worked in business environments where anyone who cannot 'hack it' can be perceived as weak. However, for all of us there are periods of our lives when internal or external pressures affect our performance: this is not right or wrong. It just has to be managed. Those who criticize may not have experienced this yet but it does not mean to say that they will not do so in the future.

It is therefore important to encourage people to be objective and non-judgemental. Older workers are equally capable, able to work efficiently, effectively, productively and make a huge contribution to your business.

The need to maintain stamina

One of the reasons why work–life balance is important at this stage of life is physiological change. The fact is that there are cellular changes that occur in the body over time and these affect different people in different ways. Statements such as 'I am always so tired – but what do you expect at 50!' are frequently based more on beliefs than on reality. (See Chapter 5 Changing Attitudes and Stereotypes.) However, for many people as they become older they find that they do become more tired at the end of a working day and are less able to sustain twelve hours a day working, five days a week.

Some of this can be due to lack of motivation or boredom because of the repetitiveness of their working activity, length of commute and no new stimulation. People say to us, 'I've been doing this commute for 30 years and I don't think I can face doing it for another ten! If I could work from home a couple of days a week it would make a real difference.'

It may be that your older workers will not raise these issues with you of their own accord for fear of being seen as weak. Take the initiative, therefore, to explore this situation. This requires some sensitivity and observation of the law – for example, not saying: 'Oh you are getting old now so maybe you'd like to work from home', but perhaps asking: 'Can you identify any ways of working that would help you to perform more effectively?'

3. CARING RESPONSIBILITIES

People aged in their 40s and 50s, as mentioned earlier, are often sandwiched between children and ageing parents. When things are working well this can be a great pleasure but when ageing parents become ill, as in our scenario, it increases the pressure, often for a number of years. This can affect mental, emotional and physical ability to function well.

Parents, grandparents, aunts and uncles are living considerably longer than in previous times. With more frequent divorce and remarriage it can mean that a person has several sets of elderly parents and family members to support. With forecasts predicting that there will be a 25 per cent increase in people over the age of 85 in the next five years, this means that an additional 25 per cent of your workforce are likely to be dealing with caring issues. At the same time the trend towards having children at a later age means that 50–60 year olds may also be having to find the energy to manage adolescents and/or young children. Having watched two of our politicians manage young children we can see that although Tony Blair was the older father, even the relatively youthful Charles Kennedy found the lack of sleep difficult to manage!

Already in 2005 there are three million working carers who have to deal with the stresses and responsibilities of what might seem like two jobs – one paid and one unpaid. At present 13 per cent of full-time workers are carers and 17 per cent of part-time workers are carers. This figure will only increase and talented staff may feel that, unless working practices change, they cannot combine work and caring. It is therefore beneficial to the organization to redesign policies and practices to meet this need.

Make policies available to all

People often imagine that these problems only relate to female staff. This is not the case. Several men we have worked with have confided that they are stressed by looking after elderly parents, particularly if they are the only child and therefore the sole person responsible for a parent's welfare. They also find it very difficult to discuss their problems with their managers.

These social changes are not the responsibility of your organization but they are a reality. Most organizations today are functioning in the area of knowledge, service and intelligence and require their staff to maintain clarity of thought, concentration and creativity far more than the organizations of the past who were not having to compete in a global environment. The shareholders and stakeholders of your organization need the staff to be able to work at their optimum in order to maintain continued innovation and competitive edge. Where organizations are able to offer practical support to their staff they are able to demonstrate real savings in recruitment and training costs, reduced sickness absence, and real profits in terms of increased productivity.

4. FLEXIBLE WORKING

✎ Exercise 14.3

Flexibility is often the key and work–life balance policies and practices can provide solutions for these individuals. The policies are now usually in place but the practices are taking time to be integrated because of the long-hours culture in many organizations in the UK.

Even the Department of Trade and Industry (DTI) legislation offering flexible working for parents of children under six has not proved infallible in practical terms. Senior managers, in particular, report that they find it difficult to ask for flexible options because they believe that it will have an adverse affect on their career prospects. We have worked with several senior women in the older age brackets who say that being able to go home early just one day a week to pick up their child from school would make life easier for them emotionally. However, working culture and the fear of being judged negatively prohibits them asking. This is one of the main reasons why organizations are losing their skilled women.

HR initiatives must therefore not only put policies in place but will also need to address cultural and behavioural issues.

Working options

A number of initiatives have been introduced in companies which, as we stated above, have been shown to have some real business benefits. There are a variety of working options available and it is not always necessary to introduce sweeping reforms in order to maintain morale and motivation within your workforce. Sometimes the allowance, or provision, of emergency care is enough to allow people to relax and concentrate on the job. At other times enabling someone to work at home one day a week, or stagger their hours to miss the rush hour can ease the burden and help someone to work more effectively.

Some of the flexible working options available to you are:

*   flexible start and finishing times

*   core hours

*   home working

*   annualized hours

*   term-time hours

*   compressed hours

*   job sharing

- job splitting

- part-time working

- tele-working

- nine-day fortnight

- flexible holidays to fit in with alternative care arrangements

- hours shaped to volume and customer needs.

You will need to analyse the roles within your organization to identify what is feasible in the way of both permanent and short-term flexible options. These options have to be seen within the needs of your business.

Each team and each organization are unique and yet many of the pressures of today's life affect people in a similar way across the globe. No-one is exactly sure how to manage the present situation, so one of the main responsibilities of any executive is to keep reviewing current practices.

Some individuals and teams would find flexible working harder than others. There are roles which dictate face-to-face contact with clients. Whilst it is possible that these jobs can be shared and rotated it is obvious that it is necessary for someone to be present.

Other roles can easily be carried out from home or at different times of the day to the 'norm'.

The world can change in a moment and your business or life priorities can change with it. Encourage managers to make the art of balancing life for themselves and their team a priority. Help them realize that if someone feels fulfilled and content with their home arrangements they are more likely to perform better in the workplace. This may seem obvious to someone working in HR but no doubt you realize that managers often have a different set of skills and expertise and will rely on you to give them guidance on people issues.

5. TRAINING MANAGERS

If your work–life balance policies are to be integrated effectively into practice in your workplace, managers will only be able to do this effectively with training and support.

Many can also perceive it to be more difficult and complex to manage flexible workers and to measure outputs rather than hours-at-work. There are various strategies that can assist them make a success of new ways of working.

Make managers aware of the options

Managers are not aware of all the options available to them in how they build teams to achieve required results. The managing director of an energy consultancy mentioned to us recently that he was losing several young women in one of his departments and could see no way that he could attract them back to post because of the hours involved. Interestingly until talking with us he had neither thought of breaking up the shift patterns to be more manageable; nor considered the possibility of hiring older people for this area of his business.

Involve the team in brainstorming solutions

Teams usually hold the solutions to their problems themselves but will need the forum to share their ideas. Teams with whom we have worked have generated some really creative ways of working that have enhanced team morale as well as performance. They know how their jobs function and can analyse the needs of customers and operational requirements. They know the downtimes – which they may not share with their manager unless given the opportunity but with which they can work to gain leeway for rostering or flexi-working. An example was a finance group who had struggled to produce figures by 2.30pm every day and who suggested to their manager that if they came in earlier than 9am it would make this easier. So they changed their hours to work from 7.30am – 3pm and this eased the situation for all concerned.

Another example is in the NHS where recruitment of staff is a common problem. Their Improving Working Lives policy has encouraged staff of all ages to be able to participate in their own way and at their convenience. In one NHS Primary Care Trust where there was a shortage of district nurses the only applicants for a particular post were those that wanted term-time working. Although this is not ideal as patients' needs are relatively constant and certainly don't change around school holidays, a management decision was made that it was better to have a nurse for approximately 40 weeks a year, leaving 12 weeks of understaffing, than having 52 weeks understaffed.

Some of the team found this an extremely difficult decision and felt that it would just leave them burdened in holiday times, with other people's work. For a period of time the new workers felt isolated within the team and considered leaving. At this point the team was offered support where the effect of them leaving was both analysed and the emotional feelings within the group acknowledged.

The team agreed that they would accept this way of working for a period of six months and then review the effects. During this period the team started to pull together and this change in policy has now reduced the staffing shortage and increased the patient quality of life beyond any of their expectations.

Also, the flexible workers, having had their needs acknowledged and met, are very aware of times of pressure for other members of staff and will work extra hours whenever it is at all possible so that all members of the team feel supported.

6. SENIOR MANAGERS AS ROLE MODELS

It is essential that senior management 'walk the talk'. Without their participation it is very unlikely that your work–life policies will be successful. We have heard some companies argue that if the policy is in place then it does not matter whether senior managers participate in changing or shortening their hours. However, in our experience there is a mismatch here and people become both nervous and cynical when a policy is not upheld by management behaviours.

You may find different opinions on these issues even within your older workforce. There will be those, as we mentioned earlier, who really want to have some flexible way of working. There will be others who think that 9–5 is the 'norm' and this is the way working life is because this is how they have been doing it all their lives. Your role will be to enlighten these people. You may need to help them to see that flexible working could be a way of reducing their stress and motivating them to stay and be positive in the workplace. Case studies and examples of best practice in other organizations can help them to recognize the value both to the business and to the individuals within it.

It is really important that you are able to help management and staff to see tangible business benefits to work-life policies and to recognize that unless you flex to the demands of your workforce in these areas then you could experience skill shortages in the coming years. This is not some fanciful idea but will make a real difference to productivity.

Encouraging discussion and honesty

People are fearful of the consequences of being honest. They say they are ill rather than telling their manager that they have to take a child to the doctor or attend a meeting at the care home. Much sickness absence relates to other commitments if the person does not feel they can ask for this time off. If you make it difficult for people to be honest about their external commitments and responsibilities they may find it easier to be less than straight about other crucial business areas. Once team members understand each other's pressures and responsibilities they tend to be more co-operative and supportive of one another. The management and HR team together can facilitate these discussions to enable each person to see the other person's point of view and work out the solutions together.

Focusing on best use of available time

Managers can often be so busy on tasks that they can make assumptions that their team know what to spend time on. Help managers to share the current vision and strategy of the department and organization with their direct reports so that everyone can identify what is important and what is not. When individuals know what their contribution is and what part they can play to achieve goals, they use time well rather than squandering precious moments on irrelevant areas of the business, or on displacement activities. This should assist each decision they make, ensuring that they focus their time on what matters most. Review and update this information frequently, as older workers may have less tolerance to having their time wasted or badly spent as it could deplete their energy unnecessarily.

7. ADJUSTING REWARDS AND BENEFITS

When you alter an employee's hours or place of work there are employment factors that you will need to take into account, such as adjusting salary, pension, rewards and incentives. If they are working from home then there are health and safety issues that you have to take into account regarding their home working environment.

Equally you can use flexible working options to enable a person to adjust to impending retirement. We know of two legal firms where senior partners in their 50s are finding the long hours too punishing and have therefore adjusted their working time to three days per week. This has led to a change of pay reward and there is a recognition that this leads them towards retirement in a phased way, whilst the company benefits from their skill and expertise at the same time. In one of these cases this has also had a very real health benefit, leading to reduced sickness absence and greater productivity at work.

Job design

Recent surveys have shown that most managers are working beyond their contracted hours. Much of this is due to unrealistic job design. Evaluate job descriptions carefully to ensure that the tasks are truly achievable within the hours contracted. If not discuss these issues with the individual and team to explore new solutions to address this problem. Older people who work long hours, take work home at weekends and take no time to refresh can end up exhausted and therefore less creative and productive.

8. INDIVIDUAL RESPONSIBILITY

The organization can play their part in introducing policies and practices that support work–life balance. The individual must also play their part and take responsibility for their own life decisions and arrangements. They may need training in the skills and strategies that will enable them to manage their work and life commitments so that they can contribute towards effective working practices.

9. SUPPORT SYSTEMS AND PRACTICES

Technology: To enable people to work from home, or on the move, it is important to provide up-to-date technology. For example, make your intranet and log-in system available from laptops and home PCs. Provide Blackberries or hand-held email systems to help those people who have roles where they are out of the office a lot.

Personal support: Investigate the excellent concierge and Internet services that are available today, for example, supermarket shopping, wait in for the service-engineer, or deliver the dry-cleaning. Many of these do not cost a great deal.

Childcare: Explore the possibilities of childcare provision such as back-up and emergency nanny services and creches.

Caring support: Allow time off for those caring for elderly or disabled relatives. Have a resource bank of helpful numbers and services for emergencies or difficult times.

Time out: Many companies are now allowing 'duvet days' or days where a person can take a certain number of days to recoup their energy and refresh themselves mentally and physically. It is important also to allow time out during the day – there is a feeling that individuals would benefit from the equivalent of a 'non-smoking' break, that is, the ability to take five to ten minutes out every so often during the day to clear the mind. Make sure people take holidays on a regular basis – those who slog on for months on end can drain their batteries to such an extent that they are no use to you or their families. Burnout can occur overnight: make sure it doesn't happen to yourself or one of your staff.

Multi-skilling: Where teams are covering for one another multi-skilling can give people greater confidence to fulfil roles more effectively.

SUMMARY AND TIPS

This section has explored work–life balance issues for the older worker and the need for new ways of working. Commitments outside work are a fact of life. Very small changes can make a huge difference to an individual. Often people are able to manage the daily routine demands and all people need is support at times of real crisis so that they can problem solve and manage the situation.

Behaviour change takes time. It can sometimes take time for people to accept the value of new ways of working. You may well find pockets of resistance within certain departments to any suggested changes. You will therefore need to be persistent and a skilled influencer if you are to open people's minds up to new possibilities. You will need to demonstrate at every level the objective business value that this will bring to your organization. Starting networks and encouraging managers and teams to meet every fortnight or every month to review progress and reinforce new behaviours will ensure that the policy works in practice. (See Chapter 5 Changing Attitudes and Stereotypes.)

Where there is a long-term requirement people are likely to need support initially but once the behaviour becomes routine it becomes possible for the individual to manage with less external support from their workplace. Measure change where possible so that you can provide tangible results to all concerned.

Six tips

1. Understand the issues that may affect older workers' performance.

2. Take time to really understand what work–life balance means to yourself and how you can be a role model.

3. Encourage people to explore new options in how they work.

4. Find ways to create an open atmosphere so that people can talk about the issues that are affecting them.

5. Audit your company's practices and policies.

6. Set up some support mechanisms and allow people to have time out for emergencies.

Exercise 14.1

BECOMING A SUPPORTIVE COMPANY

If, as an organization, you are going to help your staff to manage their life situations while actively contributing to the business goals, an area that needs to be considered is how supportive you are of their needs.

The following questionnaire will offer you an opportunity to see how far along the continuum you are with this.

Scoring

If you have scored 12–15 you are well on the way to providing support to your older workers.

If you have scored 9–15 you have obviously considered the issues and there are areas that you could still focus on.

If you have scored under 9 you really could benefit from taking these issues seriously otherwise you could really miss out on valuable older workers and leave yourself with a skills and knowledge shortage.

NEW WAYS OF
WORKING

SUPPORT AUDIT

	Yes	No
1. Does your organization have flexible working arrangements?		
2. Are they available to all your employees?		
3. Does your organization have flexible leave arrangements?		
4. Does your organization have a right to time off for emergencies? (a) unpaid (b) paid		
5. Do you offer information on flexible working options – through websites, intranets, resource packs – to your older staff?		
6. Do you have an external support programme such as an employee assistance programme (EAP) that all employees can readily access?		
7. Is there anyone in your organization that older people could talk to about their issues?		
8. Do you run focus groups for your older staff to discuss the issues affecting them and how these could be improved?		
9. Do you have a pre-retirement programme?		
10. Do you provide external confidential advice on financial planning in older age?		
11. Is it easy for someone within your organization to talk about their life responsibilities and negotiate a way forward?		
12. Is managing the older worker just left to HR?		
13. Who else supports your older workers?		
14. Do you give your staff duvet days to recover their energy?		
15. Do you allow your staff time to deal with home issues in the workplace?		

MANAGING THE WORK–LIFE BALANCE IN YOUR ORGANIZATION

Management practices, whilst shifting in some organizations to encompass flexible practices, are in the main based upon a 'presenteeist' habit and many managers feel uncomfortable managing staff who are not on site. However, as the workforce becomes proportionately older it is likely that more staff will be asking to work flexibly or from home, in order to retain energy and avoid long commutes.

The checklist below is a start point in helping managers to analyse and focus on managerial practices that support effective performance in their older workers. This can either be done on a one-to-one basis with a manager who is having difficulty in their department or it could be done in a small group as an awareness-raising exercise.

Step one: defining what balance means to you – the manager

Analyse what work–life balance means to the manager and help them develop a vision of what the achievement of work–life balance would mean to them personally. This will enable the manager to take an objective viewpoint of their own practices. Unless the manager becomes aware of what work–life balance means to them they may pay lip service to it and may not make themselves truly available or supportive of their staff. Help them to take ownership of the fact that they are a role model and that it is exceedingly difficult for their direct reports to leave early if they aren't. Their own behaviour will influence that of others.

Step two: Brainstorming what work–life balance means to the department as a group

Provide the group with a safe environment in which they can brainstorm all the possible ways that they could achieve work–life balance. Suspend judgement and criticism at this stage and allow for all contributions to be welcomed and recorded.

Step three: Reality check

Take the ideas from Step Two and group them in three lists:

1. Definitely possible

2. Possible with modification

3. Pie in the sky.

☐ Exercise 14.2   *continued*

Step four: Business benefits

Take the ideas listed in Lines 1 and 2 and identify (a) the personal benefits and (b) the business benefits that could evolve from these practices.

Step five: What has to be done to make this happen?

Allow the group time, possibly by dividing them up, to outline any actions – mental, emotional, practical – that need to be taken in order to start to make this happen.

Step six: Policies and systems

Make sure that all your ideas are typed up and given to the HR Department so that this can feed in to either the development of new policies or into existing policies.

Step seven: Action stations

Don't wait for a policy to be written and introduced before taking action as many of the possibilities that you have outlined can be introduced without major changes. Take this back to your team and begin to discuss these issues. Exercise 14.3 will help you with this process.

WHAT'S OUR LINE?

This is an exercise that can be done in a team to start to explore the need for work–life balance. Book a different room from your usual meeting room to do this exercise and lay it out so that people are sitting in a circle. If possible lighten the atmosphere by providing some music, flipcharts, juggling balls or anything that makes the setting different from the norm. This can either be run by a team leader or by the HR department/training department or by an external facilitator.

- Explain that the group are going to do some thinking around work–life balance.

- Ask them to divide into groups of three and brainstorm all the different roles they play in their life – for example, mother, father, brother, sister, pet walker, gardener, cook, carer of elderly parent (alongside all their work responsibilities).

- The group then have between them a number of different roles that they are all playing.

- They should now select six of these roles to mime to the rest of their colleagues, who have to guess what they are doing.

- Each group has ten minutes to prepare and 3 minutes to mime. All members of the group should take part.

- The 'audience' then have to guess and the team leader makes a list of all the roles on a flipchart.

- Each group takes this list and focuses on their own roles and discusses what skills and strengths they have learnt from managing these roles.

- How many of these skills and strengths are used in work?

- Which ones would you like to use?

- How are you going to do this?

- What could the company do to support you performing these roles more effectively?

- In how many different ways or in how many different places could you carry out your work roles?

 Exercise 14.3   *continued*

Plenary session

Each group feeds back their findings and the key points of their discussion.

They now prioritize the suggestions and create an action plan to changes that could be made (a) to integrate skills, strengths and talents into the workplace and (b) to support performance.

CHAPTER 15

Retirement, Pensions and Employment Issues

Simon is in the canteen eating a sandwich when he is joined by Raj and Maria, who have also worked for XYZ Organization for many years.

Raj says, 'I've just been having a conversation with Sally of HR. Isn't it great that they have increased the retirement age and that we can go on working until 65. Sally told me that with the new legislation laws we might be able to work even longer than 65 if all goes well. I just can't imagine retiring even in five years' time: there is so much more I want to do here.'

Simon retorts, 'You are lucky; you enjoy your job! I hate this place but I can't afford to leave. I still have teenage kids to support, and my mother may need to go into a care home, which is incredibly expensive. So my dream of early retirement has just gone out of the window!'

'I used to like my job,' joins in Maria, 'but don't you find that you are forever being de-selected for things? I don't think I am going to get any further here and I, like you, Simon, can't afford to leave. As you know, I am now on my own and my pension is worth a pittance so even though I could retire at 60 because I just get in in time, I can't afford to. I don't feel old but I do feel like there is a 'grey ceiling' and I am gently being shunted out and it frightens me.'

'That's why I haven't even looked for another job because nobody will look at us – we're too old,' Simon agrees.

Raj replies, 'I think you will find that attitudes will change when they bring that new law in because they are going to have to treat us all the same.'

Possible outcome

Simon and Maria fuel each other's negative feelings and this begins to pervade throughout their team and the organization. Raj, on the other hand, is likely to thrive if he does not get caught up with the politics of peer group pressure.

Institutionalized retirement programmes including social security and pensions have existed in the UK since the Second World War. The first state pension scheme was introduced in Germany in 1889. The retirement age was set at 65 but the average age of life expectancy was 45, so few people collected it. In the UK a universal state pension was introduced in 1948, when there were ten people in work for every person in retirement. Nowadays there are only four workers to every retiree; by 2050 there will be only two workers for every pensioner.

As the proportion of people over 65 is set to double in the next 45 years, with little change in numbers of those between 20–64, this situation is financially untenable. As Adair Turner, Chair of the UK Pensions Commission and Chair of the Low Pay Commission, recently commented, successive governments have been living in a fool's paradise and the UK is headed towards pensioner poverty with insufficient funds in government coffers to provide for these increased numbers. A raising of the retirement age is one solution to this problem but people's expectations have been shaped by these programmes and people have come to assume that they will be able to retire currently on a reasonable pension at the age of 60 for women and 65 for men. This will be equalized by 2015.

Working patterns in their current format, whereby people possibly work for 30 years, retire at 55 or 60, and then live for another 20–30 years is a new phenomenon. It is also unlikely to be a financially sustainable one as effectively people are living another lifetime after retirement now that people are living well into their 80s and longevity is rising two and a half years with every decade.

This will be a new challenge to you and your organization. You will need to:

- revisit and review your current retirement policies;

- link these policies with your pension provision;

- find new ways of working with your older workforce.

In this chapter we cover:

1. Retirement legislation

2. Attitudes to retirement

3. Strategies to manage retirement issues

4. Employment practices and procedures

5. Pension provision.

RETIREMENT,
PENSIONS AND
EMPLOYMENT
ISSUES

1. RETIREMENT LEGISLATION

The following points will all be modified by the Age Discrimination Regulations:

Default retirement age

The Government has proposed a national default retirement age of 65, when employers will be able to retire workers. From 1 October 2006 employers are not able to retire employees below their organization's Normal Retirement Age (NRA) or where there is no normal retirement age, below 65. If the NRA is below 65 it must be objectively justified. Employers who want to terminate the employee's employment before the Normal or the Default Retirement Age must have another fair reason for dismissal and follow the normal dismissal procedures.

The decision to have the national default retirement age of 65 will be reviewed in five years. Lobbyists had wanted to set this at 70 but this was overruled under pressure from the unions who said that 20 per cent of people (mainly men) would die before they received their pension. However, the lobbyists argue that the default age maintains the stereotype of a 'sell-by date'. In the United States, Australia and New Zealand there is no mandatory retirement age and a recent HSBC survey reported that 80 per cent of workers want to see it scrapped. Political considerations are therefore dictating the process of raising the age.

Planned retirement

This is a new concept whereby the employer must give 6–12 months' written notice of the date of retirement. All retirement will be at age 65 or at the Normal Retirement Age for the organization, unless there is an objectively justifiable reason, for example, it would be acceptable not to employ a 48 year old to play a seven-year-old child in a screenplay.

The employer must notify the employee in writing of the intended date of retirement (IDR) and of the employee's right to request not to retire. This notification must be given not more than one year and not less than six months before IDR. It is important to diarize this process.

Notification cannot be given through other means: a statement in a handbook or in the employee's engagement letter or contract is not sufficient to fulfil this duty. If the employer fails to do this, the employee can apply to the tribunal for an award of up to eight weeks' pay. If no notification of retirement is given an employee can treat this as a non-retirement issue and take appropriate action.

Employers have been charged with the duty to consider requests to work beyond the set retirement age. As with flexible working regulations an employer must provide fair business reasons for refusing an employee the right to continue to work. This must be in writing. The employee's request to work must be delivered within a certain timescale in order to trigger the employer's obligation to consider it:

- If the employer has given notification in the 12 to six months' window, then the employee must make the request between six and three months before the IDR;

- If the employer misses this window, then the employee can make the request before but not more than six months before the IDR.

There is a set procedure that the employer must follow on receiving the request. Firstly, a meeting with the employee and then a dated decision given in writing. The employee cannot be dismissed before the decision has been made. If the employee is granted permission to continue working, the decision document must be specific about the time scale, recording whether it is indefinite or there is an end date. It should be noted that the requirement to notify an employee of retirement date would still need to be adhered to when their final date approached.

In the case of the employer refusing permission they must offer an appeal and hold, if requested, an appeal meeting. The employee has a right to be accompanied at the meeting and the appeal meeting. All parties are required to take reasonable steps to attend all the necessary meetings.

Continued employment rights

Where an employee is granted leave to stay on at their post beyond the default retirement age they will still be protected by continued employment rights such as discrimination policy and unfair dismissal. An employer would have to prove that they were no longer effective, but if the employer applies performance testing they will have to demonstrate that these tests are given to all age groups and are not discriminatory towards older workers. As providing continued work-related benefits is likely to be both complex and expensive it is considered likely that employers might be deterred from keeping people on and raise spurious reasons to justify their actions.

The new provisions address two issues in respect of dismissal through compulsory retirement: the reason for the dismissal, and its fairness. Different situations are identified where the reason for dismissal is presumed to be retirement: basically where the reason for dismissal can only be retirement. It also identifies situations where the reason for dismissal cannot be retirement. The concept of 'normal retirement age' is therefore crucial to the fairness or unfairness of the dismissal.

Fairness is determined solely on procedural grounds. To ensure that the retirement dismissal is fair the employer must have notified the employee of the IDR and the right to request no later than 14 days before the date dismissal takes effect and complied with the procedures. A failure to comply results in automatic unfair dismissal. It is therefore essential that the employer is clear regarding the reason for dismissal. As this is a complex procedure it is wise to refer to the specific details of the Regulations to ensure that relevant personnel are aware of these processes and that the actions of your organization are compliant. (*EEF Summary of Final Age Regulations*, DTI Summary of Age Regulations March 2006, 13 March 2006.)

Early retirement

Towards the end of the twentieth century the retirement age actually fell to an average of 62 in the UK. Economic fluctuations and cash-flow problems resulted in employers easing the non-high-flyers out of the organization to make way for younger people to reach the top. This could be done either through early retirement proposals or through redundancies. The older worker became the easy target and long-serving employees could be rewarded with generous early retirement pay-outs. However, employers have cut back on their generosity and under the new legislation this option will no longer be possible as it could appear discriminatory.

The Age Employment Regulations will therefore impact your retirement policies, pension provision, and employment procedures. The demographic trend whereby the large cohort known as the baby boomers are approaching retirement age will increasingly mean that you will need to retain older workers to maintain the business at its present productivity rate. You could be faced with non-performing staff who can't retire, and a group of older managers who aren't retiring to open up opportunities for younger staff to get promoted.

2. ATTITUDES TO RETIREMENT

It is easy to make assumptions that all older people take the same approach towards retirement. As you can see from our scenario each person is unique in how they respond to this situation. This is borne out by a EFA Research Study (17 February 2005), which has demonstrated that:

- people in their 50s and 60s are not rushing to retire;

- 30 per cent are happy to work until they are 70;

- 13 per cent dread retirement – a feeling that increases with age;

- People are happier at work the older they get;

- 93 per cent of the over 60s like work, the highest of all age groups;

- 20 per cent of 16–19 year olds; 23 per cent of 20–29 year olds; 33 per cent of 30–39 year olds; 40 per cent of 40–49 year olds; 45 per cent of 50–59 year olds; 50 per cent of 60–69 year olds do not think that retirement makes any sense.

This research demonstrates that attitudes to retirement vary not only within an age group but also alter as one gets older.

A recent AARP Roper Report Survey found that 80 per cent of baby boomers planned to work at least part time during retirement. Only 60 per cent say that they will not work at all. A further survey reported that 55 per cent view retirement as an opportunity for a new chapter of life whereas only 27 per cent said they saw it as a time for rest and relaxation. (Harris Interactive Market Research *Sunday Times*, 22 May 2005.)

Research from HR Services Company, Reed Consulting and Age Concern London found that 48 per cent of people aged 50 or over intended to work beyond the state pension age, including 23 per cent who plan to work until 'forced to stop'. The researchers commented that this represents 'a huge shift' given that only 9.2 per cent of people over retirement age are currently still working.

Pre-retirement planning

It will be advisable for you now to introduce pre-retirement planning into your organization as it allows you to work with your older workers to consider their options. There are specific services and consultancies that specialize in this process but equally you can collaborate with your staff to help them make the best decisions for themselves and for your business.

You will find that there will be staff who cannot afford to retire, for financial reasons; others who don't want to retire because they can't imagine how to spend their time beyond work. There will be those who now have to work longer than they had previously anticipated if the occupational retirement age had been 60 and is now raised to 65. All these are both emotional and practical issues that will need to be handled carefully through good performance management processes (see Chapter 10).

Research studies have shown that the majority of people do not have adequate financial provision for their old age. The inadequacy of the state pension is evident and the UK Government are trying to remedy this through cutting back the generous final salary pension schemes common in the public sector. The pension schemes of top civil servants are rumoured to be cut by some 50–75 per cent and this should save the UK Government 50 per cent of its pension cost. Individuals are not saving sufficient sums and lack of trust in government, private and corporate schemes are fuelling this problem. Even for those who have saved £100 000, which might seem a princely sum to have saved, they will only receive approximately £5000 per annum on which to live.

Fears of pensioner poverty can paralyse people so that they hold on to their jobs for as long as possible. Financial advice and education can help them to analyse their situation and consider how best to manage it. Inevitably, you will have greater performance where you have staff who are choosing to stay with you rather than staff who are holding on out of anxiety. Working with them on this and helping them plan can reward you with motivated employees who feel more in control of their decisions and their future.

Flexible and phased retirement

One of the options available is flexible and phased retirement, which in our experience is popular with both organizations and individuals. People are looking for different ways of working – for example three days a week or possibly six months per year. Many are doing this because they need the income. However money is not the only motivator. Many people see themselves in terms of their work and want to continue to contribute and feel useful. Self-esteem and self-confidence are often linked to contribution at work and a sense of purpose in life. In the twenty-first century the workplace frequently represents an opportunity both for fulfilling work and also for access to a social life. As people get older the prospect of a lonely retirement raises fears and anxieties, especially in a society where more people are living alone. Companies frequently felt comforted by the fact that a demotivated, non-performing worker would be forced to leave at some stage in the near future so that they did not need to address the issue. Now you will need to find methods to ensure that all your staff are working well up to retirement. (See Chapter 10 Performance Management.)

In devising your retirement policies it will therefore be helpful to understand that the concept of a one-off retirement package may no longer be relevant either to the needs of your employees or to the needs of your business. Chapter 14 on New Ways of Working helps you to consider whether there are more lateral ways for you to ease people into the next stage of their lives. Equally it will be valuable to you to encourage retirees to stay in touch so that you can re-employ them for short-term contracts such as maternity leave, sickness and holiday absence. Better to have temporary help from someone who knows your organization than have to train up a new person.

3. STRATEGIES TO MANAGE RETIREMENT ISSUES

The exercises in this next section will give you some suggestions regarding the management of your retirement policies and how to help your older workers continue to feel engaged and motivated by their work.

Once the individual has completed the exercises you or the manager can work with them to help them re-engage with work. They can do this by looking at specific examples of changes they can make in attitude, behaviour and practice. Although it is easy to imagine that older employees want to remain in the role they have known for some time, our own research demonstrates that many older workers actually want a new challenge. Discuss with the manager whether there are new projects they could be given or changes that could be made within their department that could meet their motivational needs. Refer back to the Section on Motivation in Chapter 6 on People Management to understand what their personal motivators are.

The exercise, Re-Engaging Your Interest, stimulates the individual to identify these actions.

Exercise 15.1

Exercise 15.2

Exercise 15.3

Exercise 15.4

4. EMPLOYMENT PRACTICES AND PROCEDURES

You will also need to review your current policies and procedures in a number of employment areas such as:

*   redundancy practice;

*   pay adjustments for flexible retirement;

*   benefits adjustment for flexible working;

- health insurance;

- dismissal policies;

- early retirement policies;

- pension provision.

Pay and benefits

Your pay and benefits will need to be adjusted. Pay scales that allow employees to reach top of the scale within five years will remain whatever their age; and service-related benefits can continue if objectively justifiable by reference to, for example, rewarding loyalty or experience of some or all workers, or for motivational purposes. However, age-related benefits will need to be justified by employers as fulfilling a 'business need' and this may be difficult. It is acceptable to reward five years' service with an extra day's holiday, but it will no longer be permissible to give extra holiday when an employee reaches a certain age unless exceptional justification can be proved.

✎ Exercise 15.5

Insurance and health insurance benefits

Provision of income protection, permanent health insurance and sick pay schemes have frequently previously been age-related. The Regulations now state that any ill-health scheme based on a cut-off age is likely to be discriminatory. This will significantly add to employment costs as employers will face much higher premiums in order to ensure their older workers are covered.

You will need to carry out a full audit of all schemes and policies and consider whether they are justifiable. Insured benefits must be age-neutral and equal. You will need to analyse and review your current health insurance policy in the light of the fact that you are likely now to have a higher proportion of older workers. Currently insurance companies greatly increase their premiums for older people and this can become a significant proportion of an employer's costs. It is more expensive to provide health insurance for those over 65, but cost alone will not be an acceptable reason for withdrawing a benefit under the new regulations. This could act as a disincentive to retaining or recruiting older workers.

There are options such as discussing the situation with your staff and seeing whether they would be prepared to fund a percentage of the premium when they stay on (although you will need to make it clear that this is not a discriminatory suggestion). You might also discuss this situation with your health insurance provider and with increased competition in this area you may be able to come to a better deal so as to cover all staff. There is a proposal that health insurance should be transferable from one employer to another. The alternative is that you do not, in future, provide this cover.

The Regulations permit employers to stop paying life assurance cover to workers who have retired early on grounds of ill health when the workers reach the NRA or if no NRA, aged 65. This, however, is not a general exemption allowing employers to stop providing life assurance to employees who are working beyond 65 or their NRA.

5. PENSION PROVISION

The state has provided a percentage towards people's pension provision and the individual and organization have provided the rest. In the light of the current fiscal deficit with regard to all types of pension the, UK Government are likely to seek to review their proportion and try to encourage individuals and organizations to bear more of the financial burden of the retirement years.

One of the problems has been that the pension system has been very inflexible and worked out on earnings. Private pension schemes were not available to all and those earning over £30 000 were barred from taking any other pension provision. We now have Sipps (Self-invested personal pension plans) and tax-efficient ways of saving such as individual savings accounts (ISAs). Even these, set up by the UK Government as flagship savings schemes have been shown to be at risk, for example when the Chancellor threatened to remove the tax benefits of ISAs in 2006.

The Government introduced Stakeholder Pensions which charged any company employing five or more staff to set up a pension scheme. However, only 4 per cent of small employers pay any cash into the schemes and small-to medium-sized businesses find the burden of contribution too high to maintain. Those who are self-employed fare even worse and most cannot afford adequate pension schemes and therefore are shown in surveys to intend to continuing work well into their 70s because they cannot afford to retire.

The baby boomer women are particularly badly hit. Some of those who took time out to have children missed paying National Insurance contributions and therefore have greatly reduced benefits. Others who continued to work or to pay contributions often took married women's allowance, which again reduced their state pension considerably. Divorce has also left many women in very difficult financial positions. Those who divorced before 1999 did not receive a proportion of their husband's pensions and many divorced since will still find themselves with less provision. Divorce has also affected men whose pension will not be sufficient for them to support themselves and possibly more than one family.

Advisers state that people should contribute a percentage of their salary equivalent to half the age – for example at 40 years old you should put away 20 per cent of your earnings. However if you only start saving at 30 years old your pension will be 40 per cent less than if you had started saving at 25.

One of the issues has become lack of trust as government schemes have not benefited individuals, the stock market decline has emptied coffers, and many occupational pensions have failed to provide promised sums to their staff. This is resulting in people shying away from putting their money into pension funds and going for low-risk savings such as cash or a fixed-interest fund. Actuaries and government alike have miscalculated the impact of the ageing baby boomers, increased longevity and risks such as stock market fluctuations, which have resulted in the current pension crisis.

On 6 April 2006, known as A-Day, new pension regulations were introduced. This is a major shake-up and includes:

- Single tax treatment on pensions.

- Allowances instead of limits: current limits on pensions contributions and benefits will cease. Tax relief will be available up to the stated allowance.

- Personal contributions into a pension scheme will be subject to 'annual allowance' rules. Tax relief will be given for a contribution in any tax year. Earnings will include salary, bonus, benefits-in-kind and self-employed earnings.

- All current benefit limits will be replaced by a 'lifetime allowance' – the total pension savings that can benefit from tax relief.

- There will be a limit on the amount of pension benefit that can be taken as a tax-free cash lump sum – 25 per cent of the fund, subject to a maximum of 25 per cent of the lifetime allowance.

- Greater options regarding assets available as investments for pension funds. Cash can be used from within the fund to buy anything from residential property to works of art and fine wines.

- Members of occupational pension schemes will no longer have to retire from employment to draw their pensions.

- The minimum age at which pension benefits can be taken will be increased from 50–55.

- Greater choice of retirement options. An Alternatively Secured Pension is to be available to individuals from 75 years enabling a form of income drawdown as an alternative to the purchase of an annuity. It may be possible to include relatives in a scheme to provide a tax-efficient means of passing on unused pension funds.

Exercise 15.6

SUMMARY AND TIPS

This section has highlighted the fact that everybody will be affected by the changes in the way retirement is managed. This is an issue that is high on the agenda of both the UK Government and internationally. It will therefore be subjected to continuous review and it will be important for you to remain observant of the situation as it evolves and develops.

As the unprecedented shift in the world's demography becomes apparent it is likely that the concept of 'old age' will change. This will result in what will appear to us from today's perspective as a very old workforce! Each of the stages will present different retirement issues for the working population. These will need to be continuously reviewed and managed because you will be breaking new ground.

Six tips

1. Keep abreast of retirement legislation.

2. Explore best practice on pay, benefits, pensions and employment practices.

3. Analyse and modify your organization's retirement policy.

4. Identify those people who may be affected by changes in retirement policy and offer them opportunities to discuss these issues.

5. Brainstorm solutions within specific departments.

6. Help managers to support potential retirees to re-examine their views on their work.

RETIREMENT OPTIONS

Review your current retirement policies in the light of the new Regulations and consider what options are open to you with regard to how you manage this new situation.

Find the answers to the following questions:

- Is your current retirement policy aligned to the Regulations?

- Do you have a mandatory retirement age that may need to be changed?

- Are your performance testing practices equal to all age groups?

- Do you help people plan during their pre-retirement years?

- Do you keep a database of retired staff on whom you could call during busy periods or periods of staff absence?

- Are you prepared to give the period of notice required for retirement? For example, you will need to know date of birth and also have a system to alert you at the correct period so that you issue notice in time.

- Do you have a system whereby you can manage requests to stay on beyond 65? Will these situations be managed by the HR department or by line managers? Do they have adequate information to ensure that you follow compliance requirements?

- Do all your managers know about the Age Discrimination Regulations and realize that they will not be able to offer early retirement or redundancy on the basis of age?

- Have you investigated the business benefits of retaining older staff in your business beyond your current retirement age?

MANAGING THE DEMOTIVATED OLDER WORKER

The consequences of the older worker being unsupported in their attitudes to retirement can lead to productivity problems for the business. This exercise provides ways to manage an older worker who is demotivated, either for work-related reasons, personal or financial considerations that do not allow them to retire although they would prefer to do so.

You can take an individual through the following exercises, either directly yourself, or provide them as handouts to help managers to manage their staff.

Aim

This series of exercises offers alternative ways of looking at this period of life and enable individuals such as Simon, in our scenario, to value what they have to offer and find ways to continue to gain from their everyday experience at work.

WAITING FOR RETIREMENT

The following questionnaire can be completed by the individual in order to highlight and discuss their feelings and attitudes towards work and retirement.

Are you just waiting for the magic date?

Aim: To identify if this description fits you
Time: Five to ten minutes to complete the section

Tick the box that most reflects your experience	Yes	No	Don't know
1. Do you look forward to coming to work?			
2. Does your work interest you?			
3. Are you only here for the money?			
4. Would you willingly go on training?			
5. Can you see promotion potential?			
6. Are there hobbies you would rather pursue?			
7. Do you welcome change?			
8. Do you prefer the status quo?			
9. Do you feel valued?			
10. Do you feel past your sell-by date?			
Score:			

For Questions 1, 2, 4, 5, 7, 9: score 3 for yes, 1 for no, 2 for don't know.
For Questions 3, 6, 8, 10: score 1 for yes, 3 for no, 2 for don't know.

If you scored 1–10, you are obviously still enjoying your work.

If you scored 11–20, things aren't brilliant, it may be worth looking at Chapter 15.

If you scored 21–30, you need this now, don't waste your life!

RETIREMENT, PENSIONS AND EMPLOYMENT ISSUES

 Exercise 15.3

FOCUSING ON THE POSITIVES

There is always a choice about the way you do your work, even if there is not a choice about the work itself (Lundin, 2000).

Different people are motivated by different things. To re-engage their interest at work you need to help them to identify what makes them feel good and gives them a buzz. You could ask them the question 'How can you do this task AND enjoy it?' For example, an employee we knew hated forms and figures, dreaded the end of the month when they had to fill in expense and mileage forms, and used to spend hours moaning about it and procrastinating. They then realized that this was a task that had to be done and had a financial reward. They began to visualize how they would feel when the task was completed and how they would use this money. Once they had a positive picture they began to discover that the task took less time, felt more enjoyable and they did not talk about it; they just did it.

FOCUSING ON THE POSITIVES

Take a few moments to identify what motivates and demotivates you both inside and outside work. Fill in the lines on the branches with your responses:

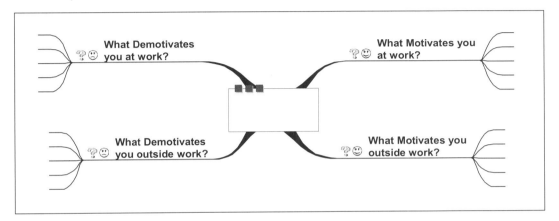

Motivation

Now reflect on your current position and tick the bubbles that apply to you:

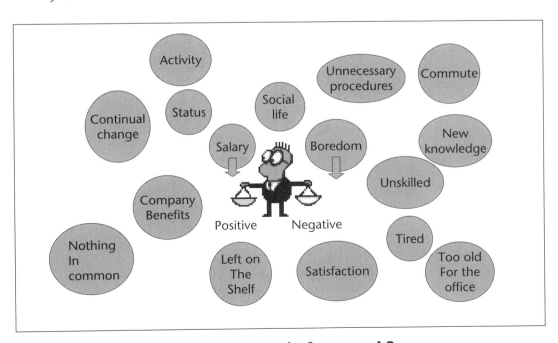

What do you gain from work?

RETIREMENT,
PENSIONS AND
EMPLOYMENT
ISSUES

RE-ENGAGING WITH WORK

Once the individual has completed the previous exercises you or the manager can work with them to help them re-engage with work. They can do this by looking at specific examples of changes they can make in attitude, behaviour and practice. Refer back to the Section on Motivation in Chapter 6 on People Management to understand what their personal motivators are.

This exercise, Re-Engaging Your Interest, stimulates the indivual to identify these actions.

RE-ENGAGING YOUR INTEREST

Aim: To find ways to feel positive about work

Having thought about this subject you will now need to make some decisions and take some action. Complete the exercise below:

Which aspects of work make you feel good?

What would make you look forward to coming to work?

What changes could realistically be made?

Who can help you make these changes?

How are you going to go about doing this?

Exercise 15.5

PAY AND BENEFITS

Review your current practices and consider what changes you will need to make to policies such as:

- flexible and phased retirement policies;

- new ways of working such as flexible or part-time working;

- pay scales and benefits.

Make a list below of what actions you will need to take and create a plan for implementation. (Note that you will need to continue to review these as the legislation unfolds in practice.)

PENSION PROVISION

Review your current pension provision in the light of the 6 April 2006 changes and consider what options you are able to offer your staff. Staff who feel secure about their future are likely to be able to focus more effectively on their work. Currently there are four pension options:

- occupational final salary

- money purchase

- group personal pension scheme

- stakeholder pension.

You will need to analyse your current pension provision in the light of the fact that you are likely to have many older staff who may be able to claim pension payments at pensionable age, while still working. This could prove expensive and you will need to review this situation with your pension provider. It is likely that individuals will need to be encouraged to save more themselves.

One of the most important factors is to make your pension scheme as transparent as possible. Current practices are very difficult for people to understand and the more individuals can view forecasts of annual provision the more likely it is that the importance of saving will dawn on them.

When you communicate information about pensions ensure that it reaches everyone. Putting a notice only on your intranet may not be helpful as people of different ages, roles and personal circumstances may not feel that their needs are understood.

It is very important that your pensions policy is not discriminatory to any person on the basis of age. Many older workers are concerned that their pensions will be affected by the changes in legislation, so particular care needs to be taken in the light of this, to avoid litigation.

Training and Implementation

16

Awareness-Raising Session:
Influencing Senior Management

Aim   To introduce the topic of Age Discrimination and the requirements of the Age Discrimination Regulations October 2006 to your decision makers, and to agree the way forward for the organization. Refer back to relevant chapters in the book as you prepare your session.

Format   30-minute interactive presentation.

Target group   Chief Executive, Directors and Senior Managers.

Equipment   Flipchart
Powerpoint
Handouts to be chosen depending on the relevance to your group.

SUGGESTED SESSION OUTLINE

Introduction

Introduce the group to:

1. The Age Discrimination Regulations

This means that it is illegal to discriminate on the basis of age. This is a European Directive. Explain that this impacts all areas of employment for compliance reasons. These include:

- recruitment
- retirement
- pay, benefits and pensions
- health and sickness

- harassment and discrimination
- performance management
- succession planning, career development and promotion
- training and lifelong learning
- work–life balance and flexible working.

2.   Demographic change means that:

- there will be a significantly larger number of older people in the workforce;
- insufficient numbers of young people to replace them;
- pension poverty will result in people continuing their working life;
- longevity can lead to people working longer.

3.   Business impact and benefits:

- older workers can fill skills gaps;
- continue corporate knowledge and memory;
- bring access to wider customer base;
- improve the organization's public image;
- increase staff morale;
- increase staff retention;
- lower staff absence.

THE LAW

The Law is based on the familiar concepts found in existing discrimination laws and will cover direct and indirect discrimination, harrassment and victimization. The Law refers to employment in the broadest sense possible. It includes apprentices, trainees and vocational training. This law will be treated in the same way as all other discriminatory laws and as an organization you will want to avoid litigation by treating your employees fairly.

Take each aspect of employment law and give a brief overview of key points.

Recruitment

All current recruitment practices will need reviewing and updating to ensure age-neutral processes. This includes:

- advertising strategy and remit;

- age-neutral application forms;

- short-listing using competencies, not experience as criteria;

- non-stereotypical interviews.

Retirement

Retirement procedures are changing:

- National default retirement age of 65.

- Employers' duty to consider requests to stay on to work beyond 65.

- Employers' obligation to give adequate reason to refuse such requests.

- All employees to be given at least six months' notice of their retirement date.

Pay, benefits and pensions

- Organizational policies and pay and benefit structures will need to be reviewed.

Training and lifelong learning

- Training to be available equally to all workers of all age groups.

- Exclusion from long-term training courses only when they would be completed after the agreed retirement date.

DEMOGRAPHY

Chapter 3, Demographic Changes, has statistics and graphs that you can photocopy and use as handouts in your presentation to explain the current situation.

BUSINESS CASE

Older workers can fill skills gaps

There will be a shortage of replacement younger workers to maintain productivity and profitability. They can therefore use older workers to fill these gaps.

Maintaining corporate knowledge and memory

Organizational knowledge is held by long-serving workers. You can use your older workers to share this knowledge with new members of staff.

Bring access to a wider customer base

Demographic change is affecting the worldwide population. Therefore your customer base will have an increased proportion of over 50s. This is an opportunity to look at your products and services to leverage this situation.

Improve the organization's public image

Organizations showing that they embrace diversity are seen as employers-of-choice.

Increase staff morale

Older workers who choose to stay on have been shown to be happier, loyal and motivated.

Increase staff retention

Recruitment costs time, energy and money. Retaining staff makes business sense.

Lower staff absence

It is a myth that just because a worker is older they take more sickness leave. Lack of motivation is a far greater factor in absence.

Succession planning, career development and promotion

The demographic change could lead to leadership gaps at all levels. It can lead to blockage for younger staff so flexibility in role change needs to be introduced through good career development processes.

Performance management

Competence-based performance management is essential to ensure that all workers' goals and aspirations are met to ensure peak performance. Performance management is particularly important where you may have disaffected staff or staff not meeting targets.

Work–life balance and flexible working

Flexible working practices will enable staff to work in new ways to meet their own and business demands.

CREATING THE AGE-INCLUSIVE ORGANIZATION

Ask the group individually to draw an 'old person' and a 'young person'. Give them two minutes.

Ask them to share the features of each and capture points on flipchart.

Ask them where these images came from and explain that people develop such stereotypical thinking from parents and it becomes fixed and automatic. Remind the group that this stereotypical attitude and behaviour will be common within the organization and will need addressing.

Introduce the age-inclusive model.

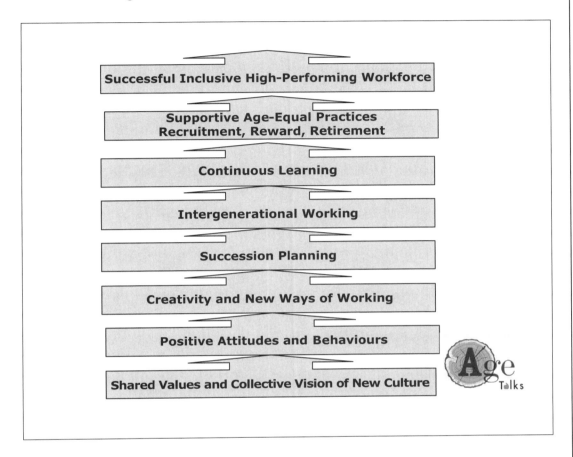

Figure 16.1   Age-inclusive model

This will lead you into explaining your own proposed plan of action for your organization. This needs to include commitment from the group with regard to shared responsibility for the success of this implementation.

Ensure agreement of the first phase of your action plan.

17

Awareness-Raising Session:
Cascading Awareness on Age Discrimination Throughout the Organization

Aim	To introduce the topic of age discrimination and the requirements of the Age Discrimination Regulations October 2006 to all your staff, and to agree the way forward for the organization. Refer back to relevant chapters in the book to prepare your session.
Format	Two-hour interactive presentation.
Target group	All levels of staff.
Equipment	Flipcharts Powerpoint Handouts to be chosen depending on the relevance to your group.

SUGGESTED SESSION OUTLINE

Introduction

Introduce the group to:

1. The Age Discrimination Regulations

This means that it is illegal to discriminate on the basis of age. This is a European Directive. Explain that this impacts all areas of employment for compliance reasons. These include:

- recruitment

- retirement

- pay, benefits and pensions

- health and sickness

- harassment and discrimination

- performance management

- succession planning, career development and promotion

- training and lifelong learning

- work–life balance and flexible working.

2.   Demographic change means that:

- there will be a significantly larger number of older people in the workforce;

- insufficient numbers of young people to replace them;

- pension poverty will result in people continuing their working life;

- longevity can lead to people working longer.

The figure below shows an overview of the session.

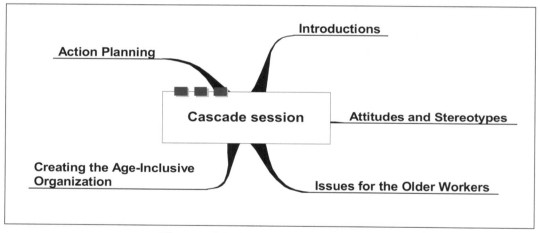

Figure 17.1   Cascade session

Session one: Attitudes and stereotypes

✎ Exercise 17.1: Drawing exercise

Ask each person to take two pieces of A4 paper and a pen and draw an older person on one sheet and a younger person on the other. Remind them that these need not be perfect pictures but the first thing that comes into their head. Give them two to three minutes to complete these.

Ask them to share with someone what they have drawn and why.

Plenary session

Ask the group to share findings. Questions you could ask:

- Would they have drawn the same picture if they were 20 years older, or younger?

- Where do they feel these ideas came from?

- Were the pictures based on family or work?

- What does it say about attitudes?

- Were they positive or negative pictures? Which was the most positive?

Theory input on stereotypes

See Chapter 5, section 2: Stereotypes and section 3: Beliefs and Habits for background information. Figures 5.1 and 5.2 can be used as handouts or to be drawn on a flipchart. Lead people on from the drawing exercise to discuss how beliefs and habits might influence behaviours in your organizational culture.

Issues for the older workers

Refer back to Chapter 4 on Understanding Your Older Workforce in order to get some background on this topic.

✎ Exercise 17.2: What are the pressures facing older workers today?

In groups of six brainstorm all the different pressures you think this group might be under at the moment, for example, having teenage children and elderly parents.

Ask each group to prepare a short charade where they act out for the other group at least five issues that are affecting older workers. Give the group 15 minutes to prepare a four-minute 'act'.

The 'audience' group has to guess which issues they are depicting.

The group exchanges roles and the 'audience' group has to act out the issues to the first group.

Plenary session

- What themes did you notice?

- How do you feel about this situation?

- How might these issues impact performance and team working?

- What ideas do you have to resolve these issues for yourself and your team?

Reproduced from *Age Matters* by Keren Smedley and Helen Whitten, Gower Publishing, 2006.

Creating the age-inclusive organization

Introduce the age-inclusive model and identify which policies and practices will need to be changed within the organization.

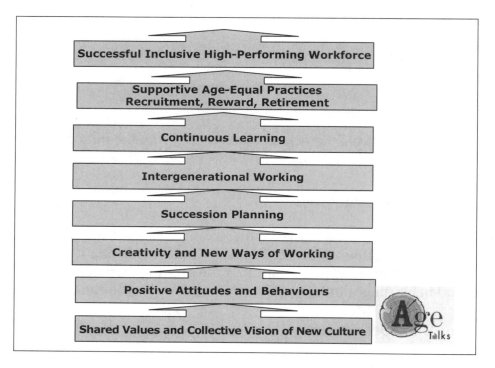

Figure 17.2   Age-inclusive model

✎ Exercise 17.3: Identifying behaviour changes

In fours ask the group to consider what working practices and behaviours need to be changed within this organization to achieve an age-inclusive culture and ensure that there is no direct or indirect discrimination, harassment or victimization. Suggest they consider language, body language, activities (for example, giving birthday cards) and HR procedures.

Give them 15 minutes.

Plenary session

Capture key points on a flipchart as these are areas that HR and line managers will need to continue to work on.

Produce copies of the flipchart information and send to each participant.

✎ Exercise 17.4: Personal actions

Ask each person to identify one or two actions they will personally take to make sure that they are not ageist.

Reproduced from Age Matters by Keren Smedley and Helen Whitten, Gower Publishing, 2006.

CHAPTER 18

Implementation:
One-day Training Programme to Introduce Age-Inclusive Working Practices into your Organization

Aim
To enable HR and line managers to identify the issues of Age Discrimination and the requirements of the Age Employment Regulations 2006, explore how to manage this new situation, and develop skills to ensure that managers are able to motivate and make the most of the wisdom and experience that lies within their older workforce. By the end of the programme delegates will have identified:

- the likely impact of an ageing workforce on business performance;

- the advantages and disadvantages of the 2006 regulations;

- how to be prepared for the demographic changes;

- how to demonstrate the value placed in their older workforce;

- how to ensure continued motivation across the workforce;

- intergenerational communication and knowledge sharing;

- action points to ensure peak performance in the workforce.

Refer back to relevant chapters in the book both for background information, interactive exercises and handouts.

Format	One-day interactive workshop

Target group	HR, training, and line managers
	8–12 people per programme.

Equipment	Flipchart
	Powerpoint
	Handouts to be chosen depending on the relevance to your group
	Plain paper and pens.

Room layout	Provide tables or desks either in U-shape or cabaret-style
	Space for break-out sessions
	Ideally, break-out rooms.

SUGGESTED PROGRAMME OUTLINE

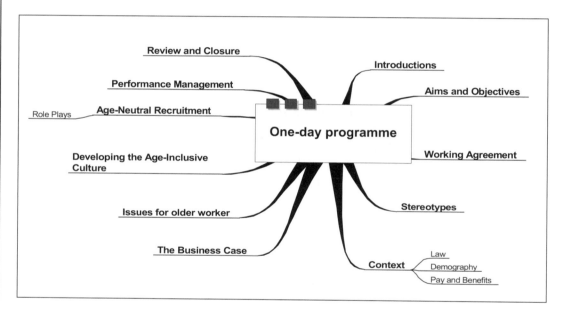

Figure 18.1   Programme outline

Introduction

1. Welcome the group and introduce yourself.

2. Overview of session. Emphasize that the reason you are running this programme is because the introduction of the Age Discrimination Regulations 2006 will demand that you change policies and working practices in your organization.

3. Reiterate the aims of the programme, as listed above. These aims can be done as a flipchart sheet, a handout or a PowerPoint® slide so that all are able to see them.

4. Explain then overview of the programme by showing them the MindMap®.

5. Aims and objectives: Each individual to consider personal goals for the course. Ask them to identify two goals they would like to have achieved by the end of the programme. Ask them to share this with one other person.

Facilitator to ask each individual for their goals and write them up on the flipchart.

6. Working agreement: Explain to the group that in order to achieve their objectives they will need to identify specific behaviours and values that will help them to do so. Ask them to share their views on this. Ensure they have on the list:

Confidentiality and an agreement of what this means to the group.

Session one: Attitudes and stereotypes

✏ Exercise 18.1: Drawing exercise

Ask each person to take two pieces of A4 paper and a pen and draw an older person on one sheet and a younger person on the other. Remind them that these need not be perfect pictures but the first thing that comes into their head. Give them two to three minutes to complete these.

Ask them to share with someone what they have drawn and why.

Plenary session

Ask the group to share findings. Questions you could ask:

- Would they have drawn the same picture if they were 20 years older, or younger?

- Where do they feel these ideas came from?

- Were the pictures based on family or work?

- What does it say about attitudes?

- Were they positive or negative pictures? Which was the most positive?

Theory input on stereotypes

See Chapter 5, section 2: Stereotypes and section 3: Beliefs and Habits for background information. Figures 5.1 and 5.2 (page 68 and 69)can be used as handouts or drawn on a flipchart.

Context

Explain that The Age Discrimination Regulations mean that it will be illegal to discriminate on the basis of age. This is a European Directive. Read Chapter 2 on the law and prepare a short presentation on the main issues that will impact your organization.

The law

The law is based on the familiar concepts found in existing discrimination laws and will cover direct and indirect discrimination, harassment and victimization. The law refers to employment in the broadest sense possible. It includes apprentices and trainees. This law will be treated in the same way as all other discriminatory laws and as an organization you will want to avoid litigation.

Take each aspect of employment law and give a brief overview of key points.

Recruitment

All current recruitment practices will need review and updating to ensure age-neutral processes. This includes:

- advertising strategy and remit;

- age-neutral application forms;

- short-listing using competencies, not experience as criteria;

- non-stereotypical interviews.

Retirement

- Retirement procedures are changing.

- National Default Retirement age of 65.

- Employers' duty to consider requests to stay on to work beyond 65.

- Employers' obligation to give adequate reason to refuse such requests.

- All employees to be given at least 6 months' notice of their retirement date.

Pay, benefits and pensions

- Organizational policies and pay and benefit structures need to be reviewed.

Training and lifelong learning

- Training to be available equally to all workers of all age groups.

- Exclusion only regarding long-term training courses that complete after the agreed retirement.

Allow a short question and answer session to respond to delegates' questions on the law.

Demographic change

Read Chapter 3 on Demographic Changes and prepare a short presentation on the business impact of demographic changes.

Chapter 3, Demographic Changes, has statistics and graphs that you can photocopy and use as handouts in your presentation to explain the current situation.

Demographic change means that:

- there will be a significantly larger number of older people in the workforce;

- insufficient numbers of young people to replace them;

- pension poverty will result in people continuing their working life;

- longevity can lead to people working longer.

Allow a short question and answer session to respond to delegates' questions on the demographic changes.

Business impact and benefits

Prepare a short presentation on the business benefits to your organization. You can include the following ideas:

Business case

- Older workers can fill skills gaps: There will be a shortage of replacement younger workers to maintain productivity and profitability. They can therefore use older workers to fill these gaps.

- Maintaining corporate knowledge and memory: Organizational knowledge is held by long-serving workers. You can use your older workers to share this knowledge with new members of staff.

- Bring access to a wider customer base: Demographic change affects the whole worldwide population. Therefore your customer base will have an increased proportion of over 50s. This is an opportunity to look at your products and services to leverage this situation.

- Improve the organization's public image: Demonstrates that they embrace diversity are seen as employers-of-choice.

- Increase staff morale: Older workers who choose to stay on have been shown to be happier, loyal and motivated.

- Increase staff retention: Recruitment costs time, energy and money. Retaining staff makes business sense.

- Lower staff absence: It is a myth that just because a worker is older they take more sickness leave. Low motivation is generally the cause of absence.

- Succession planning, career development and promotion: The demographic change could lead to leadership gaps at all levels. It can lead to blockage for younger staff, so flexibility in changing roles needs to be introduced through good career development processes.

- Performance management: Competence-based performance management is essential to ensure that all workers' goals and aspirations are met to support peak performance. Performance management is particularly important where you may have disaffected staff or staff not meeting targets.

- Work–life balance and flexible working: Flexible working practices will enable staff to work in new ways to meet their own and business demands.

Allow a short question and answer session to respond to delegates' questions on the business impact and benefits to your organization.

Issues for the older workers

Refer back to Chapter 4 on Understanding Your Older Workforce in order to get some background on this topic.

✎ Exercise 18.3: What are the pressures facing older workers today?

In groups of six brainstorm all the different pressures you think this group might be under at the moment, for example having teenage children and elderly parents.

Ask each group to prepare a short charade where they act out for the other group at least five issues that are affecting older workers.

Give the group 15 minutes to prepare a four-minute 'act'.

The 'audience' group has to guess which issues they are depicting.

The group exchanges roles and the 'audience' group has to act out the issues to the first group.

Plenary session

- What themes did you notice?

- How do you feel about this situation?

- How might these issues impact performance and team working?

- What ideas do you have to resolve these issues for yourself and your team?

Developing an age-inclusive organization

Explain that all the issues raised will impact the business and will need to be addressed.

AgeTalks age-inclusive model

Introduce the age-inclusive model (Figure 18.2) and identify which specific policies and practices will need to be changed within your organization.

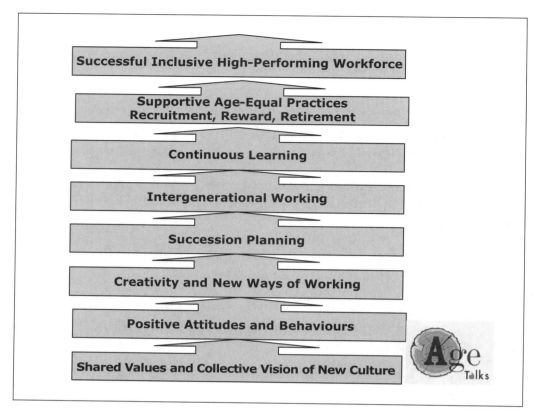

Figure 18.2   Age-inclusive model

Age-neutral role play

A selection of role plays relating to interviews and performance management can be found in Exercise 9.5 (page 181) and Exercise 10.4 (page 201). You can choose which of these is the most relevant to your group.

Exercise 18.5: Interview role plays

Refer back to Chapter 9 on Recruiting Older Workers and refer specifically to section 3. Look back to Chapter 2 on the Age Discrimination Regulations to identify compliance areas.

Follow the instructions for the role plays in Exercise 9.5 and Exercise 10.4. Choose from this selection (on pages 181 and 201) which are relevant to your group.

Divide the group into threes. One person plays the older person, one plays the manager and one is an observer.

Allow ten minutes for the role play.

Ask the observer to feedback what they observed; then the old person; then the manager. Discuss briefly the issues raised and any learning points.

Each person should play each role.

If participants have their own role play situation they would like to use do allow them to use those instead of the ones suggested in the book.

Plenary session

Refer back to the exercise for specific questions.

Performance management

Refer back to Chapter 10 for background information on this topic.

Exercise 18.6: Performance management issues

Ask the group to brainstorm the kind of issues they may face in performance management as a result of the changes in demography, the legislation, retirement age and pensions. Give them five minutes for this exercise.

Flipchart their points.

Reproduced from *Age Matters* by Keren Smedley and Helen Whitten, Gower Publishing, 2006.

Exercise 18.7: Performance management role plays

Put the group into threes. Refer to Exercise 10.4 (page 201). Choose any three of the role play topics for this exercise.

Ensure that one of the group takes an observer role and that each person in the group to have a turn as (a) the reviewer (b) the reviewee and (c) the observer.

Allow ten minutes for the role play.

Ask the observer to feedback what they observed; then the reviewee; then the reviewer. Discuss briefly the issues raised and any learning points. Each person should play each role.

If participants have their own role play situation they would like to use do allow them to use those instead of the ones suggested in the book.

Plenary session

Have a discussion and share what they find difficult when giving feedback to an older worker.

Develop with the group some strategies to help them and some reasons why this is essential to performance and productivity.

You can photocopy the handout on giving and receiving feedback (page 200) in Chapter 10 Performance Management.

Exercise 18.8: Action planning

Give individuals five minutes to write down what they have learnt and considered and at least three actions they will take to implement the age-inclusive culture.

In pairs, ask them to discuss what might hinder them taking this action and to add into the action plan strategies to break through these barriers.

Ask each participant to share one thing they will act upon.

Reproduced from *Age Matters* by Keren Smedley and Helen Whitten, Gower Publishing, 2006.

CHAPTER 19

Implementation:
Two-day Training Programme to Introduce Age-Inclusive Working Practices into your Organization

Aim

To enable HR and line managers to identify the issues of Age Discrimination and the requirements of the Age Discrimination Regulations October 2006, explore how to manage this new situation, and develop skills to ensure that managers are able to motivate and make the most of the wisdom and experience that lies within their older workforce. By the end of the programme delegates will have identified:

- the likely impact of an ageing workforce on business performance;

- the advantages and disadvantages of the 2006 Regulations;

- how to be prepared for the demographic changes;

- how to demonstrate the value placed in their older workforce;

- how to ensure continued motivation for across the workforce;

- intergenerational communication and knowledge sharing;

- action points to ensure peak performance in the workforce.

Refer back to relevant chapters in the book both for background information, interactive exercises and handouts.

Format	Two-day interactive workshop.
Target group	HR, training, and line managers 8–12 people per programme.
Equipment	Flipchart PowerPoint® Handouts to be chosen depending on the relevance to your group Plain paper and pens.
Room layout	Provide tables or desks either in U-shape or cabaret-style Space for break-out sessions Ideally, break-out rooms.

SUGGESTED PROGRAMME OUTLINE: DAY ONE

Introduction

1. Welcome the group and introduce yourself.

2. Overview of session. Emphasize that the reason you are running this programme is because of the introduction of the Age Discrimination Regulations in October 2006 which demand that you change policies and working practices in your organization.

3. Reiterate the aims of the programme, as listed above. These aims can be done as a flipchart, a handout or a PowerPoint® slide so that all are able to see them.

4. Explain the overview of the programme by showing them the MindMaps®.

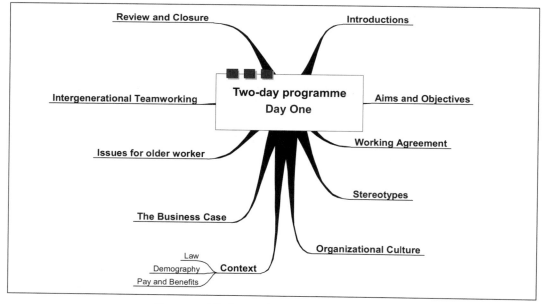

Figure 19.1   MindMap® day one

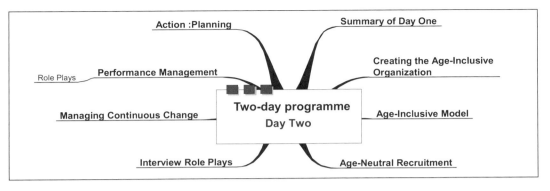

Figure 19.2 MindMap® day two

5. Aims and objectives: Each individual to consider the course. Ask them to identify two goals they would like to have achieved by the end of the second day. Ask them to share this with one other person.

6. Facilitator to ask each individual for their goals and write them up on the flipchart.

7. Working agreement: Explain to the group that in order to achieve their objectives they will need to identify specific behaviours and values that will help them to do so. Ask them to share their views on this. Ensure they have on the list:

Discuss confidentiality and make an agreement of what this means to the group.

Session one: Attitudes and stereotypes

✎ Exercise 19.1: Drawing exercise

Ask each person to take two pieces of A4 paper and a pen and draw an older person on one sheet and a younger person on the other. Remind them that these need not be perfect pictures but the first thing that comes into their head. Give them two to three minutes to complete these.

Ask them to share with someone different what they have drawn and why.

Plenary session

Ask the group to share findings. Questions you could ask:

- Would they have drawn the same picture if they were 20 years older, or younger?

- Where do they feel these ideas came from?

- Were the pictures based on family or work?

- What does it say about attitudes?

- Were they positive or negative pictures? Which was the most positive?

Theory input on stereotypes

See Chapter 5 section 2: Stereotypes and section 3: Beliefs and Habits for background information. Figures 5.1 and 5.2 can be used as handouts or to be drawn on a flipchart.

✎ Exercise 19.2: Considering your organizational culture

Photocopy the questionnaire from page and give this to each delegate.

Once they have completed the questionnaire, ask them to share their answers in threes and offer them further questions from Exercise 5.1 (page 73) to focus their conversation.

Having explored the stereotypes in your organization, introduce the theory on beliefs in Chapter 5, section 3, Beliefs and Habits (page 67).

Ask the group to do Exercise 5.3 (page 79), 'Challenging Beliefs'.

Plenary session

What stereotypes and assumptions exist in your organization that may need challenging?

How do you envisage enabling your staff to make this shift?

Context

Explain that The Age Discrimination Regulations introduced in October 2006 mean that it is illegal to discriminate on the basis of age. This is a European Directive. Read Chapter 2 on the law and prepare a short presentation on the main issues that will impact your organization.

The law

The law is based on the familiar concepts found in existing discrimination laws and will cover direct and indirect discrimination, harassment and victimization. The law refers to employment in the broadest sense possible. It includes apprentices and trainees. This law will be treated in the same way as all other discriminatory laws and as an organization you will want to avoid litigation.

Take each aspect of employment Law and give a brief overview of key points.

Recruitment

All current recruitment practices will need review and updating to ensure age-neutral processes. This includes:

- advertising strategy and remit;

- age-neutral application forms;

- short-listing using competencies, not experience as criteria;

- non-stereotypical interviews.

Retirement

- Retirement procedures are changing.

- National Default Retirement age of 65.

- Employers duty to consider requests to stay on to work beyond 65.

- Employers' obligation to give adequate reason to refuse such requests.

- All employees to be given at least 6 months' notice of their retirement date.

Pay, benefits and pensions

- Organizational policies and pay and benefit structures need to be reviewed.

Training and lifelong learning

- Training to be available equally to all workers of all age groups.

- Exclusion only regarding long-term training courses that complete after the agreed retirement.

Allow a short question and answer session to respond to delegates' questions on the law.

Demographic change

Read Chapter 3 on Demographic Changes (pp.37–46) and prepare a short presentation on the business impact of demographic changes.

Chapter 3, Demographic Changes, has statistics and graphs that you can photocopy and use as handouts in your presentation to explain the current situation.

Demographic change means that:

- there will be a significantly larger number of older people in the workforce;

- insufficient numbers of young people to replace them;

- pension poverty will result in people continuing their working life;

- longevity can lead to people working longer.

Allow a short question and answer session to respond to delegates' questions on the demographic changes.

Business impact and benefits

Prepare a short presentation on the business benefits to your organization. You can include the following ideas:

Business case

- Older workers can fill skills gaps: There will be a shortage of replacement younger workers to maintain productivity and profitability. They can therefore use older workers to fill these gaps.

- Maintaining corporate knowledge and memory: Organizational knowledge is held by long-serving workers. You can use your older workers to share this knowledge with new members of staff.

- Bring access to wider customer base: Demographic change affects the whole worldwide population. Therefore your customer base will have increased proportion of over 50s. This is an opportunity to look at your products and services to leverage this situation.

- Improve the organization's public image: Organizations showing that they embrace diversity are seen as employers-of-choice.

- Increase staff morale: Older workers who choose to stay on have been shown to be happier, loyal and motivated.

- Increase staff retention: Recruitment costs time, energy and money. Retaining staff makes business sense.

- Lower staff absence: It is a myth that just because a worker is older they take more sickness leave. Low motivation is generally the cause of absence.

- Succession planning, career development and promotion: The demo-graphic change could lead to leadership gaps at all levels. It can lead to blockage for younger staff, so flexibility in role change needs to be introduced through good career development processes.

- Performance management: Competence-based performance management is essential to ensure that all workers' goals and aspirations are met to support peak performance. Performance management is particularly important where you may have disaffected staff or staff not meeting targets.

- Work–life balance and flexible working: Flexible working practices will enable staff to work in new ways to meet their own and business demands.

Allow a short question and answer session to respond to delegates' questions on the business impact and benefits to your organization.

Reproduced from *Age Matters* by Keren Smedley and Helen Whitten, Gower Publishing, 2006.

Issues for the older workers

Refer back to Chapter 4 on Understanding Your Older Workforce (pp.47–62) in order to get some background on this topic.

 Exercise 19.3: What are the pressures facing older workers today?

In groups of six brainstorm all the different pressures you think this group might be under at the moment, for example having teenage children and elderly parents.

Ask each group to prepare a short charade where they act out for the other group at least five issues that are affecting older workers.

Give the group 15 minutes to prepare a four-minute 'act'.

The 'audience' group has to guess which issues they are depicting.

The group exchanges roles and the 'audience' group has to act out the issues to the first group.

Plenary session

- What themes did you notice?

- How do you feel about this situation?

- How might these issues impact performance and team working?

- What ideas do you have to resolve these issues for yourself and your team?

Intergenerational teamworking

Refer back to Chapter 13 for background information. Introduce the Relationship Map, Figure 13:1, and the theories of Transactional Analysis in Chapter 6 on People Management. You can do one or other of the following exercises, or both if you have time.

 Exercise 19.4: Relationship mapping

Photocopy the handout from Exercise 13.2 (page 254), and follow instructions for the exercise.

Plenary session

Does age affect relationships?

If so, in what way?

Reproduced from *Age Matters* by Keren Smedley and Helen Whitten, Gower Publishing, 2006.

Exercise 19.5: Creative intergenerational working

Follow the instructions for Exercise 13.3 (page 257) on Creative Intergenerational Working.

When completed have a plenary session discussing what would help your organization.

Review and round-up of the day

Ask each participant to share one thing they have learnt or taken away from the day.

Suggest that the group observe themselves and those around them during the evening and notice any age-related issues and assumptions.

DAY TWO: CREATING THE AGE-INCLUSIVE ORGANIZATION

Welcome the participants back.

Ask them to get into pairs, preferably with someone they didn't work with yesterday, and discuss whether they noticed anything about age-related issues and assumptions while they journeyed home and during the evening. Give them five minutes

Group feedback

What did they notice?

Has anyone any questions based on yesterday's course?

Developing an age-inclusive organization

Explain that all the issues raised will impact the business and will need to be addressed. Introduce the MindMap® overview of day two and explain that today is about making the implementation successful.

 Reproduced from *Age Matters* by Keren Smedley and Helen Whitten, Gower Publishing, 2006.

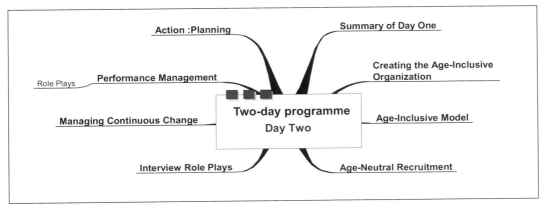

Figure 19.2 MindMap® day two

AgeTalks age-inclusive model

Introduce the age-inclusive model and identify which specific policies and practices will need to be changed within your organization.

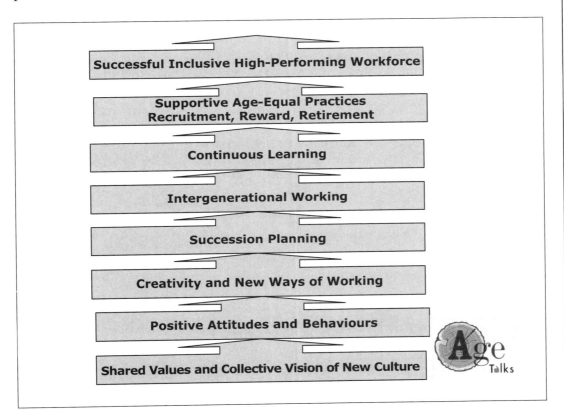

Figure 19.3 Age-inclusive model

Reproduced from *Age Matters* by Keren Smedley and Helen Whitten, Gower Publishing, 2006.

Exercise 19.6: Identifying action areas

In fours ask the group to consider what aspects of their own working practices will be affected. Give them ten minutes.

The areas that are essential for every manager to address are:

- Recruitment

- Managing change

- Performance management.

Plenary session

Capture key points on the flipchart and give a copy to each participant.

Age-neutral recruitment

Refer back to Chapter 9 on Recruiting Older Workers and refer specifically to section 3. Look back to Chapter 2 on the Age Legislation to identify compliance areas.

Exercise 19.7: Age-neutral language

Follow the instructions for Exercises 9.2 (page 176) and 9.3 (page 177).

Plenary session

Discuss the change in language.

Exercise 19.8 Interview role plays

Follow the instructions for the role plays in Exercise 9.5 (page 181). Choose from this selection which are relevant to your group.

- Divide the group into threes. One person plays the older person, one plays the manager and one is an observer.

- Allow ten minutes for the role play.

- Ask the observer to feedback what they observed; then the old person; then the manager. Discuss briefly the issues raised and any learning points.

- Each person should play each role.

If participants have their own role play situation they would like to use allow them to use those instead of the ones suggested in the book.

Plenary session

Refer back to the exercise for specific questions.

Managing continuous change

Refer back to Chapter 7 (page 121) for background information on this topic.

Exercise 19.9: Change preference

Photocopy the Change Preference questionnaire (Exercise 7.1, page 135) (Rupert Eales-White) and scoresheets. Prepare some materials to help the group to understand the model.

Introduce the topic of continuous change and its impact on people of all age groups. Ask each person to do the Change Preference questionnaire, from Chapter 7.

Put them in pairs to discuss their own profile and which profiles they think they would find difficulty with.

Plenary session

What did the participants notice?

How does this affect teamworking?

Performance management

Refer back to Chapter 10 (page 183–204) for background information on this topic.

Exercise 19.10: Performance management issues

Ask the group to brainstorm the kind of issues they may face in performance management as a result of the changes in demography, the legislation, retirement age and pensions. Give them five minutes for this exercise.

Flipchart their points.

✎ Exercise 19.11: Performance management role plays

Put the group into threes. Refer to Exercise 10.4 (page 201). Choose any three of the role play topics for this exercise.

Ensure that one of the group takes an observer role and that each person in the group has a turn as (a) the reviewer (b) the reviewee and (c) the observer.

Allow ten minutes for the role play.

Ask the observer to feedback what they observed; then the reviewee; then the reviewer. Discuss briefly the issues raised and any learning points.

Each person should play each role.

If participants have their own role play situation they would like to use do allow them to use those instead of the ones suggested in the book.

Plenary session

Have a discussion and share what they find difficult when giving feedback to an older worker.

Develop with the group some strategies to help them and some reasons why this is essential to performance and productivity.

You can photocopy the handout on giving and receiving feedback in Chapter 10, Performance Management.

✎ Exercise 19.12: Action planning

Give individuals five minutes to write down what they have learnt and considered and at least three actions they will take to implement the age-inclusive culture.

In pairs, ask them to discuss what might hinder them taking this action and to add into the action plan strategies to break through these barriers.

Ask each participant to share one thing they will act upon.

Reproduced from *Age Matters* by Keren Smedley and Helen Whitten, Gower Publishing, 2006.

CHAPTER 20

Monitoring and Evaluating Progress

It is important when trying to change an organization's culture to remember that this is a slow process and cannot be done overnight. In our experience too many organizations introduce an initiative once and assume that it will be achieved immediately. It is worth remembering that when you learnt to read it was a slow process and needed constant repetition and reinforcement.

It is therefore necessary for you to set up an implementation programme where you can evaluate the effects of your work and reassess and modify your plan. In our experience, if an organization is truly going to change this can take three to five years before all workers adopt the supportive behaviours instinctively.

CONTINUOUS ASSESSMENT

There are three exercises in Chapter 1, Age Discrimination: The Next Diversity Issue, to assess where your organization is in the implementation of anti-age-discriminatory practices. This indicates how far your organization has become an age-inclusive culture.

Our suggestion is that these exercises are undertaken with random groups on a yearly basis. The results should be monitored and compared.

Once you have undertaken this process it is important that you, as the implementers, modify your action plan according to the results.

Conclusion

The world is changing and will continue to do so. The population worldwide is ageing and governments have responded by introducing the Age Discrimination Regulations. This directly affects the UK from October 2006. Businesses need to be aware of these changes and actively respond to this situation if they wish to continue to have a competitive edge.

This book has provided new ways to consider these issues. It has presented a number of different concepts and theories intended to make you think about how this will impact your own organization. Alongside this it has also offered straightforward, practical steps and exercises that can be taken to move your organization to be age-inclusive.

It is important to remember that the older person is no better or worse than any other. We do not wish to say that we are favouring older people over any other age group. However, it is true to say that up until now the older person has been marginalized both in the workplace and in society and so our aim is to re-address this balance.

Society and organizations are faced with an unprecedented situation. Our belief is that with careful thought and creativity this will offer the world an opportunity for true intergenerational communication. We hope you agree!

Keren Smedley and Helen Whitten

Bibliography

Adair, Joh, *Effective Leadership*, Gower,1983.

Atkingson, Philip, *Creating Cultural Change*, IFS, 1987.

Barmby, T., Ercolani, M. and Treble, J. *Sickness and Absence in the UK 1984–2002*, September 2003, http://www.swan.ac.uk/welmerc/ Sickness%20and%20absence.pdf.

Basadur M. S., *The Power of Innovation*, London UK Pitman Professional Publishing, 1995.

Bennis, Warren, Biederman, Patricia Ward, *Organising Genius*, Nicholas Brealey

Publishing, 1997.

Berne, Eric, *Games People Play*, Penguin, 1964.

Berne, Eric, *What do you say after you say Hello?* Corgi, 1990.

Birren, J.E., Birren, B.A., *The Concepts, Models and History in the Psychology of Ageing (3rd edition)*. San Diego Academic Press, 1990.

Buzan, Tony, *How to Mind Map*, Thorsons, 2002.

Buzan, Tony, *Make the Most of your Mind*, Pan, 1988.

Buzan, Tony, *The Age Heresy,* Ebury Press, 1996.

Buzan, Tony, *The Mind Map Book*, BBC Books, 2003.

Buzan, Tony, Tony Dottino, Richard Israel, *The BrainSmart Leader*, Gower, 1999.

Cabinet Office Performance and Innovation Unit, Report; *Winning the Generation Game: Improving Opportunities for People Aged 50-65 in Work and Community Activity,* 2000.

Cameron, Julia, *The Artist's Way*, Pan, 1995.

Campbell, D. *National Longitudinal Survey of Youth*, London School of Economics, 2001.

Carter, Rita, *Mapping the Mind,* Seven Dials, 1999.

Covey, Stephen R., *The Seven Habits of Highly Effective People*, Simon & Schuster, 1989.

De Bono, Edward, *Six Thinking Hats*, Penguin, 1990.

Department for Education and Employment (DfEE), Quality, Prevalence and Indicator Database (QPID), *Training Older Workers*, 2000.

Department of Trade and Industry (DTI), *Equality and Diversity: Age Matters.* Report; Age Consultation 2003, Summary of Responses.

Department of Work and Pensions: Green Paper, *Simplicity, Security and Choice, Working and Saving for Retirement,* 2002.

Ditts, Robert, *Changing Belief Systems* with NLP, Meta Publications, 1990.

Dryden, Windy: *Peak Performance*, Mercury, 1993.

Eales-White, Rupert, *How to be a Better Teambuilder*, Kogan Page, 1996.

Eales-White, Rupert, *The Effective Leader*, Kogan Page, 2003.

EU Council Directive; *Establishing a General Framework for Equal Treatment in Employment and Occupation*, 2000/78/EC.

Finkelstein, Sydney, *Why Smart Executives Fail: and What you can Learn from their Mistakes,* Portfolio (Penguin Putnam) 2003.

Fletcher, Winston: *Beating the 24/7: How Business Leaders Achieve a Successful Work-Life Balance*, Wiley, 2003.

Gardner, Howard, *Creating Minds*, BasicBooks, 1993.;

Garratt, Bob, *Thin on Top*, Nicholas Brealey, 2003.

Gawain, Shakti, *Creative Visualisation*, New World Library, 1978.

Goleman, Daniel, *Emotional Intelligence*, Bloomsbury, 1996.

Greenfield, Susan, *The Human Mind Explained*, Cassell, 1996.

Handy, Charles, *The Hungry Spirit*, Hutchinson, 1997.

Herrmann, Ned, *The Whole Brain Business Book*, McGraw Hill, 1996.

Holden, Robert, *Happiness Now*, Hodder & Stoughton, 1998.

Holden, Robert, *Laughter, the Best Medicine*, Thorsons, 1993.

Howard, Pierce J., *The Owner's Manual for the Brain*, 2nd Edition, Bard Press, 2000.

Itzin, Philipson, extract from a report: *Practical Tips and Guidance on Training a Mixed-Age Workforce* by Newton, B., Hurstfield, J., Miller, J. and Bates, P. for *Extending Working Lives*. Department for Work and Pensions, Age Partnership Group.

James, Jennifer, *Thinking in the Future Tense*, Touchstone Books, New York, 1997.

James, Muriel, Dorothy Jongeward, *Born to Win,* Perseus Books, 1996.

Jeffers, Susan, *Feel the Fear and Do it Anyway*, Arrow, 1991.

Jones, Benjamin F., National Bureau of Economic Research, *Age and Great Invention,* National Bureau of Economic Research working paper No. 11359, 2005, NBER Program(s).

Kodz J, Kersley B, Bates P., *The Fifties Revival*, IES Report 359, Institute of Employment Studies, 1999.

Langdon, Ken, *52 Brilliant Ideas to Cultivate a Cool Career*, Infinite Ideas, 2004.

Lundin, Stephen, *Fish*, Hodder & Stoughton, 2000.

McDaniels, Carl, *The Changing Workplace: Career Counseling Strategies for the 1990s and Beyond*, Josey-Bass, 1990.

Manton, K.G., Stallard, E., Corder, L., 'Changes in Morbidity and Chronic Disability in the US Elderly Population', *Journal of Gerontology*, 50, 194–204, 1995.

Meadows, P., Extract from a report: page 7, *Practical Tips and Guidance on Training a Mixed-Age Workforce* by Newton, B., Hurstfield, J., Miller, J. and Bates, P. for *Extending Working Lives*. Department for Work and Pensions, Age Partnership Group.

Mehrabian, Albert, Mehrabian Communication Research, *Albert Mehrabian's Communications Model*.

Merlevede, Patrick E., Denis Brideoux, Rudy Vandamme, *7 Steps to Emotional Intelligence*, Crown House Publishing Limited, 2002.

Mitchell, J., *Vision at Work,* McGraw-Hill, 1996.

Moir, Anne and Jessel, David, *Brainsex*, Mandarin, 1992.

Neumann, et al. *Achieving Excellence on Professional Excellence*, Canadian Nurses Association, ISBN: 1-55119-7, 1997.

Newman, Sally, Christopher R. Ward, Thomas B. Smith, Janet O. Wilson, James M. McCrea, Gary Calham, Eric Kingson, *Intergenerational Programs Past, Present and Future,* Taylor & Francis, 1997.

O'Brien, Dominic, *How to Develop a Perfect Memory*, Pavilion, 1993.

O'Connor, Joseph and Seymour, John, *Introducing Neuro-Linguistic Programming*, Mandala, 1990.

O'Neill, Mary Beth, *Executive Coaching with Backbone and Heart*, Jossey-Bass, 2000.

Office for National Statistics, *Population Trends*, 2001.

Palmer, Stephen and Lynda Strickland, *Stress Management: A Quick Guide*, Folens, Dunstable, 1996.

Parikh, Jagdish, *Developmental Management,* Blackwell Business, 1991.

Pert, Candida, *Molecules of Emotion*, Simon & Schuster, 1998.

Pinker, Steven, *How The Mind Works*, W.W. Norton, New York, 1997.

Pinker, Steven, *The Blank Slate*, Penguin Allen Lane, 2002.

Prashing, Barbara, *The Power of Diversity*, Network Education Press, 1998.

Rae, Leslie, *The Skills of Training*, Gower, 1991.

Ramsden, Pamela and Jody Zacharias, *Action Profiling*, Gower, 1993.

Reid, Stephen, *How to Think,* Pearson Education, 2002.

Richardson, Robert J., S. Katharine Thayer, *The Charisma Factor*, Prentice Hall, 1993.

Rose, Colin, *Accelerated Learning*, Dell, 1987.

Russell, Peter, *The Brain Book*, Routledge & Kegan Paul, 1979.

Savickas, Mark L, Walsh, W. Bruce; *Handbook of Career Counseling Theory and Practice*, David Black Publishing, 1996.

Schaie, K.W., Giewitz, J. *Adult Development and Ageing*, LittleBrown & Company, Boston, 1982.

Seligman, Martin Dr., *Learned Optimism*, Pocket Books, 1990.

Senge, Peter, *The 5th Discipline Field Book*, Nicholas Brearley, 1984

Sihera, Elaine and Kerry Hughes, *Managing the Diversity Maze,* AnSer Publishing, 2002.

Siler, Todd, *Think Like A Genius*, Bantam, New York, 1997.

Smith, Alistair, *The Brain's Behind It*, Network Educational Press, 2002.

Snyder, C.R. and Shane J. Lopez, *Handbook of Positive Psychology*, Oxford University Press, New York, 2002.

Whithnall et al., extract from a report: *Practical Tips and Guidance on Training a Mixed-Age Workforce* by Newton, B., Hurstfield, J., Miller, J. and Bates, P. for *Extending Working Lives*. Department for Work and Pensions, Age Partnership Group.

Whitten, Helen, Richard Israel, Cliff Shaffran, *Your Mind at Work*, Kogan Page, 2000.

Whitten, Helen, Diane Carrigton, *Future Directions, Practical Ways to Develop Emotional Intelligence and Confidence in Young People*, Network Educational Press, 2005.

Williamson, G.M., Dooley, W.K. 'Ageing and coping', in C.R. Snyder, *Coping and Stress: Effective People and Processes*, Oxford University Press, New York, 2001.

Wise, Anna, *The High Performance Mind*, Jeremy P. Tarcher, 1997.

INTERNET RESOURCES

www.agetalks.com – consultancy on age inclusion and Age Discrimination

www.positiveworks.com – coaching and training on Positive Life and Work Strategies

www.ksa.org.uk – consultancy, coaching, training on management and personal solutions.

www.hbdi-uk.com – information on the Herrmann Brain Dominance Instrument

www.success-dynamics.com – information on the Success Dynamics DiSC Personality Survey

www.givemeajob.co.uk

www.jobsunlimited.co.uk

www.icg-uk.org – career guidance

www.networkeducationpress.org.uk

www.gower.com

www.buzancentres.com

www.eef.org.uk

www.efa.org.uk

www.cipd.co.uk

www.iod.com

www.ageconcern.org.uk

www.apsoc.ox.ac.uk

www.e-wc.co.uk

www.pra.org.uk

www.taen.org.uk

www.lewissilkin.com

www.businessballs.com

www.dti.gov.uk

www.fiftyon.co.uk

Index

Page numbers in bold indicate an exercise, bold and italic indicates an exercise used in a training programme. Figures are indicated by an f after the page number, followed by a number if there is more than one figure on the page.

historical perspective, 245–6
Rentokil Initial, 55
reputation of a company, 249
resourcing skills and knowledge, 229–30
retirement
    attitudes to, 286–7
    average age of, 232
    continued employment rights, 285
    default age, 34, 284
    early, 232, 286
    employment practices and
        procedures, 288–90
    flexible/phased, 287–8
    forced early, 58
    insurance benefits, 289–90
    options, **293**
    pay and benefits, 289, **300**
    and pensions, 55–6, 283
    planned, 284–5
    planning for, 56, 287
    requests to work beyond set age,
        284–5
    return to work following, 55–6
    waiting for, **295**
retirement and sickness absence, 188–9
return on investment in training, 208,
    210, **213**
role change and promotion, 232–3
role models, senior managers as, 271–2
role plays, **180, 201**

Sainsbury's, 250
sandwich generation, 52–3
self-employment, 232–3
self-knowledge, 85–93
self-management, 93–8
senior managers as role models, 271–2
sickness absence
    evaluation of, **154**
    of older people, 144
    and retirement, 188–9
sideways moves, 234, 235
Sihera, Elaine, 11
*Simplicity, Security and Choice, Working
    and Saving for Retirement, 27–8*
sixties, social change in the, 48–9
skills and experience of older people,
    229–30
skills and knowledge
    audit, 230, **237**
    resourcing of, 229–30
SMART objectives, **204**
social change in the sixties, 48–9
social implications of age
    discrimination, 13–14
Stakeholder Pensions, 290
stamina, 266–7
Statutory Redundancy Payments
    scheme, 36
Stephenson, Adelaide, 70
stereotypes

awareness raising, 308–9, 312–13
challenging beliefs, **80,** *332*
drawing, **77, 312–13**
and older people, 66–7
one-day training programme,
    317–18
organizational culture, **74, 317–18,
    328**
two-day training programme, 328
values and attitudes, **82**
straw travel, **259**
stress
    age-related sources for individuals,
        158–60
    cultural audit, **155**
    effect on time management, 149–50
    factors at work, **155**
    fight or flight response, 149, 149f
    health effects of, 148f2
    and mental performance, 149–51
    and negative thinking, 150f
    and older people, 150
    and positive thinking, 151f
    symptoms of, 147–9, 148f1
    see also health
succession planning, 230–1
support audit, **275**

teams, intergenerational, 132–3, **133**
technology supporting flexible working,
    272
Tesco, 250
Thinking Preference model, Herrmann,
    86–8, **105**
thoughts and behaviour, 70–1, 70f
time management, 149–50, 271–2
time out, encouragement of, 273
training and development
    confidence, 57, 209–10
    continuous professional
        development, 208
    discrimination, 57–8, 207–8
    evaluation of, **213**
    learning skills, 209–10
    learning styles, 211, **215**
    memory skills, 57, 211–12, **223**
    multiple intelligences, 211, **215**
    performance appraisal reviews, 186
    return on investment, 208, 210, **213**
    vocational education and training,
        209
training for performance appraisal
    reviews, 190
training programmes
    one day, **311**
    two day, **325**
transactional analysis (TA), 88–91, 90f
twenty practical steps to take for a
    healthy workplace, 146–7
two-day training programme
    action planning, 336